MORTGAGES
101

MORTGAGES 101

Quick Answers to Over
250 Critical Questions
About Your Home Loan

THIRD EDITION

David Reed

HARPERCOLLINS
LEADERSHIP

AN IMPRINT OF HARPERCOLLINS

Mortgages 101

Published by HarperCollins Leadership, an imprint of HarperCollins Focus LLC.

Any internet addresses, phone numbers, or company or product information printed in this book are offered as a resource and are not intended in any way to be or to imply an endorsement by HarperCollins Leadership, nor does HarperCollins Leadership vouch for the existence, content, or services of these sites, phone numbers, companies, or products beyond the life of this book.

Bulk discounts available. For details visit:
www.harpercollinsleadership.com/bulkquotes
Email: customercare@harpercollins.com

ISBN 978-0-8144-3874-9 (TP)

Printed in the United States of America

CONTENTS

CHAPTER 2
How to Know How Much Home to Buy

CHAPTER 3
Getting Your Finances Together

CHAPTER 6

SECTION II
THE RIGHT MORTGAGE

CHAPTER 7

FINDING YOUR HOME LOAN

SECTION III
THE RIGHT LENDER AND RATE   197

CHAPTER 11
FINDING THE BEST LENDER   199

CHAPTER 12

FINDING THE BEST LOAN OFFICER

CHAPTER 13

FINDING THE BEST INTEREST RATE

CHAPTER 15

CHAPTER 15

USING THE INTERNET THE RIGHT WAY

APPENDIX

MONTHLY PAYMENT SCHEDULES

GLOSSARY

INDEX

Preface

With more than 20 years in mortgage lending, counseling home buyers from New York to California, I've certainly seen it all. The first edition of this book, published back in 2004, helped thousands understand, in plain English, the home loan process. It's a confusing industry, mortgage lending. Heck, even the name sounds a little funny. And speaking of, the word itself has two roots with origins in both Latin and Old French. Literally it's translated as "dead pledge." Sounds fun, doesn't it? But by reading this book, you will find some fun explanations on how mortgage loans are approved and learn about the differences in home loan programs. We bust a few myths along the way, as well.

The second edition was published in 2008. You remember that time, don't you? Or maybe you erased it from your mind, just like mortgage companies and "no document" loans were erased from the industry. The old joke was that all lenders did leading up to 2008 was to make sure someone could fog up a mirror, and if there wasn't any fog they'd make an exception. It wasn't very fun being in the mortgage business back then. A lot of loan programs simply vanished almost overnight along with the lenders who made them.

The backlash was almost immediate. While it was too easy to get a mortgage loan for years with little regard for risk, suddenly it was nearly impossible to get a mortgage. Lending guidelines tightened up so fast that many mortgage companies simply appeared to be too afraid to approve a loan application, thinking they'd have to buy it back later due to some sort of compliance or documentation issue.

Slowly, however, the industry returned to its commonsense roots. Yet the mortgage landscape today looks different compared to just a few years ago. Congress stepped in and amended the Home Ownership and Equity Protection Act, first passed in 1994. The amendments took effect in 2009 and lenders are approving loans in a brand-new world. But they're getting much better at it. In fact, loan quality today rivals any other period in recent memory. Mortgage lenders are approving loans for those with a job, verifiable income, decent credit, and enough money in the bank to close on a home purchase. These same standards apply to anyone refinancing an existing loan as well.

But for those who are thinking of buying their first home, they may also carry no shortage of anxiety. After all, will another financial meltdown happen yet again? This trepidation is certainly understandable and in fact healthy. However, loans being approved today are being evaluated in ways that make sure those who apply for a mortgage loan are in the right loan program, can comfortably afford their monthly payments each month, and that the mortgage company follows proper lending guidelines throughout the loan approval process.

What remain today are the stalwarts of mortgage lending, yet with a whole new set of rules. And with this new set of rules, combined with traditional guidelines and protocol, come new questions, new scenarios, and a host of compliance issues.

Yet by reading this book, and referring to it as you move through the approval process, you'll know more about the mortgage industry than many of the loan officers out there. I've been where you are now and I know how the industry works and I know the questions you might have. In fact, the answers to more than 250 of them are in your very hands.

David Reed

MORTGAGE FUNDAMENTALS

Introduction to Mortgages

There's a lot more to buying a home than just picking one out and moving in. If you don't have a wad of cash stuffed in your sofa cushions, chances are you'll need a mortgage. Mortgage lending has been around for a long, long time, and some things haven't changed, while other parts of the mortgage process are brand new. Knowing what you're getting into can help you to make the right decisions.

1.1 HOW HAS THE MORTGAGE MARKET CHANGED SINCE THE LAST EDITION OF MORTGAGES 101?

Wow. A lot, and that's what we'll be covering in this new third edition. Yet we appear to have come somewhat full circle dating back to 2004 when the first *Mortgages 101* was published. It's really been interesting to watch, and very much so if you follow the mortgage market like I do.

TELL ME MORE

If we go back to 2004 and look at the mortgage market then, it was made primarily of two classes of mortgage loans, conventional and government-backed. Conventional loans are those underwritten to standards issued by Fannie Mae and Freddie Mac, while government-backed loans are those carrying a government guarantee and include

3

VA, FHA, and USDA loans. We'll explore in more detail these two mortgage types in Chapter 7.

Yet the subprime mortgage market was just getting started. Subprime loans, mortgages issued to those with damaged credit, began to enter the mortgage market with swagger. Lenders made a lot of money with subprime loans and soon new lenders entered the market going after the subprime borrower. Within a few years of this overheating subprime market, the foreclosure crisis began and lenders mostly stopped lending—at least those who were still in business.

The second edition of *Mortgages 101* exposed these new players in the mortgage market, yet the mortgage landscape has changed dramatically since then. Today, lenders are offering a very tight range of mortgage products. The subprime loan has essentially vanished. And because mortgage lenders have the same basic set of loan programs, they can all make subtle changes in their own internal lending guidelines. Two lenders can offer the very same mortgage but due to the introduction of "overlays" (see Chapter 7) a borrower can be declined at one lender yet approved at another.

This third edition explains how the new lending landscape works and how it should continue to work in the future. The "cowboy" days of mortgage lending have long since ridden off into the sunset.

1.2 WHAT'S THE DIFFERENCE BETWEEN BUYING AND RENTING?

One way you own the roof over your head, and the other way, you don't. If you've always rented or otherwise never owned a home, one of the things you'll discover is that when things go wrong with your house there's no landlord to yell at. There's no superintendent to come fix your leaky faucet. If your hot-water heater is busted, you're the one who has to make the trip to your appliance store to shell out another thousand bucks or so just so you can take a hot shower in the morning.

When you rent, you can pretty much walk away as long as your lease agreement has been fulfilled. Want a change of scenery? Pack up and move across town. Want a swimming pool and fitness center without the hassles of owning either? Rent. Want new carpet or drapes every year? Rent. Want your utility bills paid? Rent. Free cable? Ditto. You get the point. Renting has its perks. Much less responsibility and no hassles of ownership.

1.3 HOW DO I KNOW IF IT'S BETTER TO BUY A HOME OR CONTINUE RENTING?

Perhaps one of the easiest ways to determine if it's better to buy or rent is to sit down and calculate the financial advantages of owning versus renting. This is commonly done online with a "rent versus buy" calculator found on the web.

TELL ME MORE

These calculators compare your current or probable rent situation with a projected home ownership number. They're easy to find. I ran a Google search for the term "mortgage + calculator" and retrieved more than 56 million websites that had those two terms in combination.

But the kicker is that these calculators rarely will tell you, "No, it's not a good idea to buy." That's because of the tax benefits of home ownership. The interest and property taxes associated with a mortgage are generally tax deductible. You can deduct them from your gross income when you file your taxes. With rent, you can't.

Yeah, I know. When you're a renter you don't pay property taxes or mortgage payments. Instead you give money to someone else for the privilege of living there. But you can't write off your rent. It's just that. Rent.

When might a "rent versus buy" calculator suggest it's better to rent? When you intend to own your next home for only a year or so. Buying a home incurs other expenses, such as money for the down payment, property taxes, and *hazard insurance* (which is much higher than a renter's policy). Many apartment complexes pay your electric bills along with water and other utilities. When you own, you pay all these expenses. Owning a home with all its tax benefits doesn't outweigh the acquisition costs to buy the home if you're only going to own it for a short period. Short term, rent. Longer term, buy. Are your rent payments the same or less than what a mortgage payment would be? Depending upon where you live, they may be the same. Especially if interest rates are relatively low.

Let's say you're renting a nice 3,000-square-foot, three-bedroom home close to schools in a friendly neighborhood. You might be paying $1,800 each month in rent. A similar three-bedroom home might cost $150,000. If you put 5 percent down to buy the home, your monthly house payment, including taxes and insurance, would be close to $800 using a 30-year fixed rate at 4 percent.

If rent payments in the area in which you want to buy are near what a mortgage payment would be, it makes sense to buy. If you can save $1,000 per month and you also get to write off the mortgage interest and property taxes, then it's truly a no-brainer.

Another reason buying is generally better than renting is simply a matter of appreciation and equity. When you rent and property values increase, your landlord will probably raise your rent again. And, of course, each time you make a rent payment you're not increasing your equity in anything; you're just helping your landlord increase his stake in your house or apartment. I'll give you an example.

Your rent is currently $1,000 per month, and you're thinking about buying a $150,000 home. If you put 20 percent down and borrow $120,000 at 4.50 percent on a 30-year fixed rate, your principal and interest payment are about $600 a month. Let's also assume that property values are increasing in your area by about 5 percent per year. What's the situation after two years?

If you rented, you paid someone else $24,000. But if you owned and itemized your federal income taxes, you likely deducted over $10,600 in mortgage interest on your income taxes. You also paid your loan down by over $4,000 while at the same time increasing your equity position in the house by nearly $20,000.

Now you see why those calculators always tell you to buy a home.

Through all of these calculations, remember the real reason for buying: You buy a home because you want to. Because you like the place. It's your home. A home is one of the largest single financial commitments someone can make. And while I agree with that statement, let's not go overboard here. Buy a house because you want to, not because some calculator told you so.

1.4 HOW SHOULD I SEARCH FOR A HOUSE?

That's easy. Start doing some research on your own on the Internet, even before contacting a real estate agent. If the Internet was invented for any particular industry it has to have been for real estate. Before the World Wide Web was born, one could typically locate houses only in the newspaper on the weekend. If you saw a house that you liked, you'd contact the agent selling the home. Then came the endless cycle of driving around in a real estate agent's car looking at houses until—finally, finally—you found a home you wanted to buy.

TELL ME MORE

The Internet has helped agents become more productive by letting consumers do a little shopping first before they get serious enough to use an agent. An agent who advertises a house is called the "listing" agent, because he puts the house for sale on the *multiple listing service,* or MLS.

The agent will show you the home and ask if you are using another agent. If you aren't, the agent will ask if you would like to see other homes for sale. You of course say "yes," and the agent then becomes a "buyer's" agent as well, helping you find a home to buy and not just listing a house for sale. You give your agent your requirements for your dream home, such as four bedrooms on a cul-de-sac with a swimming pool. Your agent would then scour the MLS to search for such homes. After the search, you'd both get in the agent's car and go see the homes.

Today, however, there seems to be no end to the ways you can search for homes. Too many, it seems, and it can be a bit overwhelming. But what all of these sites have in common is they access the very same database—the local multiple listing service.

For instance, Redfin, Zillow, and Trulia are all portals where prospective homebuyers can visit online to search for homes. Most people now find interesting homes on their own before even contacting an agent. This way, the agent's not dragging you all over town to look at homes you'd never buy. Your agent spends more time selling or listing homes and less time driving all over the place.

You can start with *www.realtor.com,* or get their app for your mobile phone. At this official site of the National Association of Realtors, you can search for homes anywhere in the country or across town. It also has access to every single agent-sponsored multiple listing service database in the country. It is easy to log onto the site, select your desired location, preferences, like four bedrooms in this zip code in this price range with a pool or without, and so on. Many properties offer "virtual" tours showing video of different views of the house. All of the pricing info is there as well so you can see what homes are selling for and what's generally available.

But don't get too much further into the process without the help of a real estate agent. In fact, don't even make contact with any sellers without an agent at your side.

1.4A WHY DO I NEED AN AGENT, ANYWAY?

For one, real estate agents do this full-time; it's not something an agent does once every seven or eight years or so, typically the life cycle of owning a particular home. Real estate agents know the background of the neighborhood, appreciation, schools, and when homes are over-priced or when a home is a great bargain. Real estate agents are professionals and it doesn't cost you anything to tap into that knowledge.

TELL ME MORE

Real estate agents work on a commission. When a homeowner decides it's time to sell, or is at least thinking about it, they'll contact a good real estate agent who will then prepare a Comparative Market Analysis, or CMA. The CMA is a report that pulls up recent sales in the area. This provides the agent with the data he or she needs to determine how long it will take to sell the home and how much it will sell for.

In return, the agent charges a commission payable when the home actually closes. The amount of the sales commission varies by locale but a 5 percent or 6 percent commission is common. When the agent who lists the home finds a buyer for that property, the agent gets the entire commission. However, when another real estate agent brings a buyer to the deal, the commission is split between both agents. In essence, it is the property owner who pays your real estate agent—you don't. Essentially, it's a free service. Can you think of any other industry where the professional works at no charge to you?

1.4B HOW DO I FIND A GOOD REAL ESTATE AGENT?

Once word gets out that you're thinking about buying a home, you might soon discover there are more than a few agents who suddenly get wind of your intentions. There are a lot of real estate agents, many of them part-time, while a select few are full-time. You want the full-time agent with lots of experience. Top-notch real estate agents bring in lots of business, both from the buyer's and seller's side of the transaction. You want a successful agent, not just a referral from a coworker, family member, or friend.

TELL ME MORE

Every real estate agent you come across will typically tout how good they are. And that makes a lot of sense because who would advertise they're not really very good and only work part-time? No one, really. So if every agent is "the best," how do you sort through all the marketing? It's really very easy—you look to see how many listings the agent has.

When someone agrees to list a home for sale with an agent, they want the best they can get. That means someone who is experienced with a solid track record. Sure, there are some real estate agents new to the industry who are also very motivated and hungry for business, but you must do everything you can to find the right one to help you find and buy your next home.

Top-level real estate agents have lots of listings. They've built a reputation in the community, and with lots of listings that means a lot of other people have chosen that very same agent. If there are three agents you're considering and two of them have just one active listing while the third has 10, who do you think you should choose? The heavy hitter. The one with the most listings.

1.5 WHEN IS A GOOD TIME TO BUY A HOME?

Have you ever heard a real estate agent say that it's a bad time to buy? I haven't. It's either "The market's hot, buy now before prices go up even further," or "It's a buyer's market right now, make an offer while the deals are good." Come on, agents need to make money, too, right? A good time to buy is when you, and only you, decide that it's right.

TELL ME MORE

When I moved from San Diego, California, to Austin, Texas, I knew I wanted to live in Austin, but I really had no idea about where to live within the area. Austin's a great town with a lot going on, but I knew nothing about the area's traffic, schools, or where the best dry cleaners were. I know that there are plenty of tools out there to help make decisions and there are many relocation experts who can help. But I picked out a house to rent for about a year instead of buying. I wasn't ready to buy. Why? While I knew Austin, I didn't *know* Austin. I couldn't have known certain things without living there. I also knew that if I bought in Austin, I would most likely soon be moving out of that house to the area where I determined I really wanted to live.

It worked out great. Now when I go to work in the mornings, my commute is quick, the kids are in a blue-ribbon school district, and we're close to downtown while in a nice, quiet neighborhood. Lucky me, right? Maybe, but I don't think I would have been so lucky if I had tried to buy a house in a city right off the bat without living there first. Life's like that.

Sometimes just reading a book about something doesn't make it feel real. Living it does. Is there something that tells you, "Wham! Buy a house!"? No, of course not. But perhaps one of the best ways to know if it's a good time to buy or not is the fact that you're even thinking about it in the first place. It's a good time to buy if you're ready, and a bad time to buy if you're not. Don't get pushed into home ownership.

Too many people get caught up in real estate valuations, home price cycles, the number of homes listed, buying in the winter instead of the summer, and so on. While these are all useful considerations, they shouldn't make that much of a difference when all is said and done. Yes, it's easier to buy in the summer and move if you have kids and you want them to start a brand-new school at the beginning of the new school year. Yes, home prices might be a little softer in the wintertime than in the spring or summer because of seasonal demand. And yes, it might be a good time to buy a home because the market is soft and values will certainly appreciate. But don't get caught up in all of that. At least not to the point of paralysis. There is no right answer.

Certainly, these things should be taken into consideration at some point, even more so if you're a real estate investor who studies market trends and buys and sells homes for income. But if you're just looking for your first home, don't get bewildered by such facts.

Buy a home because you want to, rather than for an investment. Buy a home that you can call your own. Begin saving for the future by building equity. But buy from the heart while using your head. Don't buy because some real estate guru told you that you could make millions in real estate. Bookstores and late-night infomercials have enough on real estate investing. If you're reading this book because you want to become a real estate tycoon, you bought the wrong book.

Renting has definite advantages, too. Renting allows you to be more portable. If you move into an apartment only to discover three months later it was a bad decision, you know that you'll soon be out of your lease and you can move on. You might even be able to sublet while you move into another space—that is, if your landlord allows you to do so.

When renting, the maintenance costs go to the landlord, not you. If the hot-water heater breaks down, you call the landlord who will dispatch maintenance and either fix the hot-water heater or install a new one. It didn't cost you anything except maybe a cold shower or two. When you own the home, you also own the water heater and it's you who bears the cost. You're the landlord.

1.6 WHAT'S THE DIFFERENCE BETWEEN BEING PREQUALIFIED AND PREAPPROVED?

Before you get into any agent's car, the first thing you'll be asked is if you've applied for a mortgage and been prequalified or preapproved. Those terms may sound similar, but it's critical that you know the difference. A *prequalification* is typically no more than a conversation with a loan officer who asks about your job, how much you make, and what kind of car payments and so on you might have. If the new house payment is below a certain percentage of your gross income and your total debts (for home, car, student loans, etc.) are under yet another certain percentage of your gross monthly income, then *voilà*, you're prequalified. It used to be that after such a conversation a loan company would issue a prequalification letter stating that, yes, you can afford the house payments. But that's pretty much about it.

If all you want to determine is whether a lender thinks you can afford a particular debt load, then that's probably all you need. But if you're getting serious about all this and are ready to shop for houses, then a prequalification means little. You need to take the next step, which means getting preapproved.

Preapproval verifies all the information you provided. At this point, your credit report is run not merely to verify the amount of total debt but to check whether your credit is up to par for a particular loan request. Your lender will request credit scores along with your report. Mortgage programs today have minimum credit score requirements. In a preapproval, the income you verbally gave to the loan officer is now verified by a third party by reviewing your paycheck stubs or a recent W-2. Your down payment and closing cost funds are verified by reviewing bank or investment statements showing that your required funds are sitting in the bank somewhere just busting to get out.

This is your preapproval. It's nothing more than a verified prequalification, but it's also nothing less than what your real estate agent or home seller wants to see. In fact, in today's real estate market, real estate agents now know not to even drive someone around to look at homes without a preapproval letter in their client's possession.

1.7 WHAT IS THE PREAPPROVAL PROCESS?

The "pre" stuff verifies two critical elements in credit approval: your *ability* and *willingness* to repay a mortgage. Ability and willingness go hand in hand. While you can make enough money to be able to afford to pay back a loan, if you don't have the willingness to do so, then it won't work. And, of course, there are certainly a lot of people out there who may have the willingness to pay someone back, but they just don't have enough money to do so.

By verifying income and the available assets to close on a house, and then reviewing the credit report, these two initial hurdles are overcome. It's no big deal, but documenting your prequalification really is your very first step. Let's examine the process a little more in detail.

TELL ME MORE

First, here's what doesn't happen: Loan applications aren't sent to some loan committee for review. Loan committees went out with leisure suits. Once upon a time, yes, that's how it happened. Potential borrowers would apply for a mortgage and extol their financial virtues; a loan committee, usually meeting once per week, would later discuss the positives and negatives of the applications. A host of old men in black suits, smoking cigars and saying things like "harrumph," would eventually approve or disapprove the loan request.

Today, your loan application is approved or not approved at the very beginning of the process—before it ever gets to an underwriter (the person who physically approves your loan). This process is now fully automated and everything is approved first, before anything is ever verified. It's different from the old days. It used to be document and verify absolutely everything before any approval whatsoever. You could go three to four weeks without really knowing if you were approved. Today, your loan is approved first, then verified later.

Decades ago, the first thing you did was to gather all your documentation—bank statements, tax returns, and paycheck stubs—whatever you could think of. Then you trotted down to your local mortgage company, bank, or savings and loan and met with a loan officer. You completed the loan application with the loan officer, who then detailed the types of documentation needed. Your credit report was also pulled and reviewed. Your debt ratios were calculated to make certain you weren't borrowing more than you—in the lender's eyes—could handle.

If there were any credit problems—say, a late payment on a car last year—the loan officer would ask for an "explanation letter." The credit report would show whether the problem was a pattern or an isolated instance. The explanation letter was a secondary requirement that had to be in the file. Many times the letter simply said, "I forget why it was late," and it would still be okay. The explanation didn't have to convince anyone or be necessarily plausible; it just had to be there.

You'd also have to address any other discrepancies, such as length of time at your current job or a gap of employment. Didn't work because you broke your leg? Provide some medical bills to prove it. Sudden deposits of money in the account? Prove where you got the funds. You needed to show that you didn't borrow the money from somewhere else and make sure it wasn't affecting your debt ratios or perhaps hiding a prior lien on the property.

And that was just from your standpoint. At the same time, an appraisal of the home you were considering buying would be ordered, along with some initial title work. Then a bevy of folks would start mailing stuff to you, explaining this and declaring that, and using words you've never heard before. Then about three weeks later, after all of the required documentation had been gathered, and only then, your complete application would be sent to a loan underwriter for approval. By then it'd been nearly a month and the mortgage company still hadn't looked at your complete application.

Your loan today is electronically submitted to an automated underwriting system. The loan application is electronically submitted to the system, which quickly, as in just a few seconds, issues a response. The response will show whether the loan is eligible for an approval and what items must be provided in order to ensure the final loan is compliant with the guidelines set forth for the loan being applied for.

This process simply means: Verify first, approve last.

1.8 WHAT ARE LOAN CONDITIONS?

When things called "loan conditions" are tagged onto your approval, they mean that your loan is approved "conditionally." For example: "Your loan is approved with these two conditions: Bring your most recent paycheck to closing and provide me with your complete divorce decree to show that you don't pay any child support each month," or "Provide evidence of insurance coverage for the new property."

If you meet the conditions, then your loan is approved and your loan papers are drawn. In all my years of doing loans, I can recall only a few loans going to underwriting without some sort of condition attached. It's almost as if underwriters have to put a condition on a loan just to prove that they actually looked at the file.

But this process can really add to the tension of the mortgage approval process. I know that you got prequalified with your loan officer and she kept nodding her head and smiling at you, saying, "Don't worry, you'll be fine," but until you hear that final word, "Congratulations," you're still waiting. And waiting.

1.9 WHAT ARE AUTOMATED UNDERWRITING SYSTEMS?

Your loan application is entered into a specialized software program that evaluates your entire application, and within a matter of moments your approval is issued. Sound easy? It is, but that doesn't mean you don't have to provide any documentation. You do, but only what the software program says to provide.

Get approved first with an *Automated Underwriting System* (AUS) before you begin the verification process. Instead of "verify first, approve last," you will get approved first and verified last.

TELL ME MORE

If you have excellent credit and a good down payment (anything over 20 percent is generally considered "good"), the approval may only ask for one paycheck stub and last year's W-2. That's pretty much about it. Under the old process you would have provided everything under the sun *just in case* you needed it. In fact, some loan officers used to list the required documentation on the back of their business cards. Some still do. The list of items needed at the time of loan application could be daunting. Paycheck stubs; two years' worth of W-2s; three months' worth of bank statements; two years' worth of tax returns (all schedules); name, phone number, and address of your landlord; a copy of your divorce decree, if applicable; tax returns for your business (for two years, including all schedules); a year-to-date profit and loss statement . . . you get the drill. Now, using an AUS, all the software program does is say, "If you can prove what you said on your loan application, then you can get a mortgage from me."

1.10 WHO USES AUTOMATED UNDERWRITING SYSTEMS?

Every lender and mortgage broker now uses an AUS. Fannie Mae and Freddie Mac (see Chapter 7) both developed their own AUS to help speed up the home-buying process. These programs tell you exactly what you need to do to get into a home. No more documenting this and tracking down that and waiting for that magic phone call. Your approval is issued first, not last. You only need to supply what the program asked for. Government-backed mortgage loans such as VA, FHA, and USDA loans are also submitted electronically for an AUS decision.

1.11 IF AN AUTOMATED UNDERWRITING SYSTEM APPROVES ME, DOES THAT MEAN I GET THE LOAN?

Not yet. There is still an appraisal to be ordered, an inspection to be performed, a title to be searched, and a review to be done of any claims on the property. That's just for starters. But in terms of an AUS, there's still the verification process you need to go through. If you said you made $5,000 per month, then you can bet your lender will want to see a W-2 and a paycheck stub showing your earnings.

In fact, there are actually degrees of approvals using these systems. Loan applicants with little or nothing down and a limited credit history can expect to be asked to provide more documentation than people with a long track record of timely payments and a large down payment. But in any case, you will know ahead of time exactly what to document and what to ignore.

TELL ME MORE

Remember that lenders expect to get paid back, and so they determine your ability and willingness to do so. Secondly, and just as important, they review their collateral—your future home—by ordering an appraisal and reviewing the chain of title on that home.

Your potential new house and the ground it sits on also have to meet some guidelines. One is its value. Is the home worth what you're going to pay for it? Is the price based upon similar properties in the same area? Are there any obvious defects in the property, like a foundation problem or leaky roof, that need repair? That affects the value of the home. And while you may be the best borrower in the world with stratospheric credit scores, if the house is a dump needing repair before you can move in, the deal won't close.

The appraisal reflects the current market value of the home you want to buy. The current market value is, hopefully, the agreed-upon sales price of the home. If you buy a home at $320,000, then an appraisal is performed to justify that value by comparing recent sales of similar homes in your area. Market value is defined by appraisal guidelines, but it is also an art, since no two homes are ever exactly alike.

When an appraisal shows the property value to be lower than the sales price, many times the deal falls through and the buyer begins the search again. This rarely happens, but it's not unheard of.

Another issue regarding the property is determining whether there are any other claims on that property prior to your buying the home. This is done by reviewing a title report, or a history of all previous ownership claims, liens, and interests. If there's any interest other than yours showing up on this report, then those issues will have to be resolved.

A title report shows the chain of ownership in the property going all the way back to, well, all the way back to the first person who legally held ownership. Title reports can show owners in a home over several years, each time listing the owner of the property as well as any other party that might lay claim, such as a lender who holds a mortgage on the property. Each time a home is bought and sold, a new name is added to the title. The buyer is listed as the new owner and the seller signs paperwork releasing all claims against the property.

A title report may also show old liens on the property taken out by the homeowner or any judgments that were attached to someone's home. When a home is transferred from one party to another, all previous owners, liens, and judgments must be released or reassigned before a new loan can be made. Your preapproval only verifies you, not the property.

1.12 WHAT ARE THE BENEFITS OF GETTING PREAPPROVED?

You know before you go. Before you ever start shopping for a home, you should first have your preapproval letter in your hand. Preapprovals speed up the entire home-buying process. You can shop with confidence, knowing that there are no "kinks" in your application, while your agent can look for homes on your behalf knowing that you've already arranged for financing. Even sellers benefit, knowing that they're selling their home to someone who has already applied for, and been approved for, a mortgage. Still, some consumers don't get this step done until after they've found a home. That's a mistake for the obvious reasons, but also a mistake for one not-so-obvious reason.

Let's say there's a home on the market for $200,000 and there are two exact offers that arrived simultaneously. One buyer hasn't seen a lender, while the other one has. One borrower hasn't reviewed his credit report, while the other one has a preapproval letter in hand.

Who do you think will get the house? Still another buyer makes an offer below the asking price but also provides a preapproval letter stating that the loan is ready to close. Do you think a preapproval letter can sweeten an offer? Of course it can. The seller knows there won't be any hitches and knows that she can move into a new home quickly.

1.13 WHAT ARE ALL THESE TERMS?

Buying a home brings in another tyrant: terminology. You'll hear terms like PMI, LTV, FICO, title exam, survey, abstract of title, and so on. Sheesh. The glossary at the end of this book is thorough, so if there's a word you don't understand, look it up and memorize it. Knowing how to speak mortgage lingo can give you the upper hand when negotiating your mortgage rate. When you hear terms you don't understand being used rapid-fire during a loan application, it can intimidate you. But understanding the language can empower you.

TELL ME MORE

A couple has saved up $15,000 to help buy their first house. They go to their bank, sit down with their loan officer, and fill out an application. The husband asks, "I only have $15,000 to put down on a house. How much do I need for everything?" Fair enough question. As the loan officer begins to answer the question, probably taking up about twenty minutes of their time doing so, their eyes glaze over.

Now imagine that same couple walking into another bank one week later and the wife says, "We want to do an 80–15–5 purchase, but are also considering a 90-percent-financed MI. What can you offer us with the least amount of money out of our pocket under your best rate and term on a 30-year conventional?"

First, your loan officer's chin will drop. But after he is mandibly enabled again, he understands that he's not dealing with a couple of idiots but with people who may in fact know more about the loan process than the loan officer himself. Knowing how to talk the talk lets everyone in the loan process know that you're not someone to screw around with, that you're educated about the process, and that you've done more than your share of mortgage homework. Knowing the terminology and knowing who everybody involved in the process is and what they do is also important to you.

1.14 WHO ARE THE KEY PEOPLE IN A TYPICAL LOAN APPROVAL PROCESS?

The key people are the loan officer, loan processor, loan underwriter, inspector, appraiser, closer, and settlement agent.

TELL ME MORE

- ❑ *Loan Officer.* This is the person who helps you complete the mortgage application and acts as a "consultant" when it comes to deciding which program might be best for you. The loan officer is typically your key contact who generally oversees your loan package throughout the process, working up monthly payments, closing costs, and funds required to close. The loan officer might sometimes help the loan processor gather information needed for your file.

- ❑ *Loan Processor.* This person assembles your documentation as it comes in for preparation to go either to the underwriter or straight to order your loan papers. You'll get to know your loan processor fairly well since this person will be collecting your errant paycheck stub or contacting your insurance agent for policy information. Loan officers also keep track of what loan items are in and which items have yet to arrive. Loans don't get processed for underwriting or closing unless all required documents are in the file.

- ❑ *Loan Underwriter.* This person is responsible for ultimately saying "yes" or "no" on a loan file. The underwriter compares loan guidelines with what you have documented in the file. If you say you make $5,000 per month, the loan underwriter verifies that you make that amount by checking your paycheck stubs. Can you afford the house? Are the credit scores in line for a particular program? The underwriter makes sure the loan conforms to loan guidelines. You'll probably never speak to an underwriter, just to the loan officer and loan processor.

❑ *Inspector.* This person makes a visual inspection of your home, looking for building defects or pests such as termites. Inspectors can find problems that need repair before the house can close, such as a cracked foundation or a faulty roof. You should get an inspection before you order the appraisal. If the inspection report comes back showing thousands of dollars worth of needed repairs, then there's no sense in ordering an appraisal if you're not going to buy the house due to its poor condition. Don't pay for an appraisal until your home has passed inspection.

❑ *Appraiser.* This person determines the market value of the home by comparing the sales prices of similar homes in the neighborhood. Appraisers aren't property inspectors, although they may notice something about the house that would affect value. If they see a crack on an inside wall, they might make note of that crack. If they do, then the lender will want to see if there are any problems with the foundation or investigate further for structural defects. They'll measure square footage and take pictures of the house, both inside and out.

❑ *Closer.* In the lender's department, this person reviews the loan and helps prepare the lender's closing documents. The closer forwards those documents to your settlement agent's office, where you will be signing closing papers.

❑ *Settlement Agent.* This person receives specific instructions from the lender explaining what the lender needs to fund the loan. The settlement agent can be called different things in different parts of the country. In some areas only attorneys can close deals, while in some states an escrow agent holds the closing. The settlement agent watches you sign all of your closing documents and verifies that the sale of the home goes according to state laws and the lender's requirements. The settlement agent also verifies that you are who you say you are.

1.15 WHAT IS THE 1003?

First, you apply for a loan. You can do that online, you can mail it in, you can do it over the phone, or you can make the application in person—but that's the very first step. Your loan application is commonly called the 1003 (ten-oh-three), which is in fact Fannie Mae's form number for a mortgage application. Freddie Mac uses the exact same form (Form 65), but I guess Fannie started first, so that's what everyone calls it. Again, it's important that you begin to use some of the lingo. Practice it. Don't say, "I would like to fill out an application for a home loan." Instead say, "Do you want me to complete a 1003?"

The 1003 is a big form. Five pages. More if needed. It has somewhere near 350 boxes or spaces that might pertain to you, and it is divided into ten sections. At the very top you'll see some tiny, tiny writing explaining that Form 1003 should be used with help from the lender (go figure). It also asks whether you're applying for the loan by yourself or with someone else. You're supposed to check those boxes if they apply. Oddly enough, even most loan officers forget this part and don't check either box because the 1003 tells the same story without checking any boxes.

The loan application asks a lot of questions and sometimes uses bizarre language. If you're not sure what the question is, simply leave it blank and ask the lender later on if it applies. Just because the 1003 has lots of boxes to be filled out doesn't mean you have to fill in every one of them. You won't, so don't be intimidated by the application at the very start. Simply complete the stuff you know about.

1.16 WHAT ARE THE TEN SECTIONS OF THE 1003?

There are ten sections to the 1003:

1. Type of Mortgage and Terms of Loan
2. Property Information and Purpose of Loan
3. Borrower Information
4. Employment Information

5. Monthly Income and Combined Housing Expense Information

6. Assets and Liabilities

7. Details of Transaction

8. Declarations

9. Acknowledgement and Agreement

10. Information for Government Monitoring Purposes

1. Type of Mortgage and Terms of Loan

The very first thing the 1003 asks you is what type of mortgage you're applying for, be it a conventional, Federal Housing Administration (FHA), Veterans Administration (VA), or other loan. Many consumers won't know which type they need or if they're eligible for one or more of these types. That's okay. If you haven't decided, just put in the loan type you're more inclined to choose. If you're VA eligible, there will be a tad more paperwork for you and the lender to complete with "VA" stamped all over it. There are also two boxes marked "Agency Case Number" and "Lender Case Number." These boxes are reserved for FHA use and will be filled in by the lender later on. It's really of no significance to you.

This section also has a place for you to choose a fixed rate, an adjustable rate, the term of the loan (how many months or years), the requested loan amount, and, of course, "other." This part of the 1003, like the other sections, can be changed throughout the application process, so if you check that you want a fixed rate and change your mind later, you won't need to complete an entire new application. Just make the changes needed.

2. Property Information and Purpose of Loan

This is the address of the property you want to buy. You can leave it blank if you haven't found a house yet, or you can put in something like "123 Main Street" just to get an address into the system. This section will also ask you if the property is a single-family house or a multiunit property, like a duplex.

There is an area for the legal description of the property. The borrower or lender typically doesn't know this information early on, so you'll probably leave this box blank. A legal description reads something like, "Lot II, Section A, 123 Main Subdivision." Your lender will get this information from the agent, from the title, or from an attorney involved in the transaction. Some AUS programs require a property address to get a preapproval; if this is your case, use a simple "123 Main Street, Anywhere USA."

This section also asks if your request is for a refinance loan, a purchase loan, or even a construction loan. Will you live in the property or is it for a rental? Either way, you must explain in this section if the property you're buying is going to be your primary residence, a vacation or second home, or an investment property.

If you are making an application for a construction loan, there are sections that itemize the land cost and the construction cost, along with final anticipated value. For a refinance, it will ask you when you bought the property, what you paid for it, what existing liens there may be, what improvements you've made, and how much they cost.

The final part of this section asks how you're going to hold title, be it individually or along with someone else, and if you're going to own the property "fee simple" (which is outright ownership of both the land and the home) or "leasehold" (where you may own the home but the land is being leased).

How can you buy a home on someone else's land? Leaseholds can work when the lease period is for an extended time, say, 99 years or so. This sounds odd, but it is not as uncommon as you think in areas where Native American tribes may own land that has been developed with houses, shopping malls, and the like. More than likely this option will never be an issue for you.

3. Borrower Information

This section is about you. It gets into the "meat" of the application and identifies who you are by way of your legal name, your Social Security number, and where you live. This is the most personal part of the application since it's used to check your credit report, address, age, and phone number.

You may be wondering, Who cares how old you are? People have to reach a certain age before they can execute a sales contract. Age information can also help identify a borrower. Someone who is 18 years old shouldn't have credit lines on her credit report that are 20 years old, for example. Sometimes this question sounds like a loan approval question, but the fact is that it is illegal to discriminate in mortgage lending and it is illegal to discriminate based upon how old you are.

This section also asks how many years of school you've had. For the life of me, I've never understood why this question is part of a loan application and I've never been given any good reason. It seems to be a carryover from older loan applications when this information was used to predict future earnings. An underwriter might let the new law school graduate borrow a little more because of the likelihood that that person will have strong earnings potential. But is a person with a GED somehow less creditworthy than someone with a PhD and an MBA? Hardly. But this box is still there on the loan application, so you can fill in that information if you want to, but it really doesn't matter one way or the other. It might mean something if you put in just 12 years of school but claim that you're a doctor or a dentist. Then you will need to further explain how you accomplished such a feat. Otherwise, don't worry about loans not being approved based upon the number of years you've gone to school.

The final section is reserved for the number of your dependents. This box really only applies to VA mortgages that calculate household and residual income numbers, but again it isn't something that is used to approve or deny your loan request.

If you've lived at your current address for less than two years, you'll also be asked to provide a previous address. But that's really about it. No pint of blood or firstborn offspring required. Once completed, this section nails down exactly who you are and where you've lived.

4. Employment Information

Now that we know who you are, we want to make sure you have a job and see how long you've been working and whom you work for, or if you're self-employed. This section asks for your employer's name, address, and phone number. Lenders will contact your employer—either by telephone, by letter, or even by email (as long as the email address can be verified)—asking them to verify how long you've worked there, what your job description is, and how much money you make.

You'll notice there are two separate boxes about your length of employment. One box asks for "Years on this job" and the other asks for "Years employed in this line of work/profession." Lenders look for a minimum of two years in the workforce at the same job as a sign of job stability. They also like to see someone in the same line of work, for the very same reason. If you haven't been at your current job for two years, don't worry, as long as you've done the same or similar line of work somewhere else.

Have you been laid off because of an economic downturn? Document the dates and reasons for the time not worked. If you've been a store manager at your current job for six months, all you need to do is document your previous jobs for at least another 18 months to make up your two-year minimum. There's another box for previous employers, asking for the same contact information along with how much money you made at your old jobs. Finally, you'll be asked about your job title and the type of business you're in and whether you're self-employed.

5. Monthly Income and Combined Housing Expense Information

Easy enough. Now, how much money do you make and how much are you paying for housing (whether it's rent, mortgage, or living payment-free)? Your income is divided into six sections plus the now-famous "other." Here you enter your base salary, commissions or bonuses, income from investments or dividends, overtime earnings, and any rental income you might have from other real estate. Below this section there is an area for you to describe "other" income. This could be anything that's verifiable, such as child support or alimony payments, note income, or lottery winnings.

Then there is another box for your current house payment or rent. Here you put your rent or mortgage payment, plus any monthly property tax, hazard insurance payment, homeowners association dues, or mortgage insurance payment.

6. Assets and Liabilities

This section covers your bank accounts, investment accounts, IRAs, or whatever other financial assets you might have. Don't let this section intimidate you. Just because there's a space for "Life Insurance Net Cash Value" or "Vested Interest in Retirement Fund" doesn't mean that you have to have either of them to get a home loan. You don't. You simply need enough money to close the deal.

The very first box describes your first asset involved in the transaction: your "earnest money" or deposit money that you gave along with your sales contract. If you gave $2,000 as earnest money, that's the first money you've put into the deal. Lenders want to know how much you gave as earnest money and who has it. They'll verify those funds as part of your down payment.

The next four sections are for your bank accounts—checking or savings—and for related account information, such as account numbers and current balances. It's not necessary to complete every single box or to divulge every single account you might have. Typically lenders only care about having enough money to close your deal and less about what your IRA balance is. The only time other balances come into question is if the lender asks for them as a condition of loan approval. These extra funds are called "reserves."

Reserves are best described as money left in various accounts after all the dust has settled, including money for your down payment and closing costs. Reserves can sometimes be a multiple of your new house payment, such as "six months' worth of housing payments," and they must be in accounts free and clear of your transaction. Reserves can also be used to beef up your application if you're on the border of obtaining a loan approval. A lender who is a little squishy on a loan may want to see some other aspects of your financial picture before issuing an approval. Reserves are an important criterion for many loans, but it's up to you to ask the lender if you in fact need to document absolutely everything in your financial portfolio or just enough to close the deal.

This section also asks for other real estate you might own, and there is even an area to list the type and value of your car. I'm serious. Again, this is a holdover from earlier loan applications, but if you leave this section blank, an underwriter might want to know how you get to work and back.

Finally, there's the question of "other" assets. Historically, they might mean expensive artwork or jewelry, but this, too, is an unnecessary question, so don't worry about leaving this box blank.

Next to the Assets is the Liabilities section, where you list your monthly bills. This section is only for items that might show up on your credit report, such as a car loan or credit card bill. It doesn't include such items as your electricity or telephone bills. Don't worry if you can't remember the exact balances or minimum monthly payment required, just give your best estimate. Your lender will fill in the application with correct numbers taken from the credit bureau later on. If you owe child support or alimony, there's a place for that information, too.

7. *Details of Transaction*

This is the most confusing piece of the application, so much so that most borrowers leave it blank for the lender or loan officer to fill in.

In fact, most loan officers don't fill it in and let their computer program do the work for them. This is an overview of your particular deal, showing the sales price of the home, your down payment amount (if any), your closing costs, and any earnest money held anywhere. It then shows how much money you're supposed to bring to the closing table.

Note that this is just an overview and not the final word on loan amount and costs, etc. It's simply a brief snapshot of the transaction. Believe me, you'll get reams of paper on this topic in other documents.

8. Declarations

These are thirteen statements that you check "yes" or "no." For example, "Are there any outstanding judgments against you?" and "Are you a party to a lawsuit?" and so on. Here you'll also declare if you've been bankrupt or had a foreclosure in the past seven years.

Actually, there is no such thing as a seven-year requirement for bankruptcies and foreclosures for conventional or government loans anymore; this is another carryover from older application processes. Nowadays, bankruptcies and foreclosures generally affect loan applications only if they're two to four years old.

9. Acknowledgement and Agreement

This is a long-winded, obviously lawyer-written section where you cross your heart and hope to die that what you put on your application is true, that you agree to have the home secured by a first mortgage or deed of trust, that you won't use the property for illegal purposes, that you didn't lie, and so on. You sign your loan application in this section and date it.

10. Information for Government Monitoring Purposes

This is an optional section that asks about your race, your national origin, and whether you are male or female. This information doesn't make any difference on your loan approval and you don't have to fill it out if you don't want to. However, the government requires, through the Home Mortgage Disclosure Act, or HMDA (hum-duh), that when borrowers opt not to complete this information, then the loan officer meeting with the applicants must make a best guess as to "guy or girl" or "black, white, Pacific Islander," or whatever. It's one of the ways the federal government can monitor the approval rates for various classes and races of borrowers and see if your bank or lender is discriminating based upon race, color, or creed. After all, how does the government know such things if they're not told? Or maybe a certain lender isn't making loans where the community may need them most. For example, the Community Reinvestment Act (CRA) requires lenders to place a certain percentage of their mortgages in specific areas, as required by the federal government.

1.17 WHAT HAPPENS IF THE INFORMATION I PUT ON MY APPLICATION IS WRONG?

One note here, gang. Don't lie on your application. This is serious stuff, which is why the loan application asks you more than once, in different ways, "You're telling the truth, right?"

Falsifying your mortgage application for the purposes of buying a home is no fun. It isn't exactly stealing an extra newspaper from the newsstand. If you get a mortgage under false pretenses, you can go to prison. Prison, folks. This is different from making a mistake on an application, such as claiming to have worked someplace for two and a half years instead of two years and three months. That's a simple mistake. The more serious issue is willfully falsifying documents in order to obtain a loan, such as lying about where you worked or how much money you made. Your lender will check.

On the flip side is the verification of the application. The lender will verify your information using third-party sources. Your loan officer won't be able to take your word for it that you have good credit. Instead your credit report will be reviewed. You make how much each month? Yes, you put it on your application and you swore up and down that you didn't lie about it, but your lender, with your permission, will call or write your employer to verify how much you make.

There are certain types of loans, called "stated loans," that require less documentation, which means that instead of verifying your income with paycheck stubs and W-2s or contacting your employer, the lender will use whatever you put on your application. If you really, really, really want a house, it can be tempting to falsify your income or your assets in order to qualify, but the problem with that is, if you falsify your income to the point you can't afford it, you could soon find yourself in foreclosure. When loans go bad, lenders do a little research on their own and compare what you put on your application to what you reported to the IRS. If there's a big discrepancy, foreclosure won't be your biggest problem.

So we've walked through the application process and at the bottom of the application your loan officer will sign. This is where it starts. Tray tables up, seat belts securely fastened.

1.18 WHAT HAPPENS AFTER I FILL OUT THE 1003?

Lenders follow a strict definition of what is and what is not considered an "application." By definition, an official loan application has a minimum of six components:

Borrower's Name
Monthly Income
Social Security Number
Subject Property Address
Estimate of Property Value
Loan Amount

Why these six? Because once the loan application is deemed "official," it triggers a host of loan disclosures the lender must provide. For example, if you submit an application but haven't picked out a property, then there is no subject property address, hence no mandated disclosures.

Within three days of an official application, your lender is required by federal mandate to send you a Loan Estimate, a three-page form providing you details about the loan you've requested and which includes potential closing costs you will encounter, property taxes and insurance, a monthly payment, interest rate on the loan, as well as the annual percentage rate, or APR.

It's important to note, these are just estimates. The interest rate listed on the Loan Estimate can change until you lock in your rate. Closing costs may also vary. This document simply provides you with an idea of what you can expect.

Should you decide to move forward, your application will be entered into an AUS for approval. Your approval will come back with your conditions and your loan officer will contact you, telling you what you need to do to complete your approval.

1.19 ARE ONLINE APPLICATIONS THE SAME AS THE FIVE-PAGE 1003?

Essentially, they are the same, but online applications are typically more user-friendly and don't take as long to complete because they will only ask for the information required to approve your loan. There are fewer boxes to complete. And the online application is also a little faster than a handwritten application.

TELL ME MORE

When you go to a lender's website to complete an application for a home loan, your file is digitized in a format that everyone in the lending industry can read. Once you complete an online application, your loan officer is sent an email notification that your file is ready.

The loan officer will either click on the link supplied in the email or log onto a website and download all new loan applications. Mortgage companies have different software programs called loan origination systems (LOS) that take your digital loan application and "drop" your information into the proper boxes to form a brand-new loan application on paper. Your file will be stored on the loan officer's and loan processor's computer while it is being processed and updated/changed as needed. When the file is ready to be reviewed by the underwriter, it is usually your electronic application (not the "paper file") that will be sent, again via secure email, to the underwriter for review.

The underwriter will approve the loan, then send the file to the closing department, which will compile your loan documents for you to sign at closing. Your final papers are again sent via email to the person handling your closing, and it's typically only at this stage that your entire loan application is printed, awaiting your signature.

In fact, your loan will most likely be converted to a digital file even if you completed a handwritten application; loan officers do just that when they enter applications into their LOS. Few lenders these days even accept a "hard" file from a loan officer and ask that the loan officer transmit files to them digitally.

Before files were digitized, a loan officer would keep a copy of the loan papers, a copy would be sent to the underwriter, and a copy would be sent to the lender's storage office (lenders must keep loan applications at least three years before they destroy them). Meanwhile, the "original" file would be sent to the person handling your closing for your signatures. Now that loan files are digitized, I guess you could say the mortgage industry has become more "green" than it used to be by printing fewer copies!

1.20 WHAT HAPPENS AFTER I MAKE AN OFFER FOR A HOUSE?

Right after your contract is accepted, you will order an inspection of the property. An inspector crawls throughout your house looking for problems in it. Is there termite damage? Is the roof in good shape? Do the faucets leak? Inspectors will even run the dishwasher to make sure it works okay.

TELL ME MORE

Upon a satisfactory inspection report, your lender will order an appraisal. Notice that the inspection and the appraisal are two entirely different things, although some people get them confused. An inspection looks for problems with the house. An appraisal, on the other hand, is a determination of the value of the home based on a comparison of similar homes in your area that have sold recently, typically within the previous 12 months.

While appraisers may indeed note the condition of the house as good or average, they don't inspect it for defects, as an inspector does.

At the same time, your title is researched and a report is prepared. Your title report reflects all previous owners of the property as well as anyone else who might have had an interest in the home, such as a lender issuing a mortgage or a contractor who placed a lien on the home during a remodeling stage. The purpose of this research is to make sure there are no other previous owners who at some point might lay claim to your property after you close on your house. For example, you don't want some long-lost heir to the house who fifty years ago never signed anything authorizing transfer of the property. Or what if there is an unsatisfied judgment on record that has never been paid? All previous liens or claims against the property have to be accounted for and properly released. When this is done, the title company will issue a title insurance policy protecting the lender and others against any previous claims, recorded or unrecorded.

Once your appraisal and title work are done, your loan then gets sent to the underwriter, who reviews all the documentation and authorizes your loan papers to be printed. Your papers are sent to the person assigned to hold your closing, at which point you show up, sign, and close your deal.

CHAPTER 2

How to Know How Much Home to Buy

Knowing how much home to buy is just as important to you as it will be to the lender. Lenders have a comfort range of how much your house payments can be, based upon current interest rates and the amount of money you want to borrow. On the other hand, what is important to you simply might be what you feel comfortable paying every month.

2.1 HOW DO I KNOW HOW MUCH I CAN BORROW?

That depends on a variety of factors, but the most common answer is that your debt ratios are in line with lending guidelines. But it may also be more than that. It may just be the amount that you feel comfortable with. Often when I've prequalified clients, typically first-time home buyers, they're surprised at how much money a lender will lend to them. "Oh gosh, no. I don't want that much money!"

Still others are disappointed that they can't borrow more than the lender feels comfortable with, using the very same loan parameters. What's good for one borrower may not be good for another.

Different mortgage programs can have different lending guidelines, but for the most part these programs decide how much you can borrow based upon debt ratios. It used to be that debt ratios were relatively strict. If a ratio were above 41, for example, the buyer would either have to borrow less or find a cheaper house.

2.2 WHAT ARE DEBT RATIOS?

This is the most significant concept in lending today. And maybe the most misunderstood as well. Consumers are told time and time again about their "debt ratios." They hear mystical numbers tossed around, like 28 percent and 41 percent "back end" (note that every lender has different debt ratios).

Debt ratios are a percentage of debt compared to income. If you have a debt ratio of 10, then your bills represent 10 percent of your gross monthly income. Over the years, lenders have relied on historical data to set guidelines that tell them which particular ratio allows the lender to make the biggest loan to someone while at the same time making it a "safe" loan for the consumer, meaning the lender won't have to foreclose on the house due to nonpayment.

TELL ME MORE

A lender is in the lending business, right? If lenders can make the biggest loan to an individual, they probably would. After all, there's a big difference between collecting the interest payments on a $10,000 auto loan and a $200,000 mortgage. So it behooves the lender to make larger loans in order to collect larger interest payments. But the lender has to be careful not to lend too much money. Sure, making a $200,000 mortgage loan yields a greater return to a lender than a $100,000 loan. But what if the higher loan made the monthly payments too high and the borrower fell behind on the mortgage?

The lender has to find a balance between making the largest loan possible and at the same time feeling comfortable about getting repaid in a timely manner. That's where ratios come into play. Instead of evaluating each and every loan application individually, lenders have determined that loans with certain debt ratios are less likely to go into default than higher debt ratios. Historically speaking, that is.

2.3 HOW DO I CALCULATE MY DEBT RATIOS?

Debt ratios are two numbers expressed as a percentage of your gross monthly income. The first debt ratio is called your *housing ratio* because it only uses your house payment (which includes your monthly tax and insurance payment) for the ratio. This ratio is often also called your "front end." The second ratio is your housing ratio plus any other debt listed on your credit report, divided by your gross monthly income. This is sometimes called the "back end" ratio or *total debt ratio*.

Common front and back ratios on conventional loans with 5 percent down are 28 percent and 36 percent, respectively. Take your gross monthly income and multiply that number by 28 percent, then use the "cost per thousand" chart in the Appendix at the back of the book to find what a lender would consider a comfortable house payment.

TELL ME MORE

For example, your gross monthly income is $5,000. Remember, this is your gross income. Income before all your taxes and withholding are deducted. Let's say that the typical housing ratio is 28 percent, historically a common housing ratio for borrowers with 5 percent down. So 28 percent of $5,000 is $1,400.

Included in that $1,400 is your monthly hazard insurance bill of $75 and your monthly tax payment of $125. Also note that if you put less than 20 percent down you'll need a private mortgage insurance premium as well, which might be $85. By subtracting these amounts from your "allowable" $1,400, you're left with $1,115 for your principal and interest payment. For a 30-year fixed payment of $1,115 and a note rate of 7 percent, the loan amount calculates to about $168,000. You're prequalified to borrow $168,000. Give or take. Again, this is your front-end or housing ratio.

Note that this has nothing to do with the sales price of your new home but only pertains to how much you're going to be able to borrow. If you have a $168,000 loan amount, that doesn't mean you have a $168,000 sales price. You can have a million-dollar home with just a $168,000 loan amount, as long as you have $832,000 in down payment, right?

The second ratio, or back-end ratio, is your total debt ratio. It includes mostly those items that would show up on your credit report, such as automobile loans, minimum credit card payments, student loans, and the like. Other things you pay for but that are not included in your ratios are your electricity, telephone, and food expenses.

If you had a car payment of $400 and student loan payments total-ing $250, then in this example your ratios would be $1,400 + $400 + $250 = $2,050. Divide that by your gross income of $5,000 and your back-end ratio is 0.41, or 41 percent. Your overall ratios would be 28/41.

2.4 HOW MUCH DO DEBT RATIOS AFFECT HOW MUCH I CAN BORROW?

There are debt ratio guidelines for almost every loan program, but they're only guidelines, not hard-and-fast rules. Different loan pro-grams have different ratio rules. Even the same loan program can have different ratios depending on the amount of the down payment. In fact, throw those "rules" out the window, because that's not how it's done any longer. Okay, maybe some rookie loan officers or the otherwise uninformed adhere strictly to the guidelines, but it is not the practice of the industry as a whole. Knowing how much home to buy can be more of a comfort factor than anything else.

TELL ME MORE

Don't make the mistake of "preapproving" yourself before you talk to a lender. If you've read or heard that a house payment needs to be one-third of your gross monthly income, don't start the process by looking at homes that fall into that price range. If you have no idea whatsoever of how to get a comfortable debt ratio, you should start out by comparing it to what you're paying now.

If your rent payment is $1,500 per month and you feel comfort-able paying it, then certainly start with that number. If you've strug-gled with paying $1,500 every month, then perhaps you need to reduce that debt load to something that doesn't make you sweat each time you write the mortgage check. On the other hand, you might be paying $1,500 per month in rent but feel as if you can comfortably pay $3,000 per month in house payments. If you feel good about that number, then by all means, start from there.

One note of caution, though: Lenders have a term called *payment shock,* which is the percentage difference between what you're paying now and what your new payment would be. Most loan programs don't have a payment shock provision, but for those that do, a com-mon percentage increase is 150 percent. For example, if you're used to paying $1,500, then your maximum payment shock amount would be 150 percent of $1,500, or $2,250. Even though you may feel comfortable paying twice what you're paying now, payment shock guidelines suggest that would be a risk.

Payment shock is an underwriting guideline. For loans that do have a payment shock provision, there is a definite shock percentage listed in the loan guidelines. To exceed the shock guideline, typically the consumer has to get a loan exception. Loans that do have a payment shock provision usually consider it only when evaluating a loan that's teetering on loan approval.

If you have absolutely no idea what your house payment should be, then you should be talking to your lender. Ask the lender to qualify you, based upon debt ratios, for a home loan. The lender will take your information and—using current interest rates, hazard insurance premiums, and property taxes—come up with your allowable loan amount. But whatever you do, don't "decline" your own loan application by not applying for what you really want. Too often people haven't made an offer on their "dream home" simply because they figured their debt ratios to be 35 rather than 33.

After taking one loan application from a woman buying her first home, I could tell before I submitted the loan that her debt ratios were too high. How high? Her back-end ratio was 55 percent. She was biting off more than she could chew; her loan amount was $250,000. I put the loan onto the system and within thirty seconds got my result: caution. But the difference lies in what happens next.

In the recent past, borrowers would sit down with their loan officer and the loan officer would run some numbers and "tell" them what they could buy. Instead, I ran different scenarios through the computer, each time gradually reducing the loan amount and her debt ratio. After about five tries, I got her approval of $230,000 and yet her debt ratios were in the high 40s.

Just a few short years ago, she would have never even gotten to the application stage because of debt ratios. Are her ratios high? Probably so, but she felt comfortable paying them, and had a good down payment and excellent credit history.

2.5 HOW CAN LENDERS APPROVE PEOPLE WITH HIGH DEBT RATIOS?

Not all of them do every time. The new sheriff in town is an Automated Underwriting System (AUS). Whereas debt ratios are used to test a historical "affordability" model, an AUS evaluates the complete picture all at once.

It used to be that if your ratios were above 38 on many loan programs, a lender might ask that you buy a smaller home or borrow less money. That's because, actuarially speaking, higher debt ratios point to a greater likelihood of default. However, with the fine-tuning of Automated Underwriting Systems, often these ratios come to mean less and less in terms of qualification. Fannie Mae and Freddie Mac own the most common Automated Underwriting Systems. Ratios aren't disregarded, but they're less of a rule and more of a guideline.

An AUS is nothing more than a sophisticated software program designed for lenders to approve loans faster and make more money. So there is no reason not to submit an application to an AUS at the very beginning of the process. If there are major discrepancies in the file, then sure, identify a potential problem like missing coborrowers or no income, but submit your application nonetheless. It's this information that's used to not only approve the loan but also determine the "degree" of approval.

A degree of approval doesn't mean "almost approved" or "maybe approved." You are approved altogether, with the difference being how much documentation is required as a condition of loan approval. Someone with very high credit scores, a down payment of 20 percent or more, and lots of money lying around will be asked for a lot less documentation than someone with marginal credit, 3 percent down, and high ratios.

TELL ME MORE

First and foremost, AUS programs place a greater consideration on a customer's credit. If your credit score is in the high 700 range, then you can expect your ratios to be relaxed.

The next most important consideration is reserves. *Reserves* are a borrower's assets after closing, and they can include things other than cash in the bank, including stocks, mutual funds, IRAs, and 401(k) accounts. The higher the estimate of your reserve balance after closing, the higher your "affordability index."

The last important consideration is your equity position in the house, or *loan-to-value (LTV) percentage*. If you only put down 5 percent, then don't expect your ratios to go beyond loan guidelines. But if you put 20 percent or more as a down payment, then you may be able to go ahead and borrow a little more than you thought you could.

I recently closed a loan where the primary borrower had a credit score in the 580 range and still got the best rates available. The main factor had to do with the equity in his home. Yes, the credit score could have been higher, but the value of the home was nearly $500,000 and his loan amount was less than half that (a strong equity position). One word of caution, though: Many times what borrowers qualify for exceeds their comfort level. Just because you can borrow with debt ratios in the 60s doesn't mean you should, especially if you can't sleep at night worrying about making the mortgage payments. If, however, you feel confident in your ability to pay, then by all means don't let a ratio guideline thwart your new home search. You may still be able to buy your dream house, even though it seems out of your range.

2.5A HOW TO LOWER YOUR DEBT RATIOS

There are ways to lower your debt ratios in order to help qualify beyond simply borrowing less or coming up with a larger down payment. First, you can adjust your loan term. Or, you can elect to switch from a fixed-rate loan to a hybrid product. Hybrid loans are a form of an adjustable-rate mortgage where there is an initial fixed-rate period before turning into a variable-rate loan that can adjust annually. Hybrid loans have lower start rates. Or, you can decide to pay a discount point and lower the starting rate on your loan. You may also look at paying down current credit obligations, reducing your overall debt ratios. We'll discuss these options in more detail in Chapter 7.

TELL ME MORE

With regard to loan terms, the longer the term, the lower the monthly payment. There are borrowers whose goal is to save on interest when they borrow so they select the shorter loan term. Paying off a loan sooner rather than later saves on long-term interest. Yet the monthly payments are higher due to the shortened term. If debt ratios are too high, look at a longer-term loan. Lenders typically offer terms in five-year increments from 10 to 30 years. If a 15 is too high but long-term interest savings is still your goal, look at a 20-year or a 25-year loan. Many consumers aren't aware of these choices primarily because lenders usually advertise their rates in 15- and 30-year terms.

Hybrids and adjustable-rate programs will have lower starting rates compared to a fixed-rate option; yet because the rate isn't fixed for the term of the loan, the rate in the future can and will vary at times. For example, with a 5/1 hybrid ARM, the rate is fixed for five years before turning into a variable rate that can adjust annually.

2.6 WHY DO LENDERS USE MONTHLY TAX AND INSURANCE PAYMENTS IN DEBT RATIOS?

If you're paying for taxes and insurance in addition to principal and interest, that indeed affects your ability to pay your bills on time.

Your monthly tax and insurance payments are also called *escrow accounts* or *impound accounts*. Each month when you make your house payment, you will also pay 1/12 of your annual tax bill and 1/12 of your annual hazard insurance premium. When your insurance comes due one year from now, your lender will automatically make your insurance payment for you. The same goes for your taxes. When determining your ability to pay your mortgage, lenders use the more realistic number, which is the total payment you actually make. Further, for loans with a monthly mortgage insurance payment, that amount is also factored into the debt ratio calculation as are any monthly homeowner's association fees.

2.6A WHAT IS AN ABILITY TO REPAY?

This is a relatively new term that describes the lender's requirement to determine whether the borrowers on the loan application have the ability to repay not only the new mortgage payment, including taxes and insurance, but also the other, additional monthly credit obligations such as a car payment. The Ability to Repay, or ATR, is mandated by the Consumer Financial Protection Bureau, or CFPB. Should lenders want to protect themselves against future lawsuits as a result of a loan dispute and the lender followed the prescribed guidelines, the lender is protected if the ATR is documented. The ATR on most loan programs represents 43 percent of the borrower's gross monthly income.

2.7 WHY IS ESCROW A REQUIREMENT FOR LOANS WITH LESS THAN 20 PERCENT DOWN?

Loans with less than 20 percent down are at a higher risk of default than those with more than 20 percent down. And from a performance standpoint, loans with escrows don't default as often as those without. Less money down means greater risk to the lender. Some of that risk is offset knowing that the collateral is always insured and that the borrower never falls behind on his property taxes.

TELL ME MORE

At the end of the year or twice a year, whenever your county collects property taxes, your taxes are paid automatically by your lender, who has an escrow account set up for you. So there's no pain when tax time arrives. If your debt ratios are in the 40s or 50s and you put 5 percent down when you bought the house, the property tax bill will be paid—no sweat. It works sort of like a Christmas club for taxes.

The same goes for your hazard insurance premium. When your home insurance premium comes up to renew your policy, the money's already there to pay your insurance agent. You've already saved it up, bit by bit, over the past year.

Lenders spend a lot of time analyzing risk. They don't want to have to make sure you have enough money to pay your taxes on time. If you don't, then tax liens start appearing on your title; ultimately, your home can be sold out from under the lender if your taxes become seriously delinquent. Your lender sleeps better at night when you have an escrow account.

In fact, they sleep so much better that they sometimes "pay" you to take escrow accounts, even if you're not required to have them if you put more than 20 percent down. How's that? In certain parts of the country, when borrowers have more than 20 percent equity in the deal, it's customary for lenders to give them a 1/4 point discount if they elect to take escrow accounts. On the flip side, lenders may charge you 1/4 point if you don't take them. This is sometimes called an "escrow waiver" fee.

When you set up an escrow account, your lender will ask for not more than two months' worth of property taxes to be deposited with them. Federal law requires that there be no more than a couple of months of payments plus fifty bucks to establish the account. This "cushion" is there in case property taxes increase during the course of the year. Some lenders, however, do not require any escrow account to be funded at the closing table and will collect only the first month's payment with no cushion required. This is completely at the discretion of the lender.

Your local appraisal district has its own army of appraisers whose job it is to evaluate property and determine your property tax bill. One word of caution here: If your home is brand new, the property valuation may have been performed prior to your home being built, when it was just raw land with no improvements. If this is the case, and your taxes appear to have been appraised just for lot value, when your tax bill comes due you may be woefully short, because property taxes will indeed be for the improved value, not just raw land.

2.8 IF I HAVE A CHOICE, ARE ESCROWS RIGHT FOR ME?

Escrow accounts are neither good nor bad. Lenders like them. Whether to take them is a different issue, and mostly a matter of personal preference. If you would rather pay your taxes and insurance on your own when due and invest the money elsewhere for the time being, go right ahead. If you feel more content having saved up your property taxes and hazard insurance in tiny chunks, then knock yourself out. It's more a matter of how you view escrows, not what a lender thinks of them.

C H A P T E R 3

Getting Your Finances Together

For purposes of getting a mortgage, your finances come in two forms: your income and your assets. Income is how much money you make, and assets are used for your down payment and closing costs. Now that you've gotten your approval, you'll need to understand how your finances will be viewed and documented by your lender.

3.1 WHAT WILL THE LENDER LOOK FOR WHEN EXAMINING MY ASSETS?

First and foremost, you need to make sure the assets belong to you and you have access to them. Sometimes first-time home buyers share a savings or money market account with their parents. Even though your name might be on the statement, a lender might split that asset between you and your mom.

Let's say you have a checking account with your mom that you used all through college, and now there's about $12,000 in the account that you plan to use for a down payment. If your mom's name is on the account, you may only get credit for $6,000. If this happens, have your mom turn over that account to you by writing a short gift letter stating, "I'm giving all these funds to my wonderful son so he can buy a house." Any asset you list needs to be all yours.

Another consideration may be how "liquid" the asset is. If you have a retirement account worth $50,000 but can't get to it unless you retire, it's not liquid. At least to a point. You can cash in that retirement account or you can leave it alone and let the lender use a partial amount that can be included in your assets for purposes of getting financing. If you're a first-time home buyer, there are provisions that allow you to withdraw funds from an IRA to be used to buy a home. A first-time home buyer is technically defined as not having owned a home in the previous three years.

Some accounts let you cash them in, but only under a penalty. If you can get that same $50,000 for the purpose of buying a home but there's a 10 percent penalty, then the lender might also deduct that 10 percent, which leaves $45,000. Be careful that you understand the tax and penalty implications of tapping retirement accounts by speaking with a good tax accountant or financial planner.

If you don't cash in the account, a lender can still use that asset to help qualify you for a home loan. In this case, the lender will typically use 70 percent of your vested balance to count toward your total assets. If you have $10,000 in a 401(k) or IRA, the lender will count 70 percent of that toward your asset requirement, or $7,000.

In addition to money used for down payments and for closing costs, there is one other asset requirement for most loans: reserves. Reserves are funds that must be present after you close on your purchase, and they are normally expressed as multiples of your new house payment. If your new mortgage payment, including taxes and insurance, is $2,000 and a loan requires two months of reserves, then the lender will verify that two months times $2,000, or $4,000, is present in reserves after all the dust has settled.

Even though you won't have to "cash in" any of your retirement accounts and take any early withdrawal and tax penalties, retirement accounts can be used as reserve assets just by your having them.

3.1A WHAT IS A FINANCIAL GIFT AND WHAT DO I NEED TO DO?

A financial gift (congratulations, by the way) can come from an acceptable source, and the funds are not expected to be paid back. The acceptable source can be from a blood relative, a spouse, a domestic partner, a qualified non-profit or what Fannie Mae describes as someone with a "clearly defined and documented interest in the borrower." But if you do expect a financial gift, you'll need to follow certain guidelines to make sure the lender will count the funds being received. Your entire down payment, along with funds for closing costs, are allowed to be given to you without the need for you to provide documentation of a minimum contribution of your own funds. This is a recent change and the documentation requirements are much less stringent than they used to be.

TELL ME MORE

It used to be that unless the gift was for at least 20 percent of the down payment, the borrowers must be able to document at least 5 percent or $500 of their own funds in the transaction, depending upon the loan program. Today, there are no such minimums. And if the donor wires the gift funds directly to the settlement agent instead of to the borrowers, it will save a lot of paperwork and headache.

If the donor sends the funds directly to the buyer's bank account, the lender will need to document the source of the deposit, which is standard practice for any loan. To avoid this paper trail of where the funds came from and where they went, the donor instead wires the funds to the settlement agent who then lists the financial gift on the final settlement statement.

Recall that the loan application (1003) asks for the source of funds for the transaction. In this case, simply reply, "Gift." You'll then need to document the relationship with the donor, which is easily done with an explanation letter. Your loan officer will walk you through this simple process.

3.2 HOW DO I DOCUMENT MY ASSETS?

To document your assets, the lender typically asks for the three most recent monthly statements or the most recent quarterly or annual statements. These documents will show a pattern of savings and help determine if the asset is viable, or the likelihood of that asset being available in the future to provide income.

Lenders like to see that you've saved up your money to buy a home and not borrowed it from anywhere else. Borrowing money from another source in order to buy a house could mean that someone else has a prior interest, called a *lien,* on the property you're about to buy.

If you make $5,000 per month and your bank statement from last month shows a $30,000 deposit, you can bet the lender will want to know where that $30,000 came from before moving any further in approving your loan. Lenders use three months of statements to help verify there were no large deposits just before buying or, if there were deposits, to be able to explain where they came from. Three months of statements will show an average balance over an extended period and not just a snapshot with a dollar figure.

3.3 HOW DO I DOCUMENT MY INCOME?

That depends on how you're employed and the nature of your job. How you're employed and how you're paid will in fact determine what kind of documentation your lender might ask for. It can also depend upon the degree of approval. This is why it's important to get your approval in the very beginning of the process, so you'll know exactly what you need to do to show income.

If your loan officer is asking you for two years' worth of tax returns, your two most recent W-2s, and all of your bank and retirement savings, ask why all of that stuff is needed. Why go through all that work when you may not need all of it? But understand that this doesn't mean you should do nothing at all before applying for a mortgage. On the contrary, you need to know what to expect to avoid any pitfalls along the way.

Documenting income simply means proving it, such as having it verified by a third party, like your boss. Begin to document your income when you begin thinking about buying a home.

3.4 IF I JUST GOT MY FIRST JOB, HOW CAN I PROVIDE A W-2 FROM LAST YEAR?

Most loan programs will require that you have been employed full-time for the previous two-year period. Why? One of the reasons is to establish a little stability. Yes, you got your first job working in the mall, but will you be doing that job two years from now? Lenders not only look at your current situation but try to predict what your future will look like. They can do that only by looking at your recent past. If you've been employed for less than two years, you may need to wait to get that loan.

That is, unless you're fresh out of school or the armed services. Lenders understand that if you went to college and got your degree, then that shows a little stability; so instead of a two-year work history, you'll need to provide only your transcript or degree, showing when you graduated and who your new employer is.

In the armed services? During peacetime, you have to wait to complete two years of service just as a civilian does. That two-year period gets reduced to as little as 90 days during a war. And if you are deployed somewhere, you're instructed to assign someone a power of attorney to enter into contracts on your behalf. We'll specifically discuss Veterans Administration (VA) loans in Chapter 7.

Do you have a "gap" in your employment history? If that gap is for more than 60 days, you'll need to document the reason. It's okay if you've been laid off; you just need to document that fact. Two years of employment means two years in the workforce.

3.5 WHAT DO YOU MEAN BY "HOW YOU'RE PAID"?

It means how much and how often you're paid. The most common and simplest form of pay is a monthly salary. If you work for someone else, you get a pay stub each pay period. This pay period can vary; it can be weekly, every other week, twice a month, monthly, or whatever you and your employer agree upon. At the beginning of each calendar year, you will receive from your employer your W-2, which shows last year's wages.

TELL ME MORE

When a lender asks you for last year's W-2 and for your most recent pay stubs covering the previous thirty days, the first thing the lender will do is match them up to see if your year-to-date earnings are similar to what you made last year.

For example, if your W-2 shows you made $24,000 last year and your current monthly pay is $2,000, your earnings have just been verified. Your pay stub matches your W-2. Or, if you made $24,000 last year and you're making $2,500 a month this year, it shows that you got a raise. Again, no problem.

Problems can occur when your W-2 indicates you made $24,000 last year, and six months into the new year you can only show $8,000 in income; this raises a red flag. According to your W-2 you made $2,000 per month last year, but your year-to-date pay stubs in June of this year show $8,000, or $1,333 per month. Either you got a pay cut, you were out of work for a period, or you had your hours reduced. That's why your loan officer asks for both your W-2 *and* your most recent pay stub(s).

3.6 WHY DO LENDERS ASK FOR THE MOST RECENT 30-DAY PAY STUBS?

Lenders need to establish, again via third-party verification, your pay frequency. Your pay stub will show your regular earnings during a particular pay period. This is important to correctly calculate gross monthly pay. If you get paid on the fifteenth and thirtieth of the month, your gross regular wages will be the same every month. If you get paid $1,500 on each of those dates, your monthly income is $3,000. This gross pay is used to calculate your debt ratios.

When calculating income, a not-uncommon mistake loan officers make is that they don't realize that some borrowers get paid every other week instead of twice per month. These borrowers will provide their two most recent pay stubs, yet it won't reflect a full month's pay. If you get paid every other week, don't make this mistake; it might hurt your ability to borrow more money.

If you get paid every other week, here's how to calculate your gross monthly income: Take your gross paycheck for one pay period, multiply that by twenty-six weeks (every other week of the year), then divide that amount by 12 (months). If your gross pay is $2,000 every other week, your gross monthly pay isn't $4,000, it's $2,000 × 26 ÷ 12, or $4,333. That's why pay stubs covering the most recent 30-day period are needed—to check both gross pay as well as frequency.

3.7 IF I GET PAID IN CASH, HOW DO I DOCUMENT THAT?

There are two things a lender can do. One is to write a letter to your employer, verifying how much you make and how much you've been paid year to date. The other way is to match up what your application says with your W-2.

If you don't get a W-2 or a pay stub and get paid in cash, you need to make certain that you don't spend any of that money until you deposit it in the bank, establishing a record of regular pay of the same or similar amount. After that, you can pull your money out of an ATM machine. But remember, without pay stubs or W-2s, verifying cash payments is difficult.

3.8 HOW DO I CALCULATE HOURLY WAGES?

If you're paid by the hour, the lender will simply look at your pay stub to see what you get paid each hour and multiply that by the number of hours worked. Remember, a lender wants to see full-time employment to calculate income. If you're just working twenty hours per week, it may not be considered full-time employment, which typically means a minimum of thirty-six hours each week. Easy enough, right?

If you make $15 per hour, multiply that times the number of hours worked—say, 40 hours—to get your weekly pay. Multiply that weekly pay by 52 (weeks in the year) and then divide by 12:

$$\$15 \times 40 \text{ hours} \times 52 \text{ weeks} \div 12 \text{ months} = \$2,600$$

3.9 HOW DO I CALCULATE OVERTIME?

You can include overtime wages in your income, but there are some important facts about overtime that you need to be aware of.

I remember a client who filled out a loan application with me and added his additional overtime income to the income he put on his loan application. His overtime had been rather significant recently: 20-plus hours each and every week for the previous four months. He had gotten some bad advice from someone who told him that by boosting his year-to-date income with extra overtime, he could qualify for a larger loan.

Bad news. A borrower must establish a two-year history of consistent part-time employment in order for those funds to be counted. Sure, there's more money for down payment because of the increased overtime, but it doesn't help to improve debt ratios. Why? Because if the borrower is counting on part-time work to pay the mortgage and then business slows down at the job, guess what? No more part-time work, only potential problems making a house payment.

TELL ME MORE

Overtime pay is verified by reviewing your pay stub showing year-to-date regular earnings and the additional space showing "overtime wages," reviewing last year's W-2, and obtaining written or verbal verification from your employer.

For instance, say you have worked overtime on your job for the past several years. In fact, one of the reasons that you took the job in the first place was that you could get overtime. You always got it, each month, every month. Your hourly wage is $20 an hour, you get paid time-and-a-half for anything above a standard 40-hour work-week, and you average ten extra hours per week. Without the overtime, your gross monthly income, for purposes of calculating ratios, would be $20 per hour times 40 hours, or $800 per week.

$$52 \text{ weeks} \times \$800 = \$41,600 \text{ per year}$$
$$\$41,600 \div 12 \text{ months} = \$3,466 \text{ per month}$$

If you use a 28 front-end housing ratio, that's 28 percent of $3,466, or $970. By subtracting $100 per month for property taxes and $50 per month for hazard insurance, you get $820 available for principal and interest payments. Based upon a 30-year fixed rate of 7 percent and a housing ratio of 28, your qualifying loan amount is around $123,000.

Now let's run the same number with 10 additional hours of time-and-a-half pay. This adds another $300 per week in usable income, or $4,766 each month. Under the same scenario you now qualify for a loan amount closer to $170,000!

Your lender will then review your pay stubs to verify consistent regular and overtime earnings year to date. Your W-2 will also be matched up with your earnings. These numbers won't match up exactly, but they must be similar and regular. If your overtime is spotty and hard to match up, it's likely your lender can't count it.

Your lender will take considerable effort to verify your overtime pay history. This information will also be verified when W-2s from the previous two years are compared with your year-to-date pay stub. Your lender may also write your current employer asking not only how much you were paid over the last two years, but also if there is a likelihood that overtime will continue in the future. Anticipating having overtime wages to pay the bills and then having your hours cut back is no happy feeling.

3.10 HOW ARE BONUSES USED TO FIGURE MY INCOME?

Bonus income is typically averaged over the most recent two-year period, with any year-to-date bonus money added in. Bonus income can vary from person to person, but lenders will take into account whether you have a history of bonus payments and how regular and frequent your payments have been.

Some loan programs try to determine whether the bonus income can be used for debt service. *Debt service* is a fancy way of saying "using the money to pay the bills." This means determining whether you will have bonus money available to you to pay your regular bills every month.

Do you get your bonus once per year or more frequently? If you get an annual bonus, your lender might want to determine whether you use that money to pay bills throughout the year—after all, you're using this income to calculate debt ratios—or whether you will use your bonus to fly to Tahiti.

Annual bonus money is sometimes more difficult to use in a debt ratio than monthly or even quarterly bonus money. Bonus money earned every month or every 90 days can conceivably be viewed as being available to pay regular bills, month in and month out.

The other consideration will be the history of your bonus payments. Just as with overtime pay, lenders might ask for verification of bonus money paid to you, and how much and how often payments were made.

If you get an occasional bonus every few months and nothing in between, don't expect those bonus funds to be used to calculate debt ratios. Instead, the lender will just count your regular wages and use the bonus income as nothing more than something nice to have. Don't plan on being able to count bonus income unless you have a history of receiving bonus checks in similar amounts, on a regular basis, with a likelihood of continuance.

3.11 HOW DO I FIGURE MY INCOME IF IT IS BASED SOLELY ON COMMISSIONS?

Carefully. If you thought lenders scrutinized your bonus income, they'll research your employment history even more than normal if you work on straight commission. They'll also examine your income tax returns to see if you have additional business expenses. Commissioned income is typically a percentage of gross sales paid to the salesperson. If sales are fantastic one month, you're a millionaire. If they're flat the next month, you're waiting for the month that follows. Commissioned folk have all heard the expression "fried chicken one month, feathers the next," meaning, of course, that one month you're living large but the next month you're living not so large.

TELL ME MORE

Commissioned income can fluctuate. One reason may be the type of product you're selling. If you get commission on back-to-school supplies, you may have a huge August and September, but your November numbers won't be as strong. Are you a real estate agent? All things being equal, spring and summer show more home sales than fall or winter. Ski boats? Bathing suits? You get the picture.

Commissioned income can be seasonal. If you have seasonal commissioned income, your lender will typically use your income from the previous two years, as verified by your income tax returns and W-2 statements, along with your year-to-date pay stubs, and then take a monthly average to calculate monthly income.

For instance, two years ago you made $55,000; last year you made $62,000; and six months into the current year you made

$40,000. How do you calculate your gross monthly income? Add $55,000, $62,000, and $40,000 to get $157,000, then divide by the number of months it took to make that, which is 30 months. Divide $157,000 by 30 and you get $5,233 per month. This is the amount your lender will use to calculate your ratios.

People who earn seasonal commissioned income are at a slight disadvantage when compared to those who earn nonseasonal commissions. Seasonal commissions need to be stretched over a longer period than monthly income. Why? If seasonal commissions come in big chunks, the borrower needs to manage that money better than someone who gets paid a similar amount every month. No "paycheck to paycheck" living here. The big check needs to go into the bank and be saved to pay future bills until the next big commission arrives.

If you haven't figured this out already, I'll lay it out for you. Are you expecting a big bonus or commission check in the near future? Did you just land a big sale but won't get paid on it for a couple of months? If this is the case, then wait to apply for your mortgage loan until your big commission is actually paid to you. A large increase in income will help your monthly average considerably. If you can wait, do so.

For nonseasonal jobs such as insurance, telephone sales, or advertising—jobs that pay a commission based upon regular sales of a product or service—lenders have an easier time averaging such income because the amounts are similar and come regularly. But note that lenders don't have a formal classification of "seasonal" and "nonseasonal" jobs. For them, it's the difference in how income is calculated and whether your commission or bonus can be used to pay the bills each and every month, and on time. Nonseasonal commissions are calculated the very same way as seasonal commissions, using a two-year plus year-to-date average.

3.12 HOW DO I CALCULATE MY PAY IF I HAVE BOTH A SALARY AND A BONUS OR A COMMISSION?

Some jobs have a base salary plus commission. Or a base salary plus a bonus. In both cases, the lender will begin by adding your commission average to your base pay. If you don't have a two-year history of commissions, then don't expect the lender to use them. Or if you got a bonus last year but not this year, then the lender won't assume any future bonuses.

There is another threshold for those with salary-plus-commission jobs. Lenders don't consider you a "commissioned" employee if your gross commissions make up no more than 25 percent of your earnings. That is important when it comes to documenting your income.

3.13 IF I CAN DEDUCT A LOT OF EXPENSES FROM MY INCOME TAXES, DOES THAT HELP GROSS MONTHLY INCOME?

Good question. And a common error. Some sales jobs require you to pay certain expenses out of your own pocket. Car payments, gasoline, and automobile maintenance are common expenses, as are taking a business prospect to lunch or taking a client to a football game. Such nonreimbursable expenses, while possibly a tax benefit come tax time, can hurt your gross monthly income. How's that?

Let's say that last month you made $8,000 in commissions. If you had no other expenses, that's the base income your lender will use. However, if you spent $500 for a company vehicle and another $1,000 for business lunches and entertainment, then the lender will deduct those expenses from your gross income. Why? Yes, you made $8,000, but you also claim you had to spend $1,500 to do so. The expenses must be netted from your gross income.

3.14 HOW DO I SHOW EXPENSES ON MY LOAN APPLICATION?

You don't. You show them on your tax returns. It's meaningless to write in any expense amount on a loan application because, for one thing, there's no space for it, and for another, your expenses will fluctuate from month to month.

Some lenders may ask for a year-to-date profit and loss statement prepared by your accountant. This shows gross income less expenses, but all lenders can get expense information from your tax returns. Specifically, federal tax Form 2106. Those who deduct nonreimbursed employee business expenses for income tax reporting use Form 2106. It is here that you deduct your actual expenses from your income, not on your application.

3.15 HOW DO I CALCULATE MY DIVIDEND AND INTEREST INCOME?

Your lender needs to determine if the asset has been around for a couple of years by looking at your tax returns. The lender will then add the two years of interest and dividend income and divide by 24, to get a monthly amount. If you have regular investment dividends that you receive on an annual basis, the lender will review the two most recent tax returns to verify whether the dividend income is consistent.

If you got a $50,000 dividend last year but none the year before, it's unlikely the lender will use it for purposes of determining gross monthly income. For interest income, it's the same question: Is it regular and is it likely to continue? Lenders feel such income is likely to continue if they can project that the asset will still be producing dividends for another three years.

3.15A WHAT IS THE 4506-T AND WHY DO I HAVE TO SIGN IT?

The 4506-T is the number assigned to the IRS form that authorizes a lender to retrieve previous years' income tax transcripts. Lenders do this to compare what is on the loan application with what is reported to the IRS. When there is a discrepancy, usually it's simply an insignificant amount but if the tax transcripts don't match, there will need to be some documentation explaining the difference.

TELL ME MORE

The 4506-T form used to only be required for self-employed borrowers but in recent years lenders use the form with most mortgage applications, regardless of the source of income. The process of requesting and obtaining the transcripts from the IRS has been streamlined and what used to take weeks can now take just a couple of days using a third-party tax retrieval service. Otherwise, delays of up to six weeks or more can occur when the request is made directly to the IRS.

On the form, the lender will list which years are being requested. You will see on this form where these years are listed but if the years aren't specified, the form would allow the lender to request as many years as it wants. If the years aren't pointed out, enter the previous two years on your own before signing and returning to the lender.

3.16 HOW DO I CALCULATE MY INCOME IF I OWN MY OWN BUSINESS?

For starters, it's similar to how someone calculates commissioned income when it comes to gross income and expenses. Take your gross income and deduct your expenses, then average for two years. Certain business types that depreciate or deplete any assets shown on the tax returns may have depreciation "added back" into their income for qualification purposes.

For example, certain tax rules allow for businesses to buy office equipment and then depreciate its value either one time or take the depreciation over a few years. Let's say a shoe shop owner paid $50,000 for a new shoe repair machine. That tax year, the owner deducted $10,000 for depreciation, which reduced his income by that same amount. But depreciation isn't a "cash item," like writing checks for supplies or services. It's merely a tax deduction. Lenders know this and allow for depreciation to be "added back" to the shoe shop owner's income when calculating ratios.

TELL ME MORE

Lenders consider you self-employed if you own more than 25 percent of a business. Own 20 percent of a business? You're not self-employed. Own 30 percent? You're self-employed. The first consideration is how your business is structured.

How your business is structured can also affect how your income is calculated. The three basic business structures are sole proprietor, corporation, and partnership.

Sole Proprietor

A *sole proprietor* is just that: a person who alone owns his own company. You don't split the proceeds with anyone else; it's all yours. When you file your income tax returns, you file them as an individual and your business income is entered on page one of Schedule C, the form you use to determine taxable income. Taxable income is your gross income minus your expenses, or your net income.

Let's say that you own a car wash and it does fairly well. Every month those quarters really do add up and you gross nearly $7,500 per month. Don't make the mistake of using this amount as your income for purposes of qualifying. Yes, it's income, but there are also expenses you need to deduct. You buy car wash soap (lots of it), you pay for insurance and maintenance, and you have a hefty water bill. You also pay for some on-site help to manage the car wash and keep it clean. After you pay your help and your bills, you may only have $3,000 left over. This $3,000 is the amount lenders will use to approve your loan.

Corporation

If your company is a *corporation*, you have one set of tax returns for yourself and another for your corporation. For review, your lender might ask for both sets of returns and all schedules. What would a lender look for? For one thing, to see whether your company is making any money. Heavy losses for the previous two years will make a lender look extra hard at your application. However, if you have a strong credit profile with high scores and low ratios, your lender may ask for nothing more than the first two pages of your personal tax returns and leave everything else alone.

Partnership

A *partnership* means you're in business with one or more other people and you split all the net income based upon your percentage of ownership. If you own 30 percent of a partnership and the partnership makes $100,000 after expenses, you'll get 30 percent of $100,000, or $30,000. A lender may also ask for partnership tax returns, but again that may depend on the relative strength of your loan file.

3.17 HOW DO LENDERS DETERMINE WHETHER MY BUSINESS INCOME WILL HAVE A LIKELIHOOD OF CONTINUANCE?

Well, the lender doesn't have a crystal ball, but the process is very much similar to someone who receives commission or bonus income. First and foremost, the income must have at least a two-year history. This history is documented with filed and signed federal income tax forms from the previous two years. This also means the borrower must have been self-employed for at least two years. This is often documented with a business license, but most lenders will accept the two years of returns.

The lender will then add the net business income from the past two years and divide by 24 (months) to arrive at a monthly amount used for qualifying. The lender wants to see consistent, year-over-year numbers, not wild swings.

TELL ME MORE

For example, say an electrician decides to go out on her own and has been in business for nearly five years. Her income after expenses last year was $78,000 while the income from the year before was $65,000. The lender adds the two together, then divides by 24 and arrives at $5,958 per month. The lender also sees that the year-over-year income is increasing and the numbers are relatively constant.

On the other hand, should the years be reversed, the lender might consider the income to be declining and may wonder if there is a problem with the business. That's a decrease that might concern an underwriter and will likely pose a few questions, primarily, "Why the decline in income?" A proper response would be to explain the dip and that it's not likely to continue. If there were such a question, an underwriter might ask to go back another year to look at income from three years ago to establish a pattern. If the income from three years ago is relatively consistent with the second year and not the income from last year, the underwriter will likely feel comfortable the dip was in fact a one-time-only event.

Lenders use this consistency to establish the likelihood that the income will continue into the future, most often conjecturing whether similar income will be found three years from now. Because they can only surmise, using recent years' returns fulfills this guideline.

There are lenders who waive this two-year requirement and use only the most recent year if the individual is considered by the lender as a licensed professional such as a doctor, dentist, or lawyer. This option is completely up to the individual lender.

Down Payments and How They Impact Your Mortgage

Down payments are in essence your very own "earnest money" in the deal. Your down payment tells a lender that you are serious about buying a home and that you're willing to pony up some cash at the beginning to prove it.

4.1 WHAT EXACTLY IS A DOWN PAYMENT?

A *down payment* is your initial money into your purchase. A down payment is one of the risk elements lenders evaluate when making a mortgage loan, and it goes a long way in helping a lender make a loan. The more down payment from the borrower, the more risk a lender might take. The less down payment from the borrower, the less risk a lender might take.

TELL ME MORE

A down payment is calculated as a percentage of the sales price. If your sales price is $100,000 and you put 10 percent down, your down payment would be $10,000. Actually, lenders use the lesser of the sales price or appraised value. If your sales price is $100,000 but your appraisal comes in at $95,000, then your lender bases your application on the $95,000 value. Allowing for a 10 percent down payment of $9,500, your loan amount would then be $85,500. Now you're in a pickle. Since you agreed to pay the seller $100,000, you now have to come up with the difference, or $14,500.

That's why most sales contracts have something in them that says, "This deal is off if the appraisal doesn't come in at or above the sales price." It's worded a little differently than that, I know, but usually if the appraisal doesn't come in, the deal either falls through or the seller reduces the price.

Conversely, if your property appraises at higher than the sales price, lenders will still base your loan amount on the lower of the sales price or appraised value. If the property appraises at $110,000 rather than the sales price of $100,000, lenders won't give you credit for the extra $10,000. After a year they will, when you've owned the home for 12 months or more, but not at the very beginning.

A down payment can come from a variety of sources, but primarily it must come from your very own funds; if given as a gift, it must come from a family member or qualified foundation. It is also your very first equity in your home and is basically whatever it takes to get an approved loan amount. As soon as you take ownership, you've already got some of your own money in the deal. And a down payment can sway an approval one way or the other.

Let's say that you really, really want this house that just came up on the market, but it is just out of your reach from a debt ratio standpoint. If you put 5 percent down and your ratios are above 50, then a lender might not approve your loan. If you put 10 percent or even 20 percent down, a lender will allow other risk elements to relax.

4.2 WHAT ARE THE RISK ELEMENTS?

Risk elements are your gross monthly income compared to your monthly obligations. It's a comparison of your debt ratios and your credit standing, plus the equity in the home. Capacity, credit, and collateral.

If your credit is less than stellar, or if you have some negative items on your credit report, such as late payments or collection accounts, you'll have a harder time qualifying for a regular loan. To offset negative credit, try putting more money down or reducing your debt load. Or simply buy a smaller home. If your debt ratios are too high for a particular loan program, you may still get approved if you have excellent credit. If one of your risk elements needs work, try offsetting it with other risk elements.

4.3 HOW DO I KNOW HOW MUCH TO IMPROVE ANOTHER RISK ELEMENT?

There's no formula. You can figure out what works with a little trial and error. If you apply for a mortgage and want to put 5 percent down and don't get an approval, try the same application with 10 percent down. If that doesn't work, then try 15 percent. While you may not immediately have those funds available, at least you will know how much you're going to need in the future.

If you've saved up 5 percent of your own money but your lender wants 10 percent, start saving for the other 5 percent, get a gift from a relative, or find other funds to make up the difference.

Remember, the method for getting a mortgage is to get approved first, get the document later. There is no sense in getting every bit of your financial data together only to find out that you can't qualify.

4.4 WHAT KINDS OF ACCOUNTS CAN I USE TO FUND THE DOWN PAYMENT?

A down payment must be your very own blood, sweat, and tears. Lenders want your down payment to come from your own savings or checking accounts. Other people can't make it for you, though they can help by giving a gift. Otherwise, it has to come from you. There are programs that require no down payment whatsoever, and loan programs that let you borrow your down payment, but most every loan available will require a down payment of some type.

TELL ME MORE

First and foremost will be the money in your checking or savings accounts. Your lender will typically ask for account statements for the preceding three or more months to verify your funds to close the deal. Why three months? A lender wants to see a pattern or history of an account. If suddenly $20,000 pops into your bank account, the lender wants to know where it came from. Did you borrow it from someone else? Are you obligated to pay it back?

By providing three or more months of statements, you can make it clear to the lender that the funds you've saved came from you and you only. Some home buyers are in fact advised by some loan officers to simply "put some money in the bank and call me back in three months," assuming that the lender won't care where the funds came from, if in fact they've been in an account for that period. Quite true. It's also quite true that lenders can ask for more than three months. They can mostly ask for whatever they want if they think they're having the wool pulled over their eyes.

Your funds can come from your job, a bonus, your regular savings, selling something, or borrowing against an asset. Your paycheck can certify that you're getting a certain amount each month, and you can verify that it's going into a bank account. Same with any bonus or commissioned income. It's documented as you make it.

Some people have assets they can sell for down payment money. Do you have a car you can sell? Artwork? Stocks? The key to selling an asset is that, first, you need to document the transaction, and, second, the object sold must be an appraisable asset.

An *appraisable asset* is an item whose value can be determined by a third-party expert. That car you want to sell? It's an appraisable asset. Its value is independently appraised by a variety of automobile pricing schedules or even classified advertising. Do you have an expensive watch or heirloom jewelry? If the item can be appraised— in this instance by a gemologist or jeweler—and sold, then you can use those funds to buy the house.

Another form of down payment can come from a *pledged asset*, which is typically a stock or investment account that you can borrow against for a down payment. The stocks aren't cashed in; you simply pledge the asset as collateral for down payment funds. If it can't be appraised, the lender may not be able to use those funds for a down payment.

If you can't document where your down payment is coming from, many loans won't allow for that. Lenders want to be absolutely certain that the money you used to buy the house is not borrowed from another source. Borrowing from another source will affect your debt ratios and your collateral. It also affects your equity in the property and increases the risk in the loan. That's why people can't take out cash from their credit cards for down payments. The money's borrowed. Lenders want to see you save your down payment.

4.5 CAN I BORROW AGAINST MY RETIREMENT ACCOUNT?

Sure you can, if your plan allows you to do so. Lenders have allowances to borrow all or part of a down payment from a retirement account, like a 401(k) plan, as long as they get to see the terms of your repayment and they are acceptable to them. Most plans are acceptable to lenders, but typically a lender wants to verify that the loan repayment won't affect your ability to repay other debts, including your new mortgage.

I've personally closed millions in deals where people used their retirement funds to help them buy the home. Another bonus is that even though you now have a 401(k) loan with a new monthly payment, your lender won't count that new payment in with your debt ratios.

Contact your employer or plan administrator and tell them you're getting ready to buy a home and would like to explore borrowing against your 401(k). There is typically a time lag of, say, two to four weeks, or even longer. So if you plan to borrow against your 401(k), start this process early. It's not something that happens overnight.

After you apply for the loan, document that you received the funds and show your lender where those funds are.

There are retirement plans that don't allow for any loan whatsoever, although those are few. Nevertheless, don't assume that it's okay to borrow against your retirement plan. Check into it before you get started.

4.6 CAN MY FAMILY HELP ME OUT WITH A DOWN PAYMENT?

Of course any family member can help you out. If you are one of the chosen few fortunate enough to have relatives who can provide you with money for down payment funds, they are certainly a great source. What a deal, right? No saving, no borrowing, just show up.

These are called, oddly enough, *gift funds*. Recent changes to "gift" requirements allow only immediate family members, churches, government agencies, and labor unions to make gifts to help with down payments and closing costs. Gift funds carry their own rules as well (go figure), but knowing in advance what a lender requires for gifts will help make your closing go a lot smoother.

TELL ME MORE

Most lenders also ask for a *gift affidavit*, a form signed by the givers swearing that the money they're giving you is indeed a gift, not a loan, and is to be used for the purchase of a home. Lenders would like to see that form as well as a paper trail of the gift funds. If Mom and Dad are giving you $10,000, lenders want to see the gift affidavit, sometimes a copy of the check or wire transfer, and a copy of the deposit showing the gift funds being added to your own funds.

Even though you're getting a gift, most loans require that you have additional funds lying around somewhere after the deal is closed. These funds, called *cash reserves*, typically require you to have up to 5 percent of the sales price of the home of your own money in addition to the gift, regardless of whether you use any of your money. If you buy a $75,000 home and get $7,500 as a present from your folks, the lender will want to verify another $3,750 of your funds in an account somewhere.

This requirement for 5 percent of your own funds is waived, however, if your gift represents 20 percent or more of the price of the home. Now that's a deal: getting your down payment in the form of a gift, without mortgage insurance or piggyback financing, and no verification of 5 percent of your own money.

4.7 WHAT DO I DO IF I DON'T HAVE A DOWN PAYMENT SAVED?

There are organizations whose job it is to assist people with their down payments. Many times these are nonprofits dedicated to getting people into their first home. Being a first-time home buyer is usually a requirement, but not always. Down payment assistance programs (DPAPs) will either loan you the money for a down payment and/or closing costs or flat out give it to you. The first place to begin looking for a DPAP is to ask your lender about sources of DPAPs in your area. They can be sponsored by a local city, county, or state organization whose sole job is to help people buy their own home.

4.8 WHAT IS A "SELLER-ASSISTED" DPAP?

Organizations that are not government agencies with their very own nonprofit status also have DPAPs. Recent IRS rulings, however, have made such entities rare, putting most out of business. Be aware of the fact that if the DPAP agency is not a government entity, it may be illegal in the IRS's mind.

TELL ME MORE

When any lender makes a loan that has a DPAP involved, the lender will review the current 501(c)(3) status of the organization to see whether its nonprofit status has been revoked. Organizations ran afoul of IRS rulings, and certain nonprofit agencies were determined to be, in fact, "for profit" enterprises when they would charge a fee to process the transaction.

Sometimes called a "seller-assisted" DPAP, the process worked like this: The sales price of a home would be, say, $200,000, but the buyer wouldn't have any money for a down payment. If the buyer needed 5 percent of the sales price, or $10,000, the seller would raise the price of the home to $210,000, pay the "nonprofit" a small fee of perhaps $500, and send the $10,000 to the nonprofit, which would forward the $10,000 to closing and keep the $500. In this fashion, the seller wasn't technically giving the down payment money directly to the buyer—which mortgage loans prohibit. But, in effect, the seller was doing just that, and the nonprofit kept the $500.

Money for these programs can vary from government bond issues that are established for first-time home buyers to participation fees paid to the DPAP by lenders, builders, or borrowers. Although the guidelines can vary from county to county, they are similar in that you either get the money in the form of a gift with no expectation of payback, a second mortgage placed on your new house with deferred payments, or a second mortgage placed on your home that you pay back only when you sell the home.

Most of the bond programs are offered in city or metropolitan areas, so your mileage may vary. That is to say, loans or gifts will usually be limited to 5 percent of the sales price of the home, but since the programs are locally run, their requirements may differ. They may also require that the borrower have a minimum investment in the property of $1,000 or perhaps 1 percent of the sales price. Many of these programs require that the borrowers enroll in and successfully complete a home-buying and home ownership course, and that they must also be approved for their main mortgage.

But in practice, here's how these programs work: Say you want to buy a $100,000 home and need money for 5 percent down, or $5,000. You make a DPAP application, and the organization will supply you with a gift or a loan that will be used for the down payment. If it's a loan, it will be in the form of a second mortgage and will remain there until you sell the home, refinance, or otherwise retire the loan. The terms for the second mortgage may differ from plan to plan, but the rates are competitive with most other second mortgages. Some require a minimum monthly payment, some defer the payment, and some have no repayment required at all. At the same time, you apply for a standard mortgage with your mortgage lender. Your lender will approve you based on the new mortgage and the DPAP.

4.9 HOW DO I KNOW IF I QUALIFY FOR A DOWN PAYMENT ASSISTANCE PROGRAM?

You have to contact one of these programs and ask. There are no universal guidelines, but most programs expect you to be a first-time home buyer and to take an educational course (some require it, some suggest it). Many ask that you fall into certain income limitations or live in a certain area, while others have no restrictions at all. Certain communities may in fact have more than one DPAP available, run by different organizations. A municipality may have one program while at the same time the county and state can have their own programs. If you don't qualify for one DPAP, find another.

4.10 IS THERE AN IDEAL AMOUNT I SHOULD PUT DOWN ON A HOME?

That depends largely on how much you have, or will have, available. The main issue concerning down payments is the amount you actually put down. Historically, mortgages required that the borrower put down a minimum of 20 percent in order to get a mortgage loan. No 20 percent down? No home. You had to wait.

As you can imagine, this requirement locked many people out of the home ownership loop. Then, in 1934, the federal government, through the Department of Housing and Urban Development, established the Federal Housing Administration, or FHA. Guaranteed by the U.S. government, FHA loans asked for only 3 percent to 5 percent down. These loans became a welcome alternative for the home-buying public. But the private sector still asked for 20 percent down. Or more.

In 1957, a private company called Mortgage Guaranty Insurance Corporation (MGIC) stepped into the fray. If a lender required 20 percent down and the borrowers had only, say, 10 percent down, MGIC would issue an insurance policy, payable to the lender, for the remaining 10 percent should the borrower default on the original loan. If the borrower only had 5 percent down, MGIC would issue a policy for the remaining 15 percent, and so on. This is an insurance policy, paid by the borrowers, to guarantee that, should they default, the lender would get the remaining difference. It only covers the difference between what you put down as your down payment and the required 20 percent down.

Mortgage insurance was a big hit, so naturally other companies joined the party. That's the way it is now. If you put down less than 20 percent, you can expect to pay mortgage insurance. That, more than anything else, can help you decide how much to pay.

4.11 HOW MUCH IS A MORTGAGE INSURANCE POLICY?

Mortgage insurance (MI), also known as *private mortgage insurance* (PMI), is simply another form of insurance. The cost is based on the type of loan program—fixed or adjustable—and the amount of the down payment. It is not insurance to pay off the mortgage in case you die or become disabled. Like any other policy, it can vary based upon a variety of other risk factors. For example, if you were looking for home insurance, your agent might ask you if your house was made of brick or made of straw. Brick houses don't burn like straw ones do and they can't be huffed and puffed and blown down by a storybook character. That's an exaggeration, I know, but the principle is the same. The more risk, the higher the policy. Rates can also be marginally different based upon geography as well.

TELL ME MORE

If you put 5 percent down, there is a greater risk to the mortgage insurance company because they're covering more in case you default. Conversely, if you put 15 percent down, the risk decreases, so the premiums are lower. There are even loan programs with nothing down, but again the insurance premium is higher.

Another risk factor is the type of mortgage loan you select. Insurers are more able to project risk if your mortgage loan payments are fixed throughout the life of the loan. If you have a mortgage where the payments can vary throughout the term, then the insurer may charge more due to that added layer of uncertainty. There are also levels of coverage to the lender that can affect price, as well as whether you pay for your insurance premiums up front or monthly.

To get an idea of how much your mortgage insurance premium would be, an average multiplier for fixed rates can help. For most 30-year fixed-rate loans with 5 percent down, the multiplier is 0.75 percent. For 10 percent down it is 0.49 percent, and with 15 percent down it is 0.29 percent. And for loans with zero down the multiplier can be 1 percent or more.

Simply take the multiplier times your total loan amount and divide by 12 to get a monthly payment amount. If your loan is $100,000, a 0.75 percent multiplier is $100,000 × .0075 = $750. Divide that by 12 and your monthly premium is $62.50. With 10 percent down on the same loan, it's $100,000 × .0049 = $490. Then $490 ÷ 12 = $40.83, which is your monthly payment.

4.12 CAN I DEDUCT MORTGAGE INSURANCE FROM MY INCOME TAXES?

Historically, no. As an insurance policy, mortgage insurance has never been tax deductible as a separate payment—until a recent law was passed making it tax deductible. There are alternatives to mortgage insurance if you have less than 20 percent down, and one of the more common choices is a "piggyback" loan or second mortgage.

A *second mortgage* is just that, a mortgage behind your first mortgage. Remember that mortgage insurance is required if your loan is greater than 80 percent of the sales price. If you only have 10 percent down, you need to cover that other 10 percent. This can be done using mortgage insurance (as described previously), or you can use a second mortgage to cover the difference. This kind of loan structure is often called by its percentages, or an 80–10–10, with 80 percent being the first loan, 10 percent being the second loan, and the last 10 percent being your down payment.

TELL ME MORE

For a $150,000 home using an 80–10–10, your first mortgage will be for 80 percent of the sales price or $120,000, the second mortgage at 10 percent will be $15,000, and then finally there's your very own 10 percent down payment of $15,000.

Rates and terms can vary, but a common comparison looks like this for a $100,000 home: For an 80–10–10, the first mortgage is at $80,000 and the second mortgage is for $10,000. Using a 30-year fixed-rate mortgage at 7 percent for the first mortgage, the payment is $532. Using a 15-year fixed-rate second mortgage at 9 percent on $10,000, the payment is $101, with a total monthly payment of $633.

Still using 10 percent down but with mortgage insurance, your first mortgage is at 90 percent of the sales price, or $90,000. A 30-year fixed-rate mortgage of 7 percent yields a $598 payment. Wow, a lot lower than $633, right? But don't forget your mortgage insurance premium. Using a .0049 multiplier on $90,000 gives you a $36 monthly payment. Now add $36 to $598 and you can compare the two programs. An 80–10–10 loan adds up to $633, while the 10 percent down loan with mortgage insurance yields $634. Hardly a difference, right?

Potential tax deductions are moot for those who do not itemize each year on their income taxes. If you don't itemize, then mortgage insurance deductions won't apply to you. If you do itemize, this example gives you an income tax deduction of $432 at the end of the year. Note that this $432 doesn't come straight off your tax bill; it's deducted from your income before taxes are calculated. It's a deduction from income, not a credit to the IRS. This example is a common one.

The 80–10–10 is the most common piggyback scenario, but another common arrangement requires a little more scrutiny. That's the 80–15–5. It's a similar transaction but with just 5 percent down from you and a 15 percent second mortgage. There are two increases in cost to the consumer for an 80–15–5 not found in the 80–10–10. The first is the mortgage insurance premium itself. With a 30-year fixed at 5 percent down, the mortgage insurance multiplier jumps from 0.49 percent to 0.75 percent on most policies. In addition, some loans increase the interest rate on the first by as much as 14 percent, so your new first payment goes to $538. Your second mortgage payment, again at 9 percent, will be $152, making your total mortgage payments $690.

Using a straight 95 percent mortgage, with 5 percent down and a mortgage insurance multiplier of .0075, your mortgage insurance payment goes to $50. Without the 80–15–5 scenario there is no add-on for the first mortgage rate, so it would stay at 7 percent but based upon a $95,000 loan amount, or $632. Your total payment with one mortgage and with mortgage insurance would then be $682, or $8 less than the 80–15–5 calculation.

It has to be noted that some lenders do not charge a premium on their rate for an 80–15–5 and instead may charge a fee, say 1 percent to 2 percent of the loan amount. It's highly important not just to compare the advantages of mortgage insurance to a piggyback, but to compare the various offerings by different lenders on those programs. The trick with mortgage insurance is that the permanent deductibility is an annual event, meaning it has to get authorized by Congress every year. There is no guarantee the deductibility will continue, but when it does there are two qualifications:

1. Your adjusted gross income can be no greater than $100,000 for full deductibility and up to $109,000 for partial deductibility.
2. The loan must be either on your primary residence or second home and not for investment properties.

One consideration when comparing piggyback mortgages and mortgage insurance is that, as mortgage rates in general rise, the attractiveness of mortgage insurance rises. Mortgage insurance rates are set by a multiplier that never changes. A 0.49 percent multiplier on a conventional loan will always be 0.49, regardless of what rates do. When mortgage rates reach 8 percent or more, it will likely be your best choice to choose a loan with mortgage insurance.

Let's look at an example using a 30-year fixed rate on a $250,000 mortgage and compare various total payments with 10 percent down.

Payment with PMI and 10 Percent Down

Loan Amount $201,000	6.00%	7.00%	8.00%	9.00%
PMI Payment $83.00	$1,205	$1,337	$1,474	$1,617
Total Payment	$1,288	$1,420	$1,557	$1,700

Payment Using 80–10–10

Loan Amount $200,000	6.00%	7.00%	8.00%	9.00%
Loan Amount $25,000	7.50%	8.50%	9.50%	10.50%
Total Payments	$1,374	$1,355	$1,540	$1,725

It used to be that, given a choice, a piggyback loan was hands down the better alternative due to the nondeductibility of mortgage insurance, but no longer.

4.13 CAN I "BORROW" MY MORTGAGE INSURANCE?

Yes, you can, on some policies. You do so by rolling your PMI into your loan. It's another alternative to piggyback mortgages and mortgage insurance, called a *financed premium,* which you should review and compare. This program allows for the borrower to buy a mortgage insurance premium and roll the cost of the premium into the loan amount in lieu of paying a mortgage insurance payment every month. The program came about just a few years ago, but for some reason it's never really gotten off the ground. However, when compared to an 80–10–10 program, it's worth examining further.

TELL ME MORE

Let's look at a typical transaction on a $200,000 home with 10 percent down. With an 80–10–10 program, the first mortgage amount would be for 80 percent of $200,000, or $160,000, with the second mortgage at 10 percent of the sales price, or $20,000.

Using a 30-year fixed rate of 7 percent on the first, and a 15-year rate of 8 percent on the second mortgage, the payments work out to be $1,058 and $189, respectively, for a total payment of $1,247. With 10 percent down and a monthly PMI premium, the mortgage payment at 7 percent on $180,000 would be $1,190, with a mortgage insurance premium of $36, for a total of $1,226.

Now look at paying for mortgage insurance with one premium and rolling that premium into your loan. With 10 percent down, the financed premium cost is around $3,780. Add this number into your principal balance of $180,000 and again use the 7 percent 30-year rate. The new loan amount will be higher, and yes, you're adding to your principal, but now you have one loan at $183,780 and a payment of $1,215 using the same 30-year rate of 7 percent. Two things are happening here. First, the payment is lower than the other two options of 10 percent down with monthly mortgage insurance, and second, the interest on the full $1,215 payment is also tax deductible.

There are some detractors of the program, but really the only drawback is that it adds to your principal balance, and the cost of that $3,780 spread over 30 years gets expensive, adding over $5,000 in additional interest. True, but there are also financed mortgage insurance programs that are refundable when the loan is refinanced. This is such a solid program I'm not certain why it's not more popular. As a matter of fact, I used this very same program to buy my first home in Austin.

4.14 WILL PMI COME OFF MY MORTGAGE AUTOMATICALLY?

If you had to put less than 20 percent down or otherwise had to come up with a PMI payment each month, it's not likely that PMI will be on your conventional loan forever. In fact, federal law requires that PMI be dropped from your loan when your loan automatically goes below 80 percent of the original value of your home. That's a gradual reduction in loan balance made simply by paying the mortgage down. It can take several years for that to happen. But there are other ways you can reach that magical "20 percent" equity position other than with a simple paydown.

As a rule of thumb, most PMI policies will stay on your loan for a minimum of two years before you can do anything; that said, here are some ways to accelerate your equity so you can get PMI off your loan.

TELL ME MORE

The first way is to increase the value of your home by remodeling or making improvements or additions. If you bought a three-bedroom home for $100,000 and a year later added another bath and bedroom, you might very well have increased the value of your home by $15,000 or more—especially if all the other houses in your area are also four-bedroom homes.

Another way to increase your equity position is by appreciation. Have home values increased since you first bought? If you could sell your home for more than what you paid for it, then that increase in appreciation can be used to help remove PMI. Still another way is to simply pay down the mortgage balance by writing a check.

Any combination of any of these methods will also work. Note that, due to seasoning requirements, you won't be able to affect the equity in any manner if it's been less than 12 months since you first bought the house. But if you've had your loan for more than a year, then the next step is up to you. You have to call your lender and ask them to begin the process to drop PMI coverage. You'll have to shell out $300 or so for a brand-new appraisal, but it's worth it if you think you can drop your coverage. If your appraisal comes back and indeed shows that your loan-to-value ratio is less than 80 percent, then your lender will begin the process to drop PMI.

There are various companies that advertise how to get PMI dropped from your loan, and they charge you a fee to disclose all their "secret" ways to drop PMI. Save your money; those secrets were just revealed here.

4.15 WHAT ABOUT "ZERO-MONEY-DOWN" LOANS?

There are two primary zero-money-down loans in today's market-place and they're both government-backed. These two mortgage programs are the VA and USDA options. Both mortgage loan programs do not require a down payment but there are specific qualification guidelines for each loan.

TELL ME MORE

We'll talk more in depth about these two zero-down loan programs in Chapter 7, but for those who qualify for the VA home loan and want to come to the closing with as little cash as possible, the VA loan is the ideal choice. No down payment, low closing costs, and extremely competitive interest rates.

The USDA loan also asks for nothing down but is restricted by zip code and also has income limitations for those who will be living in the property. Both VA and USDA mortgages are government-backed and the lender is compensated for some or all of the loss should a home go into foreclosure.

4.16 WHAT IS THE CONVENTIONAL 97 OR HOMEREADY PROGRAM?

The Conventional 97 is the conventional loan with the closest resem-blance to loans underwritten to Fannie Mae guidelines; it is a mort-gage program introduced by Fannie Mae that requires only a 3 percent down payment, even lower than the 3.5 percent down payment requirement for the FHA loan. This program is now referred to as the HomeReady program. It is still relatively little used but is an excellent option for those seeking to buy and finance a home with as little cash as possible but are not eligible for a VA or USDA loan.

TELL ME MORE

With just 3 percent down, the HomeReady program is very competitive and should be looked at as an option when an FHA loan is a consideration. There is no requirement that the borrowers need to be first-time buyers and the entire amount of the down payment and closing costs can come from a gift, a grant, or cash on hand. Most lenders require the credit score to be no lower than 620 for this program.

The loan program also allows for slightly higher debt-to-income ratios as well, even as high as 50. Mortgage insurance is required but the monthly premium is reduced and lower compared to government-backed programs. There are no income limitations for the borrowers as long as the property is located within an area considered to be in or formerly in a disaster area. In an area where minorities make up 30 percent or more of the population, borrower income is limited to 100 percent of the median income for the area.

4.17 HOW DO I BUY A HOUSE IF I NEED TO SELL MY HOUSE FOR MY DOWN PAYMENT?

Get a temporary loan on your current house, called a *bridge loan,* to cover down payment and closing costs for the new home. More on that below.

It's also common to buy a new house on a "contingency" basis, meaning "I'll buy your house if I'm able to sell the house I'm in now." If the sellers of the property you want to buy have someone who is going to give them cash right now or who doesn't have a contingency clause, then you may lose out. Much depends upon the condition of the local real estate market; in a slow market, the seller may be willing to accept such conditions. In a brisk market, maybe not, unless you ante up the price a bit.

You need to speak with a real estate agent about local market conditions and whether the market is currently accepting contingency offers. But there are ways to buy the new home without having to sell your current one simultaneously.

TELL ME MORE

For example, say you found a house you want to buy that costs $150,000. The house you're in would sell for $130,000 and you have about $30,000 in equity. If you sold your house today, you would pay off your mortgage and walk away with $30,000, less associated selling charges. But you can't sell your home right away. It might take a month or two, or even more. And the house you really, really want has just now come on the market and you don't want to lose it.

First, use your current equity. You can get what is called a bridge loan, which allows you to borrow, temporarily, on your current house in order to buy the new home. These loans "bridge" the gap between the purchase of your new home and the sale of your present one. Your bridge lender, typically your banking institution or credit union, will loan you the money to buy the new house, place a lien on your current one, and expect to be paid off when your home sells.

Next, how much should you borrow using a bridge loan? Since bridge loans are short term and carry a higher rate, borrow as little as possible, usually just enough for down payment and perhaps for closing or moving costs. If your bridge loan was for $10,000, that would be enough for your 5 percent down payment of $7,500 and leave an extra $2,500 for other expenses.

A common strategy is to use a piggyback loan. An 80–15–5 is a good strategy for the $150,000 purchase price in this example, with a first loan of 80 percent ($120,000), a second loan of 15 percent ($22,500), and the 5 percent down payment ($7,500) coming from your bridge loan. This strategy gets you into the home with minimal investment while also avoiding mortgage insurance. When your old home sells, you pay off the old mortgage, the bridge loan, and the new second mortgage you placed on your new home, leaving just the $120,000 first mortgage.

4.18 WILL I HAVE TO QUALIFY WITH TWO MORTGAGES?

You'll have to be able to afford both payments. There's no sense in using this strategy if it's nearly impossible to pay all the mortgages on time. But yes, both mortgages will be counted against you, and a lender won't let you use a bridge if your ratios zoom into the stratosphere.

An alternative would be to rent your current property to either offset or entirely pay for your old mortgage. You'll need to have a 12-month lease agreement signed by your new tenants. But without a renter, if your debt ratios jump from 28 temporarily to 55 or 60, you should still be okay as long as you have good credit. If you're concerned, the first thing you should do is ask your loan officer to send your application through an AUS using both mortgages to qualify you.

Some loan programs make individual allowances for high debt ratios and don't use an AUS. Instead, they look to see if the transaction makes sense. If you're selling your current property, the lender might want to see a copy of the listing agreement showing that your home is in fact on the market and you intend to sell soon.

Do you have solid cash reserves? Are you able to show that you can make these new payments from liquid accounts? Better still, if you can provide a sales contract on the house you're selling, the lender might not count the new mortgage at all. If this is your situation and you need to leverage your current property to buy a new one, then a bridge loan is a good alternative.

CHAPTER 5

Getting Your Credit Together

Credit is the single most important risk element when applying for a mortgage. Information about you and your payment histories is evaluated and logged each and every time you make a credit purchase, apply for credit, or even make a payment. Knowing how credit can both help and harm you when lenders look at your loan application is key.

5.1 WHAT EXACTLY IS CREDIT?

Credit means I'm going to loan you some money and you're going to pay me back. If you pay me back on time, every time, I'll be happy to lend you more money or make a loan the next time you need it.

There are several definitions of credit, but it really boils down to two terms: "ability" and "willingness." *Ability* means that you can afford the monthly payments. *Willingness* means you care about paying the loan back. Ability means that you make $5,000 per month and you can afford a $200 car payment. Willingness means you actually make the payments on time, every time they're due.

TELL ME MORE

One of my clients was a vice president of a publicly traded company, so he made lots of money. He had the "ability" to pay his bills on time. But the "willingness" was not so evident. No, he never cheated

81

anyone out of their money, but he was often late with his payments. As a result, his credit was damaged when it really didn't need to be.

On the opposite side are people who have the "willingness" to pay but not the ability. Yes, John Doe would really, really like to pay the money back for a new castle, but his pocketbook can only afford a two-bedroom condo. Willingness alone is not enough. Nor is ability. It takes both to make for a good credit profile. And it means paying when you've agreed to pay it back, not when you get good and ready.

There's a misconception some people have about paying back money lent to them. "They'll get their money, I never cheated anyone" is not necessarily the same thing as paying back a loan as agreed. Loan agreements of any type always state what the payment will be and when those payments will be made. That's the "due date." The due date can be any set time, not necessarily the first of the month, but there is indeed a specified time when you need to pay. Paying back money "sooner or later" won't cut it.

5.2 HOW WERE CREDIT BUREAUS ESTABLISHED?

In the past, when you wanted to borrow money or open a credit account, you'd sit in front of a banker or department store manager, apply for the credit, and the bank would contact other places where you might have borrowed money before to see if you paid on time. If you did, you probably got the loan. If you didn't, you probably wouldn't get the loan, or if you did get the loan, it would be at a higher interest rate. But this was still a cumbersome process, both for the prospective lender and the borrower. So credit repositories were invented.

A repository, like a library, is a place to store records. A *credit repository* is a place where credit histories are stored. Merchants and banks agree to store consumers' credit patterns in a central place that other merchants and banks can access. Instead of taking a loan application and literally writing to or calling all the listed credit references, lenders now just enter the person's name and Social Security number and pull all the credit information listed in the record bank.

Quicker loan decisions mean more loans can be made. Merchants contribute to these mutually beneficial entities as reporting members of the repository. Other repositories emerged, with the three major ones being Equifax, Experian, and TransUnion.

5.3 WHAT'S IN MY CREDIT REPORT?

It contains a list of companies where you applied for credit, what your credit limits are, and if you've paid on time. And more. There's also quite a bit of personal information. It contains not only your full name, but also any other name or nickname you might have used to apply for credit. If your name is John Q. Public you may have several different ways that your name might be listed. One creditor might have you listed as John Public while another creditor has you as John Quincy Public, or even J. Q. Public. All the various ways you may have applied for credit will show up here along with your Social Security number. Are you a Jr. or Sr.? Name variations will appear as well. Your credit report will also contain where you live now and any previous addresses as listed with creditors, along with your birth date or age and employment information.

In addition, you may find certain public records in your credit report. You won't find your driver's license number or private information, but you might find anything gleaned from public records, such as tax liens or judgments and bankruptcies. Other information found will be who else has looked at your credit report, called an "inquiry," and when they looked at it. If you applied for an automobile loan last year, then you'll see the name of your auto lender here. If you've applied at more than one mortgage company, then you'll see a list of those inquiries, too. Your credit report will list your credit scores as well as which bureau is reporting each score, along with credit scoring comments.

Your credit accounts will show any outstanding balance, when the account was first established, your credit limit, your scheduled monthly payment, and any payment due, along with your payment history.

TELL ME MORE

The payment histories are listed in groups of 30: 30 days, 60 days, and 90 days. A 1 × 30 late payment means that your payment was received 30 days after the due date. A 60-day late payment means that your payment was received 60 days after the due date, and so on.

The payment history will also show how much you borrowed, what your payments are, and how long the account has been open. If the monthly payment on your auto loan is due on the first of the month but you don't make the payment until the fifth of the month, that's not considered late for purposes of credit reporting. If your payment is made past the due date, you might be liable for late payment fees but it won't be reported as late to the credit repositories. It will only be reported if it's more than 30, 60, or 90 days *after* the due date.

If you have a minimum of three credit lines over at least a two-year period and you've made your payments each and every time they're due, then you probably have good credit. If you have those same three credit lines over a two-year period and haven't made your payments on time, or if some have even gone to collection, then you probably have bad credit. If you have no lines of credit or only one or two with little trade history, you have neither good nor bad credit—you don't have any credit.

5.4 WHAT'S NOT IN MY CREDIT REPORT?

The credit report gathers information on who you are and how you pay your bills. It doesn't list anything regarding your race or marital status. If you apply jointly for a mortgage, your marital status might be added to the report but that's because you applied jointly, as husband and wife. (Unmarried partners, of course, do not show up together on the same credit report.) Your credit report won't show debt that's more than seven years old, and it won't show a Chapter 7 bankruptcy if the discharge date is more than 10 years old. If you had a Chapter 13 bankruptcy, it will stay on your report seven years after the Chapter 13 has been filed. You also won't find anything on your credit report about your medical condition, trips to a psychiatrist, or your personal life.

5.5 WHAT'S THE DIFFERENCE BETWEEN A CHAPTER 7 AND A CHAPTER 13?

A Chapter 13 allows for repayment of your obligations over a predetermined period, whereas a Chapter 7 completely wipes out all consumer debt except for taxes and child support. It used to be that you would have a choice as to the type of bankruptcy you'd like, but now there is a "means test" that lets you know if a Chapter 7 is even an option for you.

TELL ME MORE

Recent changes in bankruptcy laws mean you have to "qualify" for a complete discharge of all your debts via the Chapter 7 option. To qualify for a Chapter 7, you need to pass a means test requiring that your income not exceed 80 percent of the median income for your area as defined by the Department of Housing and Urban Development. You can find this information on HUD's website at *www.hud.gov*.

If you pass the income test, then you have a choice between the two forms of bankruptcy. If you make more money than the bankruptcy choice allows for, then you are forced to take the Chapter 13 and take three to five years to pay back your creditors.

For instance, if you have some credit card balances, some collection accounts, and other debts, the court-appointed bankruptcy trustee would add up all those balances and work out a payment plan with the outstanding creditors. This plan would calculate your net income less everyday expenses such as utility bills, automobile transportation, insurance, gasoline, braces . . . whatever. The amount left is what's available each month to settle with your creditors. The trustee will divide that money up between all parties and give them their monthly allotment. You will make monthly payments to your trustee, who will then disperse the funds to your outstanding credit accounts.

5.6 DO LENDERS VIEW A CHAPTER 7 OR A CHAPTER 13 MORE FAVORABLY WHEN REVIEWING A MORTGAGE APPLICATION?

Neither, actually. It might sound a bit surprising, but a lender gives no more and no less credit depending upon the type of bankruptcy filing. At first glance one would think that someone who is trying to pay everyone back would do so by electing the Chapter 13 option instead of a complete debt wipeout of the Chapter 7 type. Instead, lenders who evaluate borrowers with any bankruptcy in their past treat them the very same way and use the discharge date of both bankruptcy types.

If a lender requires that a bankruptcy be discharged before four years have passed, then it doesn't matter if it's a Chapter 7 or a Chapter 13. In fact, if it takes five years to pay off a Chapter 13 and a lender requires four years to elapse before a new loan can be placed, then essentially nine years must pass to meet that particular lending guideline. Five years to pay off the debts in order for the Chapter 13 to be discharged, and four years to wait and reestablish credit. Under a Chapter 7 filing, the discharge date is usually about 60 days or less after the Chapter 7 request.

5.7 WHAT'S THE DIFFERENCE BETWEEN "GOOD" AND "BAD" CREDIT?

Good credit is obtaining credit and using it responsibly. This means keeping your debt load low compared to your available credit and paying back your loans when they're due. Bad credit means doing the opposite. There can be a gray area when it comes to mortgage loans. What's good for one lender may not be good for another. Most loans require that you have, at minimum, two full years of a credit history. If you opened up your first credit card account last month, you will not have established a credit history. Furthermore, at least three trade lines need to be established. There are three basic types of credit that can appear on your credit report: installment accounts, revolving accounts, and real estate accounts.

An *installment account* involves borrowing one lump sum and agreeing to pay back a certain amount each month until the loan is paid off. A car loan is an example of an installment loan. A *revolving account* is a department store account or credit account. You typically have a limit and don't make any payments until you charge something. A *real estate account* is a mortgage secured by real estate.

5.8 HOW DO I ESTABLISH GOOD CREDIT?

By opening up three trade lines for a minimum of two years—the more years the merrier—and making your payments on time, every time. Also, by keeping your balances low on those accounts. There isn't an exact number I can point to, but the generally accepted number is having at least 70 percent of your credit lines available to you. If you have available credit of $10,000 on three credit cards, ideal lines might be $3,000 of money owed and $7,000 unused.

More trade lines? That used to be a no-no if you wanted to have an absolutely sterling credit rating. Keeping the number of active credit accounts to a minimum used to be important, but now it's not as much of an issue as how you manage those accounts. Having eight accounts with zero balances is better than having three accounts with high balances.

Many people's first credit cards are from department stores like Sears or JCPenney. Their credit guidelines, though not designed for people with bad credit histories, are less stringent than other types of credit. There are a couple of reasons for this. First, department store or consumer goods accounts are installment loans backed by hard collateral. If you buy a sofa from a department store on credit and don't make your payments, the store comes and picks up the sofa. Your credit is issued in part on the basis of collateral. Second, most first credit accounts come with a very low credit line. Creditors will wait and see how you pay them back, eventually increasing your credit line based upon good payment history and your ability to pay them back.

5.9 I'VE GOT GREAT CREDIT. HOW DO I KEEP IT THAT WAY?

By doing the very same things that got you the good score in the first place. Keep a few trade lines open, don't max them out, and don't open up new accounts. First-time home buyers can be susceptible to their newfound potential wealth.

TELL ME MORE

A recent college graduate had a couple of credit cards in his name and also owned a car. He needed the car, and credit cards were more convenient for making purchases than writing a check or paying cash. When he checked his credit report (after getting solicitations from several credit companies offering one) he was floored to learn what excellent credit he had. And without even trying! Now that he knew he had great credit he realized that anyone and everyone would open up an account for him.

So that's what he did. He bought a new HDTV with surround sound, a bigger car, and he borrowed money to take his girlfriend on a romantic cruise around the Virgin Islands. Soon he didn't feel comfortable anymore. Soon he was sweating his monthly payments and not sleeping at night. Soon he couldn't even afford to take his girlfriend out as often as he had before. But he was okay, he wasn't late on his payments, he made sure of that. Maybe late once or twice, but not every month. Soon thereafter he decided he wanted to buy his first home and he went to check his credit report. Ouch. His scores had dropped through the floor. He had opened up too many new trade lines, was at his maximum credit limits, and had some late payments. He would have to wait and fix his credit before trying to buy a home. Now he had to concentrate on his credit profile, something he didn't have to concern himself with before he found out what good credit he had.

If you've got great credit, do what you've always been doing and don't change.

5.10 I COSIGNED ON MY BROTHER'S CAR, BUT HE'S MAKING THE PAYMENTS. WILL THIS AFFECT MY CREDIT?

You must realize that while helping out your brother, you also obligated yourself to the car lender. The car payment history will show up on your credit report as if the car belonged to you. If your brother is late, the late payment will show up on your report and will hurt your credit. It doesn't matter if you tell the credit reporting company that it's not your car. It may not be, but it's your obligation.

Anything you cosign for becomes your obligation. Especially a mortgage. If you help someone get a mortgage, then know that the mortgage payment will not just show up on your credit report, but it will also count against your debt ratios. Some lenders won't count that mortgage if you can provide 12 months' worth of canceled checks showing that the person you helped has been making the payments on his or her own without your help. Some lenders, however, won't, especially if the mortgage is new and there's no payment history. While it's a nice thing to do, if you cosign, understand that your credit reputation will be at the mercy of whomever you helped. If they're late, you'll be late.

5.11 WHAT SHOULD I DO FIRST TO IMPROVE MY CREDIT?

Get your credit report as early as you can and review it for accuracy. Although you can get your report from most anyone (according to your junk email every day), go direct to the source at Equifax, Experian, or TransUnion. The Fair and Accurate Credit Transactions Act (FACTA) of 2003 allows consumers to get one free credit report each year, regardless of whether they've been declined, approved, or have even applied for credit. Without knowing what's in your report, you won't know what to work on.

Incorrect information is, unfortunately, not an uncommon finding among credit reports. If you're not the only Bill Smith in Detroit, it's possible that other Bill Smiths have information on your report.

5.12 WHAT HAPPENS IF I FIND A MISTAKE ON MY REPORT?

The credit repositories tell you to challenge the alleged mistake, in writing, and if they can't verify that the entry is correct within 30 days then they must, by law, remove the item. Remember, there are three major credit repositories. If you find a mistake being reported to Equifax, you also need to make sure the same mistake isn't being reported to Experian or TransUnion. The FACTA of 2003 provides that if one mistake is corrected at one repository, that mistake should automatically be corrected at the other remaining repositories. And even then, get confirmation that the other bureaus received the correction. If you find a house, make a down payment, and want to close within 30 days, it's a bad time to find out there's more than one Bill Smith out there.

5.13 CAN'T I WRITE A LETTER EXPLAINING MY SIDE OF THE STORY TO THE CREDIT BUREAUS?

Sure you can. And you have the right to include any explanation you deem fit to be reported along with your credit information. Unfortunately, this type of letter carries little, if any, weight when loans use an internal AUS or credit scoring, which we'll discuss further in Chapter 6. "Explanation letters" on file at the credit agency have nothing to do with a credit score or AUS. The only thing they might be good for is when a lender is really deciding whether to approve your loan and the lender wants something handwritten by you in the file. Otherwise, consumer letters in a credit file don't have much of an impact.

5.14 CAN MY LENDER HELP FIX MISTAKES IN MY CREDIT HISTORY?

The easiest way to correct a mistake might very well be through your lender or mortgage broker, not the credit repository itself. In fact, it's the easiest way. Lenders regularly work with companies that collect credit information and provide reports to the lenders to help them make credit decisions.

TELL ME MORE

Lenders and credit agencies work together each and every day in established business relationships. Lenders are customers of the credit agencies. Credit agencies hire marketing specialists and account representatives to call on lenders and mortgage brokers and solicit their business. One of the services credit companies offer is to correct mistakes on credit reports for lenders. Not many outside of the lending industry know about this, but it's done every day.

One of my clients who was buying a loft noticed that on his credit report a previous lender had mistakenly entered multiple 30-day late payments on his credit account. This mistake was killing his credit. Fortunately, the client had copies of everything he needed to prove his case, including canceled checks and copies of statements. If he had done it the old-fashioned way and mailed his documentation to the credit bureau and waited for 30 days, it would have been too late.

Instead, he provided me with his documentation, which I promptly forwarded to my account representative at the credit company. She verified that, in fact, the credit report was in error. There were no late payments. Within minutes the mistake vanished. Within a day the credit scores were recalculated as if the damaging item never existed. This is hard to duplicate with the bureaucracy of a credit repository.

One big caveat is that the mistake needs to be verified by a third party. Your lender won't be able to fix a mistake on your credit report simply on the basis of a letter from you saying so. If it's a case of mistaken identity, simply comparing the Social Security numbers is enough. If it's a collection account that has been paid but not yet reflected as such on your credit report, then a "paid in full" letter from the creditor or collection agency is enough. Don't expect everyone to take your word, albeit earnest, to correct anything.

5.15 WHAT DO I NEED IN ORDER TO PROVE SOMETHING IS A MISTAKE ON MY CREDIT REPORT?

You'll need to have some data to back up your claims. Otherwise, the information won't leave your report. If you and the creditor have a disagreement and they're sending the credit agencies a past-due bill, get the information that's being reported and provide third-party documentation proving your side. A simple "Did not, did too, did not, did too" won't cut it.

A common problem with such a scenario is that, yes, you might have paid off the past-due balance, but there was a lingering late fee or past-due charge not reflected on the final bill. Many times such small charges won't be reported, or worse, they are ignored by the consumer. When that happens, your credit report reflects a past-due account and your refusal to pay. Credit reports are reports, not people.

5.16 WHAT ABOUT MORTGAGE COMPANIES THAT ADVERTISE "BAD CREDIT, NO CREDIT OKAY"?

There are lenders that specialize in mortgages for people with bad credit, and we'll explore those loans in detail in Chapter 7. Such loans, normally called *subprime loans,* underwrite to different guidelines from a conventional mortgage. So, yes, you can get a mortgage with a bankruptcy discharge as little as one hour ago, but with a larger down payment and higher monthly payments. Typically it's not a situation of "if" someone can get approved for a mortgage, but at what term and cost.

5.17 WHAT ABOUT A COSIGNER?

The best use of a cosigner is with an FHA loan, because they make the most liberal use of the nonoccupant coborrower's income. If you're having a hard time qualifying due to your ratios, get a cosigner and research one of these loans. Cosigners are usually relatives (although they don't have to be in all cases) who agree to pay your mortgage if you default. They also usually don't live with you. This isn't as common as it used to be, primarily because the guidelines for nonoccupant coborrowers (i.e., cosigners who don't live with you) for conventional mortgages have changed significantly over the past decade. It used to be that if someone's credit was shaky he would find a rich uncle somewhere who would agree to pay the mortgage if ever that payment became late. Or a cosigner was recruited because the buyer didn't make enough money to qualify on her own. Soon, lenders raised an obvious question: If the buyer can't qualify on his own to buy this house, why are we making the mortgage in the first place? Good question. Lenders then adopted policies that, while allowing for cosigners, also required the buyer to have debt ratios similar to those of borrowers without a cosigner whatsoever.

Not so with FHA mortgages. These loans still take into account all the qualifying income, regardless of whether it's from the owner-occupant or the nonoccupant coborrowers.

Even more misunderstood is that while cosigners may have excellent credit, that in no way makes up for the buyer's bad credit. I have gotten many calls from potential home buyers saying, "I want to warn you up front that I have terrible credit, but my folks are willing to cosign." While using cosigners still works quite effectively with automobiles and other installment debt, it's not as easy with real estate. Fall behind on the car payment, goodbye car. Fall behind on mortgage payments and hello lawyers, foreclosures, missed housing payments, and so on. Cosigners just don't have the same effect as they once did with regard to credit issues. If you have bad credit and your parents want to cosign for you, ask them instead to buy the house as an investment property, with you living there. Their good credit won't erase your bad.

5.18 CAN A SELLER ASK FOR A COPY OF MY CREDIT REPORT?

Sure they can ask, but that's about all they can do. The only thing a seller needs to know is if you've been qualified for a loan. It's none of their business what type of loan you get or what your rate and terms will be. Sometimes, if a seller thinks that the buyer is getting a mortgage from a subprime mortgage company, the seller suddenly thinks there's a problem and wants to back off from the deal.

This also applies to a seller who wants to see the terms of your loan as a condition of the sale. If you have a subprime loan and the seller notices your interest rate is a couple of percentage points higher than market, the seller might mistakenly assume there's going to be a problem with closing. Keep your credit report and your loan terms to yourself; it's none of the seller's business. Is your agent asking the same thing? Same answer. Tell him or her politely that you got a good deal and you're ready to close. Did your real estate agent refer you to a loan officer? If so, there's most likely a business relationship established there. They've done deals together before and they always talk to one another about their various closings.

Again, your real estate agent has no business nosing around in your loan file. Your mortgage application is a private document between you and the lender. It is both improper and illegal for a loan officer to divulge anything regarding credit or income status from your application. How much money do you make? What business is it of theirs, anyway? Right. None.

5.19 WHAT IS ALTERNATE CREDIT?

Alternate credit in relation to mortgage loans is sometimes called nonstandard credit. These are items you must pay each month but won't appear on your credit report.

Alternate credit accounts might include your telephone bill. You get a telephone bill every month, you pay it on time, and your phone has never been disconnected due to nonpayment. The same goes for your electricity bill or water bill. While such items aren't reported as installment or revolving credit, they can in fact establish your ability and willingness to make consistent payments in a responsible manner.

Certain loans ask for alternate credit if no credit has been established. In those cases, lenders typically want to see two to three of these accounts documented, with copies of monthly statements and copies of canceled checks showing timely payment.

5.20 I HAVE BAD CREDIT AND WAS CONTACTED BY A CREDIT COUNSELING COMPANY THAT WANTS TO HELP REESTABLISH MY CREDIT. CAN THEY DO THAT?

Sure they can. But you need to be careful in choosing the company and also understanding the impact it will have on your overall credit report.

You can find listings of credit counseling services in the telephone book or on the Internet. Many of them are nonprofit organizations that fall under the umbrella term of *credit counselors*. These companies help you sort out your credit problems and put together a program that gets everyone paid back but still gets the creditors off your back without filing for bankruptcy. Don't be fooled into thinking that all of the advertisements hawking credit repair or credit counseling services are the same. They're not. Sometimes you can find a company that claims it can settle all of your bills and get your debts reduced or even eliminated. Sometimes such companies are firms that help you file for bankruptcy. Some are nonprofit, some are not.

TELL ME MORE

A credit counselor will evaluate your current income and debt situation and recommend a budget for you to follow. In the meantime, this company has contacted your creditors and helped arrange a new payment plan for you at reduced rates or at a reduced debt balance. At the end of each month, instead of paying all your money to the various companies to which you owe money, you send the money to the credit counselor, who then takes those funds and disburses them to your creditors under the new terms.

You need to carefully research the credit counselor to make sure they're on the up-and-up and are doing what they say they're going to do. Will they take your money and make the payments on time or will they also be late? If a credit counselor takes your money yet continues to be late on your obligations, they're hurting your credit even more.

In addition, it's critical to understand that a lender can view a credit counselor plan just as harshly as they would a bankruptcy discharge or a Chapter 13 wage earner plan. If a lender sees that you're currently in credit counseling, it will affect your ability to get a mortgage. Even though credit counseling can be a good thing, it also shows the lender that you recently got yourself in financial hot water and aren't out of it yet.

If your bills are getting you down and you want to explore using a credit counselor, then by all means get going with it. Just be a wary consumer and understand the impact it will have on your credit report.

5.21 CAN I ERASE MY OLD CREDIT REPORT COMPLETELY AND START ALL OVER AGAIN?

You can, but creating a new identity can be illegal. Although some companies claim they can establish a brand-new identity for you, nothing can be "erased" from your credit report or from public records. If you have a foreclosure and it's recorded somewhere in a county courthouse, then how can some company wipe that record clean without breaking into the county recorder's office and swiping the record? They can't, of course. No company can erase something that's on your credit report.

Fix mistakes? Sure. Counsel on credit guidance? Happens every day. Help challenge credit entries? There are legitimate means to challenge any credit entry. But there is no such thing as "erasing" and starting all over unless you change your name and Social Security number and begin applying for credit at local department stores for a new revolving account.

TELL ME MORE

But let's say that you do this. Let's say that you find some sleazy company that, for a hefty fee, tells you how you can be a brand-new person. At least in the eyes of a credit bureau. You start all over, ignoring all the old bills attached to the "old" you and focusing on establishing a "new" you. After your new persona gets some accounts established over two or three years you'll begin to see some credit scores pop up. At this stage they're significantly higher than the ones you left behind. So you decide to buy a house and apply for a loan.

If you apply for a mortgage using another identity, you're committing loan fraud. The loan application Form 1003 asks you if you've ever been known by any other name. If you say "yes," they'll want to know that name and look up that person's credit report. Yuck. If you say "no," then you're lying. People go to prison for lying on mortgage applications. I'm not kidding.

5.22 I HAVE GREAT CREDIT, BUT MY SPOUSE HAS TERRIBLE CREDIT. WHAT DO I DO?

If you've got good credit and your spouse has bad credit, there's really no way to "average" your overall credit standing. One way to overcome this problem is to see if you can qualify by yourself and leave your spouse off the loan.

There's a distinction between home ownership and who's responsible for paying the loan back. You can designate almost anyone you choose to have a legal interest in the property and have their names recorded on your title report. Heck, you can have Santa Claus appear on the title of the property as long as you can get him to show up at closing to sign a deed. But that doesn't mean your lender will come after ol' Santa if you can't pay your mortgage. Title ownership, or legal interest in the property, is much different from paying back a home loan. So apply for the loan by yourself and have your spouse listed on the title report.

TELL ME MORE

The trick is being able to qualify for the mortgage while also assuming your spouse's credit obligations. Here's a for-instance.

You met the love of your life, got married, and proceeded to go on with life. Soon after, you found out that your spouse's credit was ruined long before you were married. Even though those credit accounts were opened way before you met, they'll still show up on your joint credit report. After all, if a lender is evaluating your credit application based upon your ability and willingness to repay the home loan, the lender will take your spouse's past and present loan obligations into consideration, paying no attention to whether they were paid on time. For better or worse, right?

A spouse who brings love and happiness into your life may also bring all those late payments to Nordstrom's. You can't erase this information when applying for a home loan together. But you can leave the spouse off the loan application if you can qualify by showing you are able to afford the Nordstrom's bill, even though it wasn't yours before you got married. If you can keep your debt ratios in line with guidelines while at the same time assuming responsibility for your spouse's payments, then you should be able to get a new mortgage loan. You will keep the spouse on title, but not on the note anywhere.

5.23 MY "EX" HAS SCREWED UP MY CREDIT. WHAT DO I DO?

Keep your divorce decree handy so you can show who the judge said was responsible for paying what. Getting divorced is a bad thing. What many people don't realize is that the ex-spouse can mess up your credit report long after the ink is dry on your final divorce decree. I know, I know. The judge said he could have the house and the car and you could have all the credit cards, but if you applied jointly for the house and the car, the lender, quite frankly, couldn't care less about your failed marriage. The lender agreed to make a loan to both of you, whether or not your relationship worked out. If you split up, that doesn't dissolve either person's obligations to pay.

The judge may have the ability to assign credit obligations to either party in such a case, but the judge doesn't have the authority to absolve either of you from paying someone back. Only the lender can do that. Let's say you had bought a house together and your ex-spouse got the house while you signed a piece of paper agreeing to release all interest in the property. Fine. But there's still a mortgage outstanding. Here's where you need to be careful. If your ex is responsible for the mortgage and the car, unless you get off the original loan you may still find late payments on your credit report.

Let's say you give away the home and sign a warranty deed to your former spouse. Unless your ex refinances the loan, the payment history might still appear on your credit report. That's just the way it works. To compound the problem, if you needed both incomes to qualify for the original loan, then your ex may not be able to qualify for a refinance in the first place. In this instance, not only do you need to release all interest in your old home to your ex, you must also have the original loan refinanced to get you off the mortgage completely. The same is true for the car and any other loans you might have obtained together. A divorce decree isn't sent to the credit agency when you get divorced. If you've been divorced, you need to get your ducks in a row and review your credit report long before you apply for a mortgage.

Some loans make allowances for legal assignments as to who's responsible for what, and although those obligations may not be taken off your credit report, any loans still in your name might not be considered. Keep your divorce decree. If you can't find it, get a copy of it. While a divorce decree won't erase joint obligations, for qualification purposes, at least, old credit items might be excluded from your application when it comes time to determine debt ratios.

5.24 HOW WILL LENDERS VIEW OUR CREDIT REPORT IF WE'RE NOT MARRIED?

Your application will be reviewed just like any other. It's a common misconception that unmarried couples can't apply for a mortgage loan together. They certainly can. You don't have to be married to apply for a mortgage. You can apply by yourself or with someone else. Both your credit and all of your coborrower's credit will be reviewed together. All you need to do is complete a loan application, and your joint incomes, bills, and credit profiles will be underwritten regardless. Don't worry about it. Okay, that's easy for me to say, but really, apply for the loan.

5.25 HOW LONG DO I HAVE TO WAIT IN ORDER TO GET APPROVED FOR A MORTGAGE IF I DECLARED BANKRUPTCY IN THE PAST?

You're probably not as bad off as you think. Some lenders ask that your bankruptcy be discharged for two years and still others ask that the discharge be four years old. A common misunderstanding about mortgages and bankruptcies has to do with how long a bankruptcy stays on the credit report. A Chapter 7 bankruptcy, where debts were simply wiped away, will stay on your credit report for 10 years. A Chapter 13 bankruptcy, sometimes called a "wage earner plan," can stay there for up to 10 years, but is usually wiped away seven years after the filing date. But that is only how long that information will stay on the credit report, not how soon after the discharge you can get financing. Furthermore, conventional loans will allow a discharge to be less than two years old under extenuating circumstances.

The waiting periods for FHA and VA loans are two years since the discharge of a Chapter 7 bankruptcy, three years for a USDA loan, and four years for a conventional mortgage. We'll talk more about the differences between these various loan programs in detail in Chapter 7.

I recall a client in Los Angeles who had a bankruptcy discharged about eight months before she applied with me to buy a condo. Unfortunately, she had been flat-out turned down by at least three other mortgage companies before she found my office. Since her bankruptcy was less than two years old, the loan officers she spoke with had incorrectly told her that she would have to wait another year and a half to be eligible for a mortgage loan. However, she had an extenuating circumstance that made it possible, under Fannie Mae guidelines, for a mortgage to be issued to her.

Although she was an attorney, her husband had been the primary wage earner until he unexpectedly passed away. Death to the primary breadwinner can be an exception. We took her loan and put her in her new home within a few weeks.

This case illustrates an exception. Extenuating circumstances don't include getting overextended or having your business fail. In either of those scenarios, there is some control by the borrower.

5.26 I FILED A CHAPTER 13 BANKRUPTCY AND I'M STILL MAKING THE PAYMENTS. CAN I GET A MORTGAGE NOW?

It's possible with an FHA loan. FHA allows for the purchase of a home provided that the monthly payments to the trustee are made on time (so be prepared to provide canceled checks showing timely payment) and you have the permission of the trustee to buy a new home. Why would you need permission? A trustee may wonder why, if you can garner enough money for a down payment and closing costs, you don't use those funds to pay off your Chapter 13 debt. I've not heard of a trustee denying a request like this. I'm sure there are cases where permission is not given, but usually it isn't a problem. However, if you have been late by more than 30 days on one or more of your trustee payments, you can expect some difficulties getting a loan approval. In fact, any late payments during or after a bankruptcy filing or discharge can keep a mortgage out of reach until the derogatory information falls completely off the credit report.

TELL ME MORE

Lenders want to see that those who have experienced a recent bankruptcy have returned to their responsible payment patterns. A bankruptcy is most often the result of a life-changing matter and is not expected to occur again in the future. It's a one-time event that was probably out of the individual's control. When mortgage lenders review a credit report when evaluating a mortgage request, they also want to see no more late payments on any credit account. Even if there is just one payment listed on the credit report as being more than 30 days past the due date, most lenders will turn down the loan request.

Mortgage lenders want to see credit reestablished with no payments more than 30 days past the due dates and have at least three such timely credit accounts on a credit report with at least a two-year history.

Which brings up another question: How can someone get three credit accounts so soon after a bankruptcy? This is often a classic "catch 22" where a mortgage lender will consider a mortgage application just a couple of years after a bankruptcy, but what creditors will issue credit and report it to the credit bureaus so soon after a bankruptcy has been discharged?

The answer is, there are companies who specialize in helping consumers rebuild credit. For those who want to get back into the mortgage game later on, it's important to take advantage of these offerings and be absolutely responsible with them. It won't take long to find such companies because they will find you. If you have a bankruptcy discharge, you will soon see offers to open up a credit account in your mailbox, either secured or unsecured.

A secured credit card is one where the consumer makes a cash deposit to the creditor who holds the funds for a set period while the credit card is being used. The deposit is often the same amount as the original line of credit issued but doesn't have to be. For example, a credit card might have a $500 credit limit but require a $500 deposit. The deposit isn't used to make future monthly payments—you'll still have to make those on time—but in case of default, the deposit is kept.

An unsecured card is one that does not have a deposit as security with just a limited credit line available. Such credit card accounts set the original limit at around $300 or so with reviews of your account every six months. If you've made your payments on or before the due date—not after—the creditor may increase the credit line. Once you've begun to make timely payments and the information is sent to the credit bureaus, you will begin seeing more credit offers in the mail. But be careful and don't get back in too much debt.

C H A P T E R   6

Credit Scores: What They Are, How They Work, and How to Improve Them

Credit scores, which came into full force in the late 1990s, have changed the way mortgage loan approvals are issued, much the way Automated Underwriting Systems have done. Establishing a credit history is a requirement for obtaining a mortgage, and a credit score is the number assigned to quantify the quality of credit. Understanding how credit scoring and mortgage lending work hand in hand can give you the upper hand when negotiating your loan terms.

6.1 WHAT ARE CREDIT SCORES?

Credit scores are numbers that are derived from a consumer's credit history. The number reflects the various credit details in a consumer's past. People with higher credit scores get better rates than those with low credit scores. A score also attempts to determine the likelihood of default on a loan. The higher the score, the less likelihood of missed payments. The lower the score, the greater the credit risk. At least according to the scoring model.

Credit scoring has been around for years; it was just done manually. Give so many "points" for paying loans on time, so much for job stability, more for low debt ratios, and so on. Credit scoring was used mostly for credit cards. Have you seen all those signs in the mall or at a department store advertising "instant" approval for a store

account? They use a method of scoring. Your basic information—
whether you own a home or rent, your income, where you've lived,
etc.—is entered into a database and your credit is reviewed by a
software program while you wait. A few moments later, *voilà*! Shop
till you drop.

Credit scoring for mortgages is relatively new compared to other
consumer lending, like credit cards and installment loans. Credit
scoring for mortgages was developed by a company called the FICO
Company, or FICO, formally named the Fair Isaac Corporation,
hence the FICO acronym. When you hear the term *FICO* being used
generically, such as, "What's your FICO?" it really means, "What is
the credit score that the FICO has calculated for you?" All three
credit repositories use the FICO scoring system, but their credit
scores are usually different because the three repositories pull information from different parts of the country and collect different
information.

Credit scores can be as low as 300 or as high as 850. Personally,
I've never seen a score higher than 810, and if there is someone out
there with an 840, I'd like to meet them. I'm not saying it's impossible, I've just never seen one. People with excellent credit generally
have their credit scores at 720 or above. Good credit starts around
680 and average credit is around 660. Scores below that may be
considered damaged or impaired credit.

Credit scoring is not an exact science—at least to the general
public. How credit scores are calculated is not divulged to the public
because credit reporting companies want to keep people from manip-
ulating the scores. The score itself is more of a two-year overview of
recent credit behavior.

6.2 WHAT MAKES UP A SCORE?

Numerical values are assigned to your payment patterns, available
credit, how long you've had credit, the number of credit inquiries,
and types of credit.

TELL ME MORE

Certain payment characteristics have greater weight in determining
credit scores. Your payment history and how much you owe carry the

most weight. Approximately 35 percent of the score is derived from your payment patterns and around 30 percent from the amounts owed. If you can get a handle on these two items, you'll find the other scoring factors will take care of themselves.

Your payment pattern simply means paying on time. If you've never had a late payment on a credit account, then this fact alone contributes significantly to your score. If you've had a late payment or two recently, this fact will also hit your score fairly hard, especially if this late payment is within the past two years. A recent late payment on a car loan, for example, can drop a 700 credit score to 650 in a heartbeat. Another late payment? You're in the low 600s. But if you've paid your accounts on time, you can also expect your credit score to be high. As long, of course, as your other factors aren't being damaged.

The next most important scoring characteristic is your account balances, sometimes called your "available credit." Credit scoring companies want to see that you have credit accounts, but they don't want to see your balances approach or exceed your credit limit. For instance, say you get a new MasterCard with a $10,000 credit limit. Your credit score will drop if you approach the limit, and drop further still if you exceed it. Making minimum monthly payments with high balances on your credit cards will slowly erode your score. Go over your credit line and you'll really knock your score down. Ideally, keeping your amounts owed to approximately one-third of your credit lines inflates credit scores. Interestingly, having a zero balance on a $10,000 credit card does nothing for your score compared to having a $3,000 balance on that $10,000 card and making timely payments.

6.3 WHAT THINGS IN MY PAYMENT HISTORY AFFECT MY CREDIT SCORE?

Credit scores can be affected by how often you make your payments on or before the due date. The scoring model reviews the existence of any late payments and how late they actually were in 30-day increments. A 90-day late payment will hurt your score more than a 30-day late payment. That is, unless the 30-day late payment was last month and the 90-day late payment was five years ago. Remember that scores concentrate more on recent behavior than on old behavior. Payment history also covers collection accounts or charge-offs (bad debt the original creditor has simply given up hope on collecting) and includes searches of public records for bankruptcy filings, judgments, or tax liens.

6.4 WHAT ABOUT MY AMOUNTS OWED? WHAT IS MOST IMPORTANT?

Amounts owed is relatively easy to identify: It's how much you owe compared to how much you're allowed to borrow. But here again, conventional credit wisdom and credit scoring butt heads.

Advice just a few years ago suggested closing any outstanding accounts that had zero balances, or if there were accounts with small balances, paying them off and closing them out. Why? When human beings underwrote loans to loan credit standards, this might have been good advice. Heck, it's still good advice, but the impact on a credit score could backfire. Since amounts owed account for nearly a third of your credit score, you need to be very careful how you treat this scoring factor.

Underwriters can look at available credit as a bad thing, regardless of whether you've used it. If you've got $50,000 of credit available to you among various credit cards, then who's to say you won't go out and charge every bit of that just after your home closes? If you had debt-ratio issues with simply buying the house, having all this available credit means that there's the possibility of your using every dime of it buying new drapes, carpeting, furniture, and a nifty new widescreen HDTV.

At least that's what an underwriter would take into consideration. Even though you'd never charged that amount in your entire life, the simple fact that you could would make an underwriter afraid. So in this case it's good advice: If you have old accounts you're not using, cancel them out so an underwriter won't be tempted to make you close them out before your loan approval. But that's not necessarily the case these days in the world of automated underwriting and credit scoring.

Remember that having a strong "available credit" factor can increase credit scores. If you have a $20,000 credit line on various accounts and your balances only add up to $5,000, then you have 80 percent of your credit available to you. That pushes up your score.

But if you cancel some accounts, thereby reducing your available credit limit to, say, $8,000, then you've used two-thirds of your available credit—twice as much as the magical "30 percent" guideline. Your credit score can suffer. If you have cards that haven't been used in a while, leave them alone and keep your available credit at higher amounts.

6.5 HOW DO I FIND OUT WHAT MY SCORE IS?

That's easy. It wasn't too long ago that obtaining your own credit score was nearly impossible without applying for a mortgage loan first. Now it's as simple as logging onto any of the websites of the three repositories.

www.experian.com

www.transunion.com

www.equifax.com

Or you can go to a site called AnnualCreditReport.com and get your credit score.

This service pulls your credit from all three bureaus. The credit report is free, but you must pay a small fee for your score (as you would at the individual credit sites).

The Fair and Accurate Credit Transactions Act (FACTA) is the law that allows you to get a free copy of your credit report every year, regardless of any credit declination. It also lets you see your credit score. Is it important to find out what your score is? Yes, but it's more important to review your credit report first. I know you've heard this a million times, but the first thing to do when getting ready to shop for a home is to check your credit report. The reason is not to see your score but to check for errors that are hurting your score.

However, it's important to understand that the scores you have access to are not exactly the same as what a mortgage company pulls. When consumers access their own credit score, it's most often what is referred to as a Vantage Score, the name assigned to a consumer credit-scoring model that is prepared by the three major credit repositories in an attempt to compete directly with FICO. Mortgage lenders do not use Vantage Scores and use the FICO score designed specifically for mortgage companies.

6.6 HOW DO I GET A CREDIT SCORE?

By buying things on credit. Again, these computer models need a credit history of typically two years. I've seen credit reports with no score available simply because credit hadn't been established or hadn't been established long enough. If you've got a gas station credit card and have had it only a few months, you won't have a score, even if you've used the card. But applying for credit, using it, and paying it back gets your score established. You also need to have a Social Security number.

6.7 WHAT'S THE MINIMUM CREDIT SCORE I NEED TO QUALIFY FOR A MORTGAGE LOAN?

Fannie Mae and Freddie Mac set minium credit scores at 620 while FHA loans have a minimum score of 500. There are no minimum credit scores required for VA and USDA mortgages. In order for a loan to be eligible for sale in the secondary markets, the representative score must meet these minimums. However, lenders can also have their own internal guidelines, asking for a higher credit score than what is prescribed in the lending guidelines. A mortgage company issuing a conventional loan can ask for a minimum credit score of 640 if the down payment is less than 10 percent, for example. Lenders can raise the credit score bar but cannot lower it. That is, if the lender intends to sell the loan later on.

As long as the lender applies its guidelines universally, the lender has the right to have credit score minimums higher than other lenders or require additional items in order for borrowers to qualify for a loan. These additional qualifications are called "Lender Overlays," and many lenders have them. This also means that if you apply for a mortgage at one company and the minimum credit score is 640 and yours is 630, you should find a lender that uses the 620 minimum.

I've spoken with countless customers who either didn't buy a home or put it off for a long time because when they got their credit score they took it upon themselves to "decline" and didn't even apply for a loan. Similarly, sometimes people don't apply for the mortgage they want because they think their debt ratios are too high. A recent customer called me wanting to apply for a mortgage but he knew his credit wasn't all that great. High debt load, a couple of late payments, and not much available credit. He was right; his score was low at 581. Unfortunately for many people, once they see a score they consider "low," they give up without ever trying.

The guy with the 581 credit score? He got approved for a $185,000 loan. He had some other factors that offset the low credit score—mostly a hefty down payment—but the point is that he got approved. Let the lender make the determination for you.

Today, most conventional mortgage loans ask for a minimum credit score of 620 as do government-backed loans, but again exceptions can be made.

6.8 WHAT IF MY LENDER TOLD ME I COULDN'T QUALIFY BECAUSE MY CREDIT SCORE WAS TOO LOW?

Lenders can establish almost any criteria they desire as long as they don't discriminate in doing so. If lenders decide to offer better pricing to someone with an 800 credit score, they have every right to do so. If they have a loan program that requires little or no documentation, they might also offset the risk of no documentation with a credit score, and so on. If your lender said you couldn't qualify because of a score, it was most likely due to the fact that the loan you applied for had some special characteristics that conventional loans didn't have.

In these cases, a loan officer will typically ask for an "exception" to loan guidelines and get you approved anyway. What exactly is an exception? Let's say a special loan program you want has a minimum credit score of 760, but your score is 740. Instead of calling you up and giving you the bad news, your lender will ask for "compensating factors" to be used to override the 760 credit score requirement. You will then be asked to bolster your case for the underwriting exception by providing documented details about other facets of your financial life.

Do you have a lot of money left in the bank after your loan closing? Are you upwardly mobile with higher earnings ahead? Do you have a good down payment rather than just the minimum required? Have you been in the same line of work for a long time? Such compensating factors are used when a loan officer sends your loan for an exception request to override a credit score requirement.

6.9 HOW DO I KNOW HOW MUCH TO CHARGE AND HOW MUCH TO PAY OFF?

The secret formula appears to be 30 percent. Keep your monthly credit balances around 30 percent of their limits. Is $10,000 your limit? Keep a $3,000 balance. This percentage seems to work best. Yes, you need to charge things on credit and pay them back, but keep a balance. Charge nothing and you'll never establish a payment history. Charge it all and you're approaching your credit limits, hurting your score.

The 30 percent level is sometimes looked at differently, from the perspective of "available credit" instead of your credit limit, but with the same result. Available credit is just another way of saying that your current balances are 30 percent of your limits, which means that you have 70 percent of your outstanding credit lines available to you.

Credit scores attempt to take a "snapshot" of a recent two-year period and factor in all your various payment patterns to get a true picture of your credit behavior. Don't expect that you can get any significant change in your credit score by paying off or paying down your credit balances. It would only be effective if you did so routinely over a period, which would more accurately reflect your credit habits. But don't pay everything down to 30 percent of your credit lines and expect a change in your score the next day.

6.10 WHAT ELSE AFFECTS MY CREDIT SCORE?

Your payment history and amounts owed are the biggest factors, but other items can affect your score as well. One of the more common scoring items people see is "number of credit inquiries." This scoring factor takes into account how many times you've applied for credit over the past couple of years. Lots of new credit inquiries could mean that, for whatever reason, you needed to establish new credit lines. You didn't have enough money to buy what you wanted to buy, so you put it on credit. Lots of recent credit accounts might also indicate a potential for default. A person with high debt load and lots of credit payments is a greater risk than someone with fewer accounts.

Another factor is the type of credit account you've opened. Real estate accounts (mortgages) have a more positive impact on your credit score than credit from a department store. Furthermore, credit accounts from consumer finance agencies that loan smaller amounts of money at higher interest rates can have a negative effect on your score. Finally, how long someone has had credit affects a credit score. Scores will be higher the longer a consumer has used credit.

6.11 HOW CAN I INCREASE MY AVAILABLE CREDIT WITHOUT OPENING UP NEW ACCOUNTS?

You can't. But you can ask for an increase in credit limits. Perhaps one of your current lenders will raise its maximum credit limit for you, so at the very start you might contact your credit provider and ask to have your credit line increased.

But on the whole, without opening up new accounts, it's really impossible to increase available credit without increasing both inquiries and the number of new credit accounts. New credit card accounts can hit your credit score in a bad way. If you do open up new lines of credit, it may be to your advantage to leave them alone for at least a year, to let the account season and begin to work in your favor. It doesn't make sense to open up trade lines to increase available credit. Increasing your available credit only works on existing accounts with relatively low balances.

And it works even more in your favor if you've had the account for several years. If there's a trick to this double-edged sword it would be to identify your two or three oldest credit card accounts and pay those balances down to about one-third of your available credit line.

6.12 I'VE APPLIED AT MORE THAN ONE MORTGAGE COMPANY. WILL ALL THOSE CREDIT INQUIRIES HURT MY SCORE?

Not if the inquiries are for the same mortgage. An "inquiry" occurs when someone or some business inquires about your credit by contacting the credit bureaus. Let's define what is and is not a credit inquiry. First, those reports that you request yourself to check your credit are not counted as an inquiry. For instance, you apply for automobile financing with your credit union but also let the dealer check your credit to see if you qualify for financing. This will be read as an individual inquiry, not two. The same applies to mortgages. Applying for a mortgage at more than one place because you're shopping for a mortgage won't be viewed as multiple inquiries as long as it's for the same loan and within a reasonable time frame, say, within the past month or two. A mortgage inquiry for a home improvement loan two years ago and for a refinance last month will be viewed as two separate inquiries because they're not for the same loan and they're far apart in terms of time.

So the answer is no. If different mortgage companies check your credit for the same transaction, then you should see no negative impact on your score. If you thought about refinancing earlier this year, changed your mind, then started all over again six months later, then yes, you could see your credit scores drop.

6.13 HOW DO I FIX SCORES THAT ARE ARTIFICIALLY LOW DUE TO MISTAKES?

The way you can get incorrect items off of your credit report is the very same way you get your score corrected, except for one thing: You have to literally request this score be recalculated for you, and there may be a marginal charge for doing it, say, $40 or so. Why should you have to pay for the error? Good question. I don't see why you should, but currently you can expect to have to pay a charge. Not just the $40 for the mistake, but $40 for each credit bureau that's reporting the incorrect data. You have to provide your documentation, just as with any other credit dispute, and have your credit score "rerun" as if the mistake never appeared.

TELL ME MORE

There's a service that the credit reporting agencies offer their lenders called the "rapid rescore." Even if you were successful in getting the error fixed, it could take months for the scores to rebuild themselves naturally. Instead, you need to have your scores fixed immediately and permanently.

I had a client who experienced a bankruptcy, and there were several accounts that were showing up as outstanding collection items, even though they were discharged through the Chapter 7 bankruptcy filing. The loan program she was trying to qualify for was a special program that required zero down and was for investment properties. Her credit scores, all of them, were below 620, which was the minimum score needed for the loan. She was closing in less than 30 days and either had to get her scores fixed or lose the house she wanted to buy. I asked her for the complete copy of her bankruptcy papers, which showed all the accounts that were discharged and the date they were discharged. I reviewed the papers and, sure enough, the credit reporting agencies were making some serious errors.

I contacted the credit agencies, forwarded the bankruptcy discharge papers, and asked for a rapid rescore based upon the new information. Within three business days we had our results, and her credit scores were above the minimum. In fact, her middle score, which we used for the loan, was 681.

A rapid rescore is not an automatic. Just because you ask for the rescore doesn't mean you'll automatically increase your score by 30, 40, or even 50 points or more. There are too many variables to guarantee any result, but it's worth the try.

6.14 IF THERE ARE SEVERAL MISTAKES ON MY REPORT, DO I GET THEM ALL CORRECTED? HOW DO I KNOW WHICH ONES TO CORRECT?

Your loan officer should help you with that, but you should only submit a rapid rescore to the two bureaus with the highest current scores. Why? Since lenders use the middle score and not the highest or lowest, you should try to increase scores that are already higher. Rescoring costs money, and it gets more expensive with each line item and bureau you contact requesting a score change.

Don't dispute old data that might be a mistake. Instead, ask for a rescore on the most recent item(s), since scores concentrate more on recent activity and not old activity. And remember that rescoring only works on mistakes, not disputes. If there's an item that you disagree with but don't have the documentation to back up your position, such as bankruptcy papers or copies of canceled checks showing payment, then don't bother.

It's also important to remember that rescoring is a service the credit agencies extend to the lending community; it's not a consumer service. This means you'll need to have your loan officer request a rescore on your behalf. If your loan officer doesn't know what a rapid rescore is, you'll need to find one who does.

6.15 I'M A SINGLE PARENT AND A MINORITY. DOES THIS STATUS HELP OR HURT MY CREDIT SCORE?

Credit scores have no clue as to your marital status, whether or not you have kids, your race, religion, or whatever else. The scores look at credit patterns and public records. They don't care how old you are, what kind of job you have, or on which side you part or used to part your hair. The only things that really help are the items discussed in this chapter.

6.16 HOW DO LENDERS CHOOSE WHICH CREDIT SCORES TO USE?

That's a good question. Most lenders will use the middle score, not the highest one and not the lowest one. And there's a reason. Even though scoring models from all the bureaus are mostly the same, they may not have all the exact same information. If you've always lived in Southern California, for example, you may have activity from reporting members (i.e., businesses that issue credit) in a local area that is not reported to, say, the repository in Atlanta. The way lenders use credit scores is to simply throw out the highest number and throw out the lowest number. If there is more than one borrower on the mortgage application, the lender uses the lowest middle score reported.

6.17 I HAVE GREAT CREDIT SCORES, BUT MY SPOUSE HAS LOW CREDIT SCORES. WHAT HAPPENS?

Credit scoring works like a credit report. Conventional loans use the middle credit score from the person who makes less money. Other loans use the credit score from the primary breadwinner. Contrary to popular belief, they don't average the scores together, add them up, or use the highest score.

THE RIGHT
MORTGAGE

THE RIGHT MORTGAGE

C H A P T E R · 7

Finding Your Home Loan

Finding a home loan, at first glance, is a simple process. A loan is nothing more than money you borrowed and promised to pay back, right? There are two primary mortgage types in today's marketplace, conventional and government-backed. In addition, these two programs can be offered with multiple terms.

7.1 WHAT KINDS OF LOANS ARE THERE?

Here's a brief list of the most common types of mortgage loans offered by every lender or mortgage broker:

30-year fixed	25-year fixed	20-year fixed	15-year fixed
10-year fixed	5/25 two-step	7/23 two-step	1-year ARM
3/1 ARM	5/1 ARM	7/1 ARM	10/1 ARM buydown
3/6 ARM	5/6 ARM	7/6 ARM	10/6 ARM
VA fixed	VA ARM	FHA fixed	FHA ARM HomeReady
State bonds	Seconds	HELOC	Const.-perm
Portfolio			

These loans are good for conforming loan amounts. Another set of loan programs is available for jumbo loans. With a few exceptions, most lenders offer the same programs, with the only variable being the cost of the loan itself. If one lender introduces a new program and it's successful, you can bet the other lenders will soon follow with a replica product.

But that can lead to confusion for both the borrower and the loan officer. Some mortgage brokers advertise that they have access to 40 or 50 mortgage lenders. Or more. Are lenders all that different? Do we really need that many loan programs? Of course not. But loans fall into either one of two categories: *fixed-rate loans,* where your monthly payment never changes throughout the life of the loan, and loans that can adjust over the life of the loan, called *adjustable-rate mortgages.* The only difference really is in the rate and terms of the mortgage from one place to another.

7.2 WHEN WOULD I WANT A FIXED RATE?

1. When rates are at relative lows compared to the previous two or three years. Here a fixed rate is good because it locks in that money for the remaining term. Over the past 25 years, fixed rates have been as high as 18 percent or 19 percent and as low as 2 percent. If you're buying in a high interest rate cycle, it might not be the best time to get a fixed rate. If rates are relatively low, it might be a good time to lock in the low rates.

2. When you're holding onto the property for a long time, say, more than five years. This could be the home you plan to retire in, or a home where you can say, "Enough! I'm tired of moving."

3. When you're not one of the gambling types. Fixed rates never change. Yeah, adjustable rates can start low, but they can also go much higher. Some people like to be able to plan in the long run what their house payment will be five, ten, or twenty years from now. Others can't sleep at night because they're wondering if their house payments will go up next year.

7.3 WHEN WOULD I WANT AN ADJUSTABLE RATE?

1. When rates are at relative highs compared to the previous years. If rates are currently at a high cycle, chances are rates will go down in the near future. On the other hand, if rates

are at historical lows you may want to avoid an adjustable-rate mortgage.

2. When your job has you moving a lot. Adjustable-rate mortgages typically have lower starting rates than fixed ones, and if you transfer or move often, you'll have retired your mortgage before an adjustable has time to move upward.

3. When you have a gut feeling that rates will stay the same or move lower for the long term. If your rate is in the middle of the pack compared to historic rates, an adjustable rate gives you the benefit of a lower start rate with the possibility of moving into an even lower rate later on.

7.4 HOW DO ADJUSTABLE-RATE MORTGAGES WORK?

There are four basics for an adjustable-rate mortgage (ARM): the index, the margin, the adjustment period, and rate caps.

1. *The Index.* This is what your interest rate is tied to. Your index can actually be anything you agree upon, but most ARMs are indexed to a one-year treasury, or something called a LIBOR. LIBOR stands for the London Interbank Offered Rate, and this index is quite similar to the Federal Funds rate found here in the United States. The LIBOR index is released each business day and is the index by which banks lend money to one another over the short term—for example, overnight.

   The one-year treasury is a security or treasury bill issued by the Fed to, among other things, raise money. Other indexes that ARMs might be tied to are various LIBOR and treasury maturities, like one-month or six-month LIBOR ARMs; the prime rate; or even certificates of deposit (CDs). Your index could theoretically be anything you agree to. It could be the price of a gallon of ice cream if that's the deal you come up with. Just don't bet the lender will use ice cream as your index; lenders will use one of the indexes mentioned above.

2. *The Margin.* The margin is the difference between your mortgage rate and your index. The index is what your rate is based upon, and the lender adds a margin to it (think profit margin or cushion) to arrive at your *fully indexed rate* (also called your note rate), which is the number reached when you add your index and your margin. Common margins are anywhere from 2 percent to 2.75 percent, although some loans let you pay extra fees, such as a 1/2 discount point, to get a lower margin.

3. *The Adjustment Period.* This is the period after which your rate can change. At the end of each adjustment period, your margin is added to the current index to get your new rate. Sometimes the rate won't change, but most often it will, as the index will have changed. Common adjustment periods are every six months or once a year (your anniversary date). Let's say your new loan is an ARM with the cost of a gallon of ice cream as the index. You also agree that the lender will add 2 percent (the margin) to whatever that cost (index) will be. One year from now the cost of a gallon of ice cream is $5.00. Since your margin is 2 percent, your new rate for the following year will be 5 + 2, or 7 percent. But what if there's a milk shortage and the cost of ice cream zooms to $50.00 a gallon? Will your rate then be 52 percent?

4. *Rate Caps.* This is how high your rate is permitted to change each adjustment period. There are three possible caps on an adjustable-rate mortgage: the adjustment cap, the lifetime rate cap, and the initial rate cap.

Maybe the ice cream went from $5.00 a gallon to $50.00 a gallon, but don't sweat it. An *adjustment cap* protects consumers from wild swings in their loan index by limiting the increase from period to period. When the adjustment rate cap is set for 1 percent every six months, or 2 percent every twelve months, it means that at the end of each six-month adjustment period the rate is allowed to increase only another 1 percent over the previous rate. Returning to our example, even though your fully indexed rate might be 52 percent, the rate is only allowed to jump to 6 percent because of the rate cap.

A second type of cap is called a *lifetime rate cap,* which means that, no matter what, the interest rate can never be higher than the cap. Some caps are at 5 percent above the starting rate, but most caps are at 6 percent above the starting rate. If your loan has a 5 percent lifetime cap and you started out at 5 percent, then, no matter what, your fully indexed rate will never be higher than 5 + 5, or 10 percent.

Other types of adjustables have an *initial cap,* meaning that at the very first, or initial, adjustment period the cap is 5 percent or 6 percent, or whatever the agreed-upon loan parameters actually are.

You might see some adjustable-rate mortgage cap numbers reading 2/6 or 1/5. That means the adjustment cap is 2 percent or 1 percent, respectively, and the lifetime cap of the loan is 6 percent or 5 percent. For loans with initial rate caps, it might read 5/2/5, meaning a possible 5 percent cap at the very first adjustment, 2 percent annually or at each adjustment period, and 5 percent over the life of the loan.

7.5 ARE ARMS ONLY HELPFUL IN THE VERY NEAR TERM?

Probably. For borrowers who locked in at the right time, ARMs may also help them to not only get a lower starting rate than competing fixed-rate mortgages, but to have their index actually drop over the next few years. For them, it means simply watching their mortgage payment drop every six months or so, while people who chose a fixed-rate mortgage have to refinance their loan to get a lower rate. There is actually a combination of a fixed-rate mortgage and an adjustable-rate mortgage. It's called a hybrid.

7.6 WHAT EXACTLY IS A HYBRID LOAN?

A *hybrid loan* is simply a combination of a fixed rate and an ARM where the rate is fixed for a predetermined number of years before turning into an ARM for the remaining life of the loan. Hybrids have a lower starting rate than a fixed-rate mortgage, but a slightly higher rate than an adjustable-rate mortgage. The trade-off is the rate guarantee for the near term. Most hybrids are fixed initially for three or five years. Some hybrids have fixed terms that go as high as 10 years, but if their rates are higher than comparable fixed rates, they may not make much sense. Hybrids, then, even though they're a "combination" of a fixed and an adjustable mortgage, are essentially ARMs that are fixed for the first few years.

A hybrid fixed for three years before turning into an annual adjustable-rate mortgage is called a 3/1 loan. Similarly, a 5/1 hybrid is fixed for five years before becoming an ARM, and so on. Over the past few years hybrids have become more and more popular as consumers determined that they're not very likely to own a home for 15 or 20 years but, in practice, only plan to live in the house for three, four, or five years. In these cases, hybrids are hard to beat.

Are hybrids the best choice? Not necessarily. Again, there is a risk that they can change into a semi-unpredictable ARM later on. For instance, you figure that you'll be up for a big promotion in three years, so you choose a 3/1 hybrid. But during those three years you don't get that promotion, and now you're stuck with a possible rate increase at the first adjustment period. Life's what happens when you're busy making other plans, right? Plans can change, but your note stays the same.

Some people are almost positive they'll be out of their mortgage in four years but don't choose a 5/1 ARM because they're just not comfortable with the possibility of higher payments down the road. Just understand that there is an alternative between an adjustable-rate mortgage and a fixed one. But in the long run, there really are only two basic loans: fixed loans and adjustable loans.

7.7   WHAT IS A BUYDOWN?

A *buydown* either temporarily or permanently reduces the note rate on a mortgage. A temporary buydown is sometimes called a two-step or a 2–1 buydown, where there is a lower start rate for year 1, with a higher rate for years 2 through 30. Buydowns can help borrowers who might have trouble qualifying at 8 percent, but can qualify at the lower buydown rate of 7 percent.

TELL ME MORE

Temporary buydowns are nothing more than prepaid interest to the lender expressed as a note rate. They can be applied to most any fixed-rate mortgage in the market. Temporary buydowns can also be for three years, called a 3–2–1 buydown. A 3–2–1 could have a start rate of 6 percent for year 1, 7 percent for year 2, and 8 percent for years 3 to 30. Temporary buydowns can be a good choice if you expect to have increased income in the next year or two; for example, if you are starting a new job or practice.

To calculate a temporary buydown, you take your principal balance and calculate a monthly payment using a current market rate with no points. If the current rate is 7 percent and your loan amount is $300,000, then your monthly payment would be $1,995, using a 30-year fixed rate. For a 2–1 buydown, drop the rate from 7 percent to 6 percent, then again calculate the monthly payment, which would be $1,798; subtracting that from $1,995 gives you $197. If you multiply that $197 by the 12 months you'll have the 6 percent rate, you get the amount you must pay the lender for the temporary buydown, or $2,364.

You now have a choice of paying that tax-deductible interest in the form of cash at closing, or you can adjust your interest rate to accommodate the interest. By dividing the buydown interest of $2,364 by your loan amount of $300,000, you get about 80 basis points, or almost 0.8 of a discount point. If you increase your rate by about 1/4 percent, your lender will accept the higher rate in lieu of a cash payment from you.

Temporary buydowns are effective if you're either having trouble qualifying at higher market rates or you simply want lower rates to start out with.

The other type of buydown is a *permanent buydown,* which is nothing more than paying discount points to get a lower rate. It can be applied to either a fixed rate or an adjustable one. There is a difference here. Temporary and permanent buydowns are different.

7.8 APART FROM CHOOSING FIXED OR ADJUSTABLE RATES, WHAT TYPES OF LOAN PROGRAMS SHOULD I CONSIDER?

Besides deciding between a fixed rate and an adjustable rate, you also need to examine the types of loans available to you. Most loans will fall into one of two types: conventional and government. *Conventional loans* are secured and backed by lenders, while *government loans* carry a governmental guarantee. Conventional loans are mortgages that are underwritten to Fannie Mae or Freddie Mac guidelines, as well as jumbo loans. Government mortgages are loans guaranteed by the Department of Veterans Affairs (VA), the United States Department of Agriculture (USDA), or the Federal Housing Administration (FHA).

7.9 HOW ARE LIMITS ON CONVENTIONAL LOANS SET?

Fannie Mae and Freddie Mac set conforming loan limits based upon legislation passed in 2008 using a formula presented in the Housing and Economic Recovery Act of 2008, or HERA, replacing the previous method of using the national median home value as a guide. HERA was the most sweeping piece of legislation affecting the housing and mortgage industry perhaps ever. HERA guidelines state that there will be no adjustment in the conforming loan limit; if during the previous 12-month period the housing price index decreases, the limit will stay the same. When the index increases, the adjustment will be based upon the increase over the 12-month period.

TELL ME MORE

HERA was enacted to address primarily the subprime mortgage marketplace. Subprime loans are those designed to finance properties for those with damaged credit, yet it also reined in Fannie Mae and Freddie Mac as well as government-backed programs of VA, FHA, and USDA. Aside from the VA and USDA programs, there was a move toward lessening lending guidelines in order to increase market share. The housing debacle, which technically began in 2007, wiped away billions of dollars in homeowner equity, and as home values fell, because of the HERA formula, the conforming loan limit stayed where it was at $417,000 for nearly a decade before the HERA calculation finally raised the conforming loan limit for 2017. Anything above the maximum is called a *jumbo mortgage*.

Because loans are underwritten to the same standards, competition is encouraged, which helps to drive rates lower for the consumer. Conventional mortgages are one of the most common types of mortgages. They are available from most any mortgage lender or mortgage broker. Mortgages are like any other product or service in the United States: If there are more people selling the same thing, the price will ultimately come down.

7.10 WHO OR WHAT ARE FANNIE AND FREDDIE?

We mentioned *Fannie Mae* and *Freddie Mac* earlier, but let's take a moment to see what their real purposes are. Fannie and Freddie are the familiar names of the Federal National Mortgage Association (FNMA) and the Federal Home Loan Mortgage Corporation (FHLMC) and are under the oversight of the Federal Housing Finance Agency. They provide mostly the same function. They were both formed by the federal government to provide liquidity in the mortgage marketplace.

Lenders loan money and charge you for it. That's why they're in business. But what if a lender runs out of money to lend? Fannie Mae was formed back in 1938 to purchase loans that were backed by the U.S. government's newly created Federal Housing Administration. Before there was Fannie Mae, when lenders ran out of mortgage money to lend, they had only a few choices. They could:

❑ Turn to their bank vaults and lend out money they had set aside for various other purposes.

❑ Offer higher savings account rates to attract new money.

❑ Take a certain set of HUD loans and sell them.

Typically, once a mortgage was placed, it stayed there until it was paid off. But Fannie Mae's job was to provide a little cash flow in the mortgage market by buying loans from mortgage lenders that would then free up cash for them to lend again. In 1968, Fannie Mae reorganized and began purchasing nongovernment-guaranteed loans as well as FHA ones. The government spin-off, which is called *Ginnie Mae* (Government National Mortgage Association), buys VA and FHA loans. Fannie Mae then concentrated on nongovernment or conventional mortgages.

Freddie Mac, formed in 1970, provides essentially the same function, to provide liquidity in the mortgage market. When lenders want to sell their loans to free up some capital, they can sell their loans to Fannie or Freddie, or even buy and sell from one another. This is accomplished by making mortgage loans that comply with certain rules and guidelines established by Fannie Mae and Freddie Mac.

These rules say that "if you make a mortgage that fits these parameters, we agree to buy them from you if you want." And because such loans fit these parameters, they become somewhat of a commodity, allowing banks and mortgage companies to sell to one another and not just to Fannie Mae or Freddie Mac. This buying and selling of mortgages is called the *secondary market*. When Fannie or Freddie run out of money, they package those purchased mortgages into securities and sell them on Wall Street, replenishing the nest egg.

Remember, Fannie and Freddie don't make loans, but they do provide guidelines for lenders to make them. If a loan "conforms" to all of the guidelines, it's sometimes called a *conforming loan*. That's one of the main reasons mortgage programs from different lenders are most always identical, except maybe for a little variation in price. If it's a loan conforming to Fannie Mae or Freddie Mac guidelines, you can assume it's an identical loan.

7.11 WHAT ARE SPECIAL COMMITMENTS?

There are occasions when a lender makes a special agreement with Fannie Mae and Freddie Mac and markets these loans under slightly different terms. Such arrangements are sometimes called "special commitments," whereby a lender might guarantee to provide Freddie Mac with a certain amount of loan volume in exchange for an under-writing change or a discount in price. But again, for the most part, these loans are underwritten under the very same standards. That's why lenders can buy and sell them with confidence, knowing exactly what they bought and what they're selling.

7.12 WHAT EXACTLY IS A JUMBO MORTGAGE?

It is a loan that is above the conforming loan limit. Just like conform-ing loans, jumbo mortgages may also be bought and sold in the sec-ondary market, except not by Fannie and Freddie. Private corporations buy and sell them, and they work similarly to how conforming loans work. That's also why most jumbo loans can be exactly alike at two different lenders, because they're underwritten using the same guidelines. Many jumbo loans carry guidelines that are similar to what Fannie or Freddie might have, and they can even be underwritten using Fannie and Freddie. Besides the higher loan amounts, one of the main differences between jumbo and conforming loans is usually in the interest rate. Jumbo loans usually carry an interest rate about 1/4 percent or more higher than a conforming one.

7.13 CAN I PREPAY MY MORTGAGE OR PAY IT OFF EARLY?

Of course you can. Sometimes first-time home buyers might think that they don't want a 30-year fixed rate because they don't want to be paying on a home for that long. You don't have to keep a mortgage loan to full term; it's simply that the term helps to determine the monthly payment and to amortize the loan. You can pay extra on your mortgage anytime you want, and many people do; it's a great way to build equity faster. For example, on a 30-year $100,000 loan at 4 percent, the monthly payment would be about $416. By making just one extra payment a year, you would automatically knock off nearly eight years of your loan term. You can make a lump-sum payment of $416 every year or even divide it by 12 and make smaller additional monthly payments for the same effect.

7.14 WHAT ARE PREPAYMENT PENALTIES?

A *prepayment penalty* is an agreed-upon amount the lender gets in addition to normal principal and interest payments if the borrower pays extra on the loan or pays it off ahead of time. A prepayment can mean simply making extra payments, or paying off the entire note with cash, or refinancing into another mortgage. This penalty is actually in the form of additional interest, which may be a tax deduction for most people who itemize on their tax returns. Prepayment penalties used to be much more common, but most loans now have no prepayment restrictions whatsoever. Today, prepayment penalties are typically applied to loans for people with not-so-great credit and are extremely rare. Let's first look at the two different types of prepayment penalties: hard and soft.

A *hard penalty* is one that says you can't pay anything extra at any time; you can't refinance the loan, you can't sell the house, and if you don't take it to full term, you owe the lender money. That's rough, hence the nickname. Common prepayment penalties might be six or twelve months' worth of interest, although they can be practically anything the borrower and lender agree upon, as long as the penalty is within local guidelines and lending regulations.

A *soft penalty* typically allows a borrower to make extra payments (usually no more than 20 percent of the outstanding balance each year). It doesn't apply if you sell the home, and it lasts anywhere from one to three years instead of the entire life of the loan, as with a hard penalty. For example, say that two loans for $200,000 each have a penalty, one soft and one hard. The soft penalty lets the borrower pay extra on the mortgage anytime, as long as the extra payment doesn't exceed a certain amount, usually expressed as a percentage of a remaining principal balance during any 12-month period. For a $200,000 loan with a soft penalty, the consumer may pay up to $40,000 extra without penalty. Under a hard penalty, any extra payment whatsoever can result in a penalty, typically six months' worth of interest.

7.15 WHY DO LENDERS HAVE PREPAYMENT PENALTIES ON SOME OF THEIR LOANS?

Sometimes it's to offset an additional layer of risk, while at the same time keeping the borrower's payments lower. For example, a lender agrees to make a mortgage loan to someone who has just come out of a bankruptcy. Let's also say that the lender, through interest payments, expects to make $10,000 on that loan for the first three years. The lender, while accepting a higher-risk loan, requires that they make $10,000 on the loan, which they can get if the borrower makes normal monthly payments over the course of three years. If the house is refinanced or sold in the first year, then the lender still needs to get their $10,000, but it will have to be in the form of a "penalty." Prepayment penalties, in general, are just not that easy to find anymore.

7.15A WHAT IS A QUALIFIED MORTGAGE?

As part of the recovery effort after the housing crisis, the Consumer Financial Protection Bureau, or CFPB, was created by authorization by the Dodd-Frank Wall Street Reform and Consumer Protection Act passed in 2010. This is a government agency that sets rules for extending credit to consumers. The Qualified Mortgage defined by the CFPB lists the characteristics of a mortgage a lender could issue that would conform to the new standards, thus protecting the lender from any future litigation regarding the issuance of a particular mortgage. Today, most all mortgage loans may fall into the Qualified Mortgage, or QM category. If a lender does approve a loan without QM status, the loan would be most likely held by the lender as the loan would be difficult to sell in the secondary market.

TELL ME MORE

QM loans have four basic characteristics and they are:

❏ The loan cannot have a prepayment penalty of any sort; the loan cannot negatively amortize; there cannot be balloon payments; and the loan term cannot exceed 30 years.

❏ The total points and fees for the loan cannot exceed 3 percent of the total loan amount for loans over $100,000.

❏ The borrower's income and assets must be verified and documented, and

❏ The total debt-to-income ratio cannot exceed 43 percent of the borrower's gross monthly income.

What the CFPB did was essentially eliminate the types of loans that were deemed responsible for the housing crisis. No more prepayment penalty loans, no "stated income" or "no documentation" loans, no "high ratio" loans; and, in addition, closing costs were limited.

Almost immediately after the implementation of the QM guidelines, lenders were at first wary of issuing a home loan and guidelines were very difficult to meet for many borrowers. At one point, it seemed that only those with perfect credit, 20 percent down, and single-digit debt ratios could get a loan. Over time, however, lenders reverted back to commonsense underwriting and approved loans using similar methods used prior to the introduction of so-called toxic mortgages.

7.16 WHAT ARE VA LOANS? HOW DO I GET THEM?

In 1944, as part of the GI Bill of Rights, the U.S. government established a special program that rewarded certain members and veterans of the armed forces for service to their country by providing them with loan programs with zero money down and reduced closing costs. These *VA loans* have certain underwriting characteristics that are different from conventional loans, primarily in the amount of money available to buy a house. There are several zero-money-down programs available that are not VA loans, but usually the interest rates on such products are higher than prevailing rates on VA loans, making the VA loan a hot product if you're eligible. You get a VA loan by applying for and being approved by a lender that issues VA-backed loans.

7.17 WHO'S ELIGIBLE FOR A VA LOAN?

Veterans, active duty personnel, reserve troops, and surviving spouses of veterans may be eligible. There are some requirements for each category.

All honorably discharged wartime veterans of World War II, the Korean War, and the Vietnam War are eligible if they served at least 90 days on active duty. During various peacetime periods from July 1947 to September 1980, one needed to have served 181 days of continuous active duty, or less if discharged for a service-connected disability.

For service dates after September 1980, the eligibility requirements are to have completed 24 months of continuous active duty, or 181 days of active duty with a service-connected disability. If you served after August 1990, in the Gulf War or the Iraq War, then you may be VA eligible as well.

Certain National Guard troops and reservists may also be eligible if they have completed six years in an active National Guard unit that had weekend drills and active duty training. If you're an unmarried surviving spouse of someone who died while in service or as a result of a service-related injury, you may qualify for benefits as well.

And just like Fannie or Freddie deals, it's not the VA that makes the loan. Lenders make the loans to eligible veterans and Ginnie Mae may buy or sell those loans on the secondary market. Being eligible for a VA loan doesn't mean you'll get one. Lenders make the credit decision as to whether to make a VA loan, not the VA. You still need to have good credit and be able to afford the home and so on; simply being eligible is not the same as being approved. It's a common misconception that the VA will guarantee a loan simply because a veteran is applying for one. Not so. While certain leniencies are granted—for example, allowable debt ratios are higher than for some conventional loans—good credit is still needed.

So what's the big deal about VA loans? They're a good deal, that's what, especially if you're going the "no money down" option. If you have down payment funds and money for closing costs, then you might want to explore conventional products, because all VA purchases with zero down have a *funding fee* equal to 2 percent of the sales price of the home. This funding fee, required by law, is used to offset some of the costs of the VA program but may also be included in your loan amount, as long as that loan doesn't exceed VA limits.

TELL ME MORE

Let's look at a $200,000 home with zero money down, comparing a conventional loan and a VA loan. The interest rates are going to be competitive with one another; given the same circumstances, you won't find a conventional loan at 4 percent and a VA loan at 6 percent.

For the zero-money-down VA loan, adding the funding fee of 2 percent (or $4,000) to the loan amount and using a 30-year fixed rate of 4 percent, the monthly payment is $1,176.

For the 5-percent-down conventional product, the interest rate might be 1/2 percent higher than the VA rate, or closer to 4.50 percent. On a loan amount of $190,000, the payment is $1,165; and after adding the monthly mortgage insurance payment on the conventional loan of say around $90, the payment is then $1,255, or $79 per month higher than the VA loan.

Another benefit of VA loans is apparent when comparing closing costs. Veterans only pay certain closing costs, called "allowables," in connection with a mortgage, and they don't have to pay others. This saves the veteran money at closing. A good way to remember which charges the veteran is allowed to pay is to remember the acronym ACTORS. Allowable closing costs for veterans include:

Appraisal or inspection charges
Credit report fees
Title and title-related charges
Origination fees and points
Recording charges
Survey fees, if needed

Any other fees being quoted to you must pass muster with the VA to be included. Common "nonallowables" are processing fees, administrative fees, and underwriting charges. Nonallowables are sometimes a concern—not to the buyer, but the seller. If the buyer can't pay certain lender fees, such as a processing fee or underwriting fee (we'll discuss closing costs in more detail in Chapter 14) when obtaining a VA loan, then it's the seller who typically is hit with those charges. This is something sellers don't normally like to do. For years, VA loans had this albatross, which was a deterrent in some instances. If a seller gets two offers for the same amount, which one will the seller accept? The one that hits the seller with VA nonallowables or the one that doesn't? You guessed it. Sellers could be reluctant to accept a VA offer because of the additional fees that could come into play.

Now, however, VA lenders offer a choice, and instead of charging the borrower various lender fees that the borrower wasn't allowed to pay for, the lender can replace all those charges with an origination fee in lieu of the nonallowable charges.

You may also hear of a loan called a *VA No-No*. That means you're qualified for a VA loan with no money down and there are no closing costs. The closing costs will be paid by the seller of the property, with his agreement, of course. If you have zero money down and can qualify for VA, I can find no better alternative than a VA loan.

7.18 WHAT IS A VA "ENTITLEMENT"?

A VA *entitlement* is the amount the VA will guarantee in order for a VA loan to be made. Historically, VA entitlements were based upon an archaic formula and would change once every few years. If your entitlement was $20,000, then a VA lender would make a loan to you for up to four times your entitlement amount, or in this instance a maximum loan of $80,000. Even in earlier years, $80,000 would rarely buy much of a house.

Recent changes in VA lending, however, have made the maximum amount very simple: Whatever the maximum conforming loan amount is for that year, the VA will guaranty a quarter of that amount. This is a huge benefit for VA-eligible borrowers, because now their VA home loan benefit can be used to buy properties that can compete with conventional loan limits.

7.19 HOW OFTEN CAN I USE MY VA ELIGIBILITY?

As often as you like as long as the previous VA loan was paid off and entitlement restored. If you bought a home with a VA loan and want to buy another one to live in, you can use your VA home loan benefit as long as there is enough remaining entitlement available. This is rare, however, as any remaining entitlement is typically too low to be of much use. When you refinance, you can reuse your VA eligibility, replacing your old VA loan with a new one. Your lender will take care of getting your entitlement restored during the transaction.

7.20 WHAT IS A VA STREAMLINE REFINANCE?

It's a refinance loan program that significantly cuts down on the paperwork and has relaxed credit guidelines. The VA calls it the *interest rate reduction loan* (IRRL).

Under a conventional refinance, the borrowers must qualify all over again by providing pay stubs and bank statements and maybe tax returns and everything that goes with a brand-new loan application.

With an IRRL, as long as it can be demonstrated that the veteran's interest rate is being reduced, the veteran can still qualify for the refinance, even if the credit has been damaged since the original purchase. There's one major caveat: The VA mortgage cannot have any payments that are more than 30 days late over the past six months and no more than one payment more than 30 days past the due date over the previous 12. A VA IRRL is, however, perhaps the easiest refinance to qualify for.

7.21 DO STATES HAVE VA LOAN PROGRAMS, TOO?

No, but many states do have special home-loan-related benefits. The Department of Veterans Affairs oversees the VA loan program and issues lending guidelines. Some states go one better and offer special loan programs that enhance a new VA loan. In Texas, for instance, there is the Tex-Vet program whereby the state of Texas subsidizes a VA or conventional loan purchase by offering below-market interest rates. Cal-Vet in California also has special programs for qualified veterans. You need to do the research in your own state to see if additional VA home loan benefits are offered.

7.22 WHAT ABOUT FHA LOANS?

The Federal Housing Administration (FHA) was formed in 1934 to help the country recover from its economic collapse after the Great Depression. The goal of the FHA was to get as many people owning homes as possible, and they did this by establishing lending guidelines that made it easier to get into a home than previously. Before mortgages became standardized, they were mostly handled through local banks or savings and loans. This created an array of mortgage qualification guidelines, but one of the more onerous requirements was a hefty down payment. Some mortgage loans required down payments of 50 percent or more. For many folks just coming out of the Depression, that kind of money was hard to come by. For that matter, 50 percent down is a lot of money in any economy. Owning your own home has always been the American Dream, but those early lending requirements put that dream out of reach for most Americans.

FHA loans required very little down payment. And although the FHA, as a government agency, didn't actually make loans, the FHA, like Fannie and Freddie were to do later on, established lending guidelines for the loans *and* guaranteed to buy the loan back from the lender if it went sour. Not a bad deal. In fact, it changed the way mortgages were made, and soon the FHA became the standard for those with little money for a down payment. Lenders could make an FHA mortgage, and as long as the loan was written under FHA guidelines, then the lender could sell that loan to FHA if it ever went into default. That's one of the reasons FHA loans have historically had less stringent guidelines than other mortgage programs.

FHA loans aren't really all that different from conventional or VA loans. They still offer fixed- or adjustable-rate products, but they allow people who aren't fortunate enough to have VA benefits to buy a house with less than 20 percent down. The minimum down payment required for an FHA loan is only 3.5 percent, and while you still need to pay a mortgage insurance premium, the monthly premium is less than a similar amount needed for a 3-percent-down conventional loan. In addition, the mortgage insurance premium—which is 1.5 percent of the loan amount—can be rolled into the loan and does not have to be borrowed, as long as the final loan amount doesn't exceed FHA loan limits for your area.

7.23 WHO SETS FHA LOAN LIMITS AND HOW MUCH ARE THEY?

The Department of Housing and Urban Development (HUD) establishes FHA loan limits by county each year. These loans can vary from county to county. Your FHA lender will have the maximum FHA loan limit for your area, or you can visit *www.hud.gov* and check it out on your own. Typically, FHA loan limits are approximately half of what can be found in the conventional loan market, and still higher in so-called high cost areas, such as California or Hawaii. Often, however, these limits are too low for most homes in such areas, as housing prices are much higher than the FHA loan limit for the area.

7.24 IS FHA ONLY FOR FIRST-TIME HOME BUYERS?

No, but you wouldn't know it by looking at some of the numbers. Most FHA mortgages are issued to first-timers. There are no borrower restrictions with regard to income limits, but you must occupy the property as your primary residence and you can never have more than one FHA loan at a time.

7.25 WHEN DO I CHOOSE AN FHA LOAN INSTEAD OF ANY OTHER?

When you have very little money to put down and you think your credit might not be the best. FHA loans have some advantages over other types of financing. You still get competitive rates with only 3.5 percent down, and you get a choice between fixed and adjustable. Yes, you'll have a form of private mortgage insurance (PMI), strategically labeled mortgage insurance premium (MIP), but it's at a lower rate than conventional loans with 3 percent or 5 percent down.

TELL ME MORE

Another benefit is that FHA loans relax their underwriting guidelines in certain areas, such as credit quality, allowing for people to coborrow without restrictions on their personal debt ratios, letting someone buy a house while in a Chapter 13 bankruptcy, allowing all of the down payment and closing costs to be a gift instead of having to be saved up, and restricting the amount of closing costs the buyer has to pay.

If you have little or no money down of your own, but can get 3 percent as a gift from a relative or by using a down payment assistance program, and if the loan you need is at or below the limits, then FHA is a very good alternative for you. If you do require a gift to buy a home and want an FHA loan, the FHA has restricted who can and cannot give you financial assistance. Those who can provide financial aid include family, church, and government agencies.

7.26 CAN I USE A COBORROWER TO HELP ME QUALIFY FOR AN FHA LOAN?

Yes, and this is a unique advantage to FHA loans. If you want to buy a house or condo to live in and can't quite make the monthly payments on your own, your parents or another family member can help as "nonoccupying coborrowers."

It used to be that almost every loan allowed for someone else to be on the note to help the borrower qualify from an income or credit standpoint, but recently conventional loans made the owner-occupant qualify on her own. FHA is the only program that allows for the income from nonoccupants to be used when qualifying for the loan. This is a popular program for parents who want to buy a condo or house for their college student to live in. By putting the college student on the note, suddenly it's considered an "owner occupied" property, resulting in lower rates for the loan.

7.27 DOES FHA HELP ME SAVE MONEY ON CLOSING COSTS?

It used to do so by restricting what an FHA applicant could pay in terms of closing fees, much like VA nonallowable closing costs, but it has modernized and now allows for the borrower to pay for closing costs just like on a conventional loan. Just as VA nonallowables were a hindrance when making an offer on a house, because the seller was asked to pay for some of the buyer's costs, the FHA began losing market share and revised some of its antiquated guidelines.

TELL ME MORE

Let's say there are a bunch of fees, such as attorney charges and lender fees, that add up to $1,000 and a seller is looking at identical offers. If you are asking the seller to pay $1,000 in fees and the other offer isn't, you're not getting the deal unless you're very lucky. All things being equal, of course. There's another way to have those $1,000 in fees paid on your behalf, and that's when the lender pays for them. But don't get too excited, because the lender will only do this by increasing your interest rate enough to cover the $1,000.

On a $100,000 FHA loan with $1,000 in costs to be paid, you simply divide $1,000 by $100,000 and you get .01 or 10 basis points. That's typically enough to increase your rate by around 1/8 percent. (We'll discuss this method in more detail in Chapter 14.) In short, the FHA limited which fees an FHA borrower could pay. Later, the FHA eliminated the "nonallowable" closing cost feature entirely, and is now on equal footing with conventional loans. The next step for the FHA would be to increase loan limits, just as VA loans did.

7.27A WHAT IS THE USDA MORTGAGE PROGRAM?

This is an interesting loan program because it's been around for years with different names but seldom used, which is a shame. The USDA loan program was reintroduced in 1990 and is the only other government-backed mortgage loan that does not require a down payment. However, the loan can only be used in certain areas and there are income limitations for the borrowers.

TELL ME MORE

This zero-down loan program is designed for rural and semirural areas but encompasses nearly 97 percent of the country's geography. Yet due to the mapping, you'll be surprised at areas that are deemed eligible by the USDA as an acceptable location. These maps are updated every 10 years, so some areas that were outside of suburban areas are now located within suburban areas, although the USDA still labels the area as rural.

Further, the total household income cannot exceed 115 percent of the median income for the area. These are the only two restrictions for the program; otherwise the USDA loan can be used by anyone.

The USDA loan should be a strong consideration for those who qualify in the right area seeking to finance a home purchase with as little cash as possible. Interest rates for USDA loans are typically lower than other loan programs and while there is a monthly mortgage insurance payment, it is also lower. The USDA loan carries a government-backed guarantee financed with a "guarantee fee" of 2 percent of the loan amount that is rolled into the mortgage and not paid out of pocket by the buyers.

7.28 WHAT ABOUT FIRST-TIME HOME BUYER LOANS?

It used to be that a first-time home buyer loan was maybe one or two programs designed for people who either never owned a home or hadn't owned a home in three years. Back then, the first-time home buyer status mostly meant a relaxation of debt ratios by a few percent. Instead of an allowable 36 percent housing ratio, the ratio was 41 percent or some such number. These loans were great. Now, however, there are many more programs for first-time home buyers that don't necessarily use relaxed debt ratios; they can also be loans that target certain geographic areas or loans that offer down payment assistance.

Often, certain communities and states can issue bonds and form a relationship with Fannie Mae or Freddie Mac to help increase home ownership. The recipient is typically someone who's never owned a home before.

When I have a first-time home buyer with regular credit and 3 percent to 5 percent down, I first look at both FHA and conventional loans and try to get them qualified on either of those programs. They get the best rates available whether or not they're first-time home buyers. If there's a special bond program offering lower rates for a particular segment of home buyers, then yes, I look there first to see if they qualify in terms of income or other qualifications, but in general, FHA and conventional loans are tough to beat. If the buyers have no money down, the best product is Fannie Mae's HomeReady mortgage, as described in Chapter 4.

Many people mistakenly believe that first-time home buyers automatically get a special interest rate that is way below market rate. While there may be certain bond programs in a particular city or state that offer better rates, usually first-time home buyers don't get better rates. Now, first-time home-buyer status is more of a requirement for special loan programs issued by various lenders and governments. These special programs can be designed for people with credit scores as low as 600 and who are allowed to borrow closing costs. Special first-time programs can target a specific income group or a census tract within a city.

7.29 WHAT DOES "PORTFOLIO LENDING" MEAN?

A *portfolio loan* is a loan made by a direct lender, usually a bank, that is designed to be kept in-house. This means that it is made by a lender with no intentions of selling the loan or having it underwritten to any external guidelines. Instead, the loan is made and kept in the lender's loan portfolio. Unfortunately, portfolio lending is a term that's bandied about too often, encompassing loan programs that are nothing near portfolio. Often a portfolio loan is incorrectly described as any loan that's not a conventional or government loan.

Portfolio loans go by their own guidelines and don't necessarily follow loan rules established by others. Why would someone want a portfolio loan? Perhaps when their loan application doesn't quite meet the guidelines of a conventional loan. Or when no government program will work.

TELL ME MORE

Let's say you just found an apartment building with 10 units and need financing. Conventional or government loans don't cover apartment buildings, so those loans won't work. Instead, you'll need a portfolio loan. Or maybe you found a fourplex but had no money for a down payment. If you found conventional financing at all, it might require a higher down payment or other special circumstances that you might not find attractive. Are you a real estate investor and have so many residential properties that conventional lenders think you have one too many? Go portfolio. Portfolio lending is more of a "commonsense" loan that might not fit the conventional guideline, but shucks, it looks like such a great deal.

Where do you get a portfolio loan? From your bank. But don't be surprised if your portfolio loan is of a shorter term or maybe a hybrid. Retail banks certainly like to make loans, but they also don't like to tie themselves into any one rate for an extended period. If a bank makes a portfolio loan at 6 percent, and then three years later rates are at 9 percent, they'd like to make more loans, just at the new, higher rates.

7.30 WHAT'S THE DIFFERENCE BETWEEN SECOND HOMES AND RENTAL PROPERTY?

Second homes are usually vacation homes. Someone may own a home in the North to live in during the summer and have another home in the sunny South when winter comes rolling along. *Rental* or *investment homes* are used for income purposes. You collect rent on them. No big deal, really, except that some lenders charge higher rates on loans for rental properties than for owner-occupied homes.

Rental homes require more down payment and a slightly higher interest rate than a second home. Why? Risk for investment properties is higher. If a homeowner falls on hard times and is having difficulty deciding whether to pay for the mortgage on his family's home or on the rental property across town, which one do you think that homeowner will let go first? The family's own home? Nope. It's almost always the rental properties that go first.

Interest rates for rental properties will usually increase by 150 basis points, or 1/4 percent to 3/8 percent in rate. In addition, minimum down payments for conventional investment loans start at 10 percent. And you'll have a higher mortgage insurance premium on investment loans as well. Most competitive rental rates start when the buyer has at least 20 percent to put down.

Second homes aren't rented out. They're used exclusively by the owner. There's very little increase in rates for a second home when compared to a primary residence, with a 1/4-point increase in discount point being a common charge. With some lenders, the rates for a primary and secondary home are identical.

7.31 HOW DOES THE LENDER KNOW THAT A PROPERTY IS A SECOND HOME AND NOT A RENTAL UNIT?

There are a couple of ways. The first way is to simply consider the property in question. Is it a duplex across town or is it a home about

500 miles away on a beach? Vacation homes aren't duplexes across town. If you try to convince a lender that your new purchase 15 miles away is your dream vacation home, they won't buy it.

A second way to identify the property comes during the appraisal. When the appraiser inspects the property and there are other people living there, that appraiser will most likely ask the tenants if they're renters. If they are, the appraiser is required to perform another appraisal function, called a "rent survey," which will be included with the full appraisal. Are you refinancing an existing investment property and trying to claim that it's a vacation home and not a rental property? Your lender will see that you have rental income on your tax returns.

Trying to make a rental home look like a second home to save on fees and rates rarely works. Lenders have seen all the tricks, and if they determine that your vacation home isn't a vacation home but a rental, expect the rental loan program. Don't lie on your application.

7.32 CAN I USE RENTAL INCOME TO QUALIFY FOR A MORTGAGE?

Normally, no. Unless you're a seasoned real estate investor, a lender won't count the rental income to help qualify you. This sometimes looks like a great opportunity when a potential buyer sees a nice duplex for sale and plans to use the rent from the unit next door to help offset the mortgage. While the rent next door will certainly help to do that, the lender won't normally use this rental income to offset debt ratios unless you've got some direct experience in being a landlord.

7.33 ARE LOAN LIMITS FOR RENTAL PROPERTIES THE SAME AS FOR PRIMARY RESIDENCES?

Yes, but there's also a bonus. Fannie and Freddie both have the same conforming limits, but they also set the maximum loan limits for what they call *1–4 units*. The base single-family limit as of 2007 is $417,000. The maximum loan limit for a duplex, or a two-family unit, would be $533,850. A three-unit limit would then be $645,300, and finally a four-unit purchase limit would be $801,950. If you're eyeing a nice duplex but the price is above the current conforming single-family limit, don't forget the multiunit limits are higher than for a single-family home. These limits change each year just as single-family limits do. The FHA also provides financing at higher loan amounts for apartment buildings, also called multifamily units.

7.34 WHAT ABOUT SELLER FINANCING?

Seller financing is certainly an option, as long as the seller knows about it, of course. You'll go through a lot fewer hoops to qualify than when applying with a mortgage company. Just understand that you're still applying for a mortgage loan, except that it's an individual loaning you the money instead of a mortgage lender.

Seller-financed notes almost always carry higher interest rates than conventional or government loans. Why? Well, why wouldn't they? If a buyer approaches a seller and asks for financing, there is usually a reason the buyer didn't go to a mortgage lender in the first place. Most likely it's due to a poor credit situation or hard-to-prove income. If you go for seller financing, be prepared to show not only some down payment money, but also your credit report.

The rest of the closing process will look similar to a conventional closing. Because it's an individual financing the note, that individual may or may not require the same things a lender would require, such as a title examination, title insurance, or even a flood cert-ificate. Do you want to know if your new house sits in a flood zone? Of course you do, but unless you get a flood certificate declaring your flood status, then you won't know. The same goes for title issues. Is the seller in fact bringing a clear title to the clos-ing table? Your real estate agent, if you have one, can help guide you through the process, but don't forget about title insurance and legal review. You want this sale to go through as smoothly as any other. Not only that, but when you go to sell this property or if you decide to refinance later on, you, too, will be asked to provide evi-dence of clear title, flood zone, and the property being legally recorded as yours.

Another time to ask for seller financing might be for a second mortgage. For example, you want to buy a house for $100,000. The lender agrees to finance 80 percent of the sales price, or $80,000, but no more, but you only have 5 percent available to put down. You need to find another 15 percent to close the deal. Your lender, however, may not care that you seek additional funding outside of what the lender provided, as long as the combined loan-to-value ratio doesn't exceed 95 percent. In this instance, you take an $80,000 first mortgage, you put down 5 percent, or $5,000, and the seller agrees to a second note for the remaining 15 percent. You've just secured an 80–15–5 loan, with the seller providing the 15 percent.

Often, *subprime loans* work this way, where lenders may allow higher combined loan-to-value ratios as long as they're only exposed to 80 percent or so, but they don't care if you finance the rest of it, all the way to 100 percent of the sales price.

Make sure all seller financing is recorded, just as with any other loan. Take precautions as a buyer to review the property with an appraisal, inspection, title report, and flood certificate, and use a seasoned settlement agent to help guide you through the process when you go to close. Seller financing can be a good option, but it can also be a nightmare if something isn't done properly to transfer ownership.

7.35 HOW CAN I RENT-TO-OWN OR USE A LEASE-PURCHASE TO BUY A HOUSE?

A *lease-purchase agreement,* also known as rent-to-own, is a viable option when someone wants to buy a property but isn't quite there yet. Or if they find a house they like and lease the home until they have saved up enough money for a down payment to qualify for a conventional mortgage.

There are a few key ingredients to making a successful lease-purchase. In a typical lease-purchase agreement, the renter agrees to buy the house she is living in at a particular price at a future date, say, two years from now. In addition, each month a portion of the monthly rent payment goes toward the down payment. At the end of two years, the borrower retrieves her down payment monies from the owner and then qualifies for a conventional mortgage from a mortgage company. So far so good, but if the agreement is not drawn properly, the buyer could be out both the house as well as the down payment savings.

A proper lease-purchase agreement has to set up rent payments each month independent of any portion that goes to a down payment. That portion must be above and beyond the current market rents for the area. If you're in a two-bedroom house and two-bedroom houses in the area rent for $750, then anything above the market rent can be considered yours. If you pay $950 each month, then $750 will go to rent and $200 will go to your down payment. If your monthly payment is not over and above market rent for your area, it's possible that your lender won't count any of that $200 and will instead look upon it as either rent or a $200 gift each month from the seller of the property. Gifts have to come from relatives or qualified institutions. Furthermore, extra payments need to be held in a separate account by your landlord and not commingled with his general account.

Lastly, there's the agreed-upon sales price of the home. Let's say that two years ago you agreed to buy the property at $150,000, but since then property values have steadily declined; today the home is only worth $120,000. Remember that lenders use the lower of the sales price or appraised value when making loans. You'll need to come up with the $30,000 difference or renegotiate. If the seller doesn't want to renegotiate, you're most likely out of the deal and have lost all your money in the transaction. Don't let this happen.

In your original lease-purchase agreement with the owner, don't agree upon a certain price. Instead, agree upon a price that has to be justified by an appraisal. That way the protection works both ways. It works to your favor in times of property devaluations and works in the seller's favor if values increase. Lenders can be leery of lease-purchase deals, so it's mandatory that everything you do is documented and that both you and the owner follow the prescribed procedures.

7.36 WHAT'S A WRAPAROUND MORTGAGE?

There's another way to get financing and that's called a *wraparound mortgage,* or a "wrap." A wrap mortgage is a mortgage "wrapped" around another mortgage. It works like this: A homeowner sells to someone and also acts as his mortgage lender, while never retiring the original mortgage. The buyer makes mortgage payments to the seller, who then continues to make mortgage payments to her mortgage company.

This means that borrowers don't go through a mortgage company to get a loan but instead work up terms agreeable to the seller. More often than not, the original lender never knows that the house has been sold because the lender continues to receive payments from the original customer. This can be dangerous.

Many mortgages have an *acceleration clause* that basically says, "Don't change the ownership in this property or we'll immediately ask for all of our money back." Or what if the new buyers become late on their payments to the seller, who then becomes late on the original mortgage payments? People who use a wraparound mortgage must understand all the implications of a wrap before getting involved in one. However, if all parties do what they're supposed to do, then a wrap is certainly an option.

7.37 WHAT IS A BIWEEKLY LOAN PROGRAM?

This is a loan program where you pay every two weeks instead of once per month. Such programs, which are good because they can help pay off your loan sooner, work similarly to making one extra payment per year. Using the extra payment example in Question 7.13, take that same $661 extra payment, divide it in half, to $331, and pay that amount every other week. Since there are 26 biweekly periods in a year, that works out to 13 full mortgage payments, accomplishing the same goal as if you simply made one extra payment per year. Too often, such biweekly programs are established by third-party businesses that charge fees to set up the program. If you're okay with paying $300 or $400 just to set up a biweekly, that's fine. Personally, I think it's not a very good deal if it's something you can effectively do yourself without paying anyone more money for the privilege.

7.38 ARE SUBPRIME MORTGAGES GONE?

Mostly, yes, especially compared to the era from 2000–2007. There are, however, a few fearless lenders who are making loans designed for those with damaged credit, but those lenders are difficult to find.

To offset lower credit borrowers, these lenders will require a higher down payment—at least 20 to 30 percent down—low debt ratios, and a solid explanation why credit scores are so low. Negative-amortization mortgages are also a thing of the past. Neg-am loans could actually grow rather than being paid down over time as borrowers with neg-am loans had the option of paying an amount that would not be applied to the loan balance as well as not paying the fully indexed interest each month.

7.39 WHAT ARE HAMP AND HARP?

The Home Affordable Modification Program, or HAMP, and the Home Affordable Refinance Program, HARP, were both introduced in 2009 with two different objectives. HAMP's mission was to assist homeowners who were in danger of default and HARP was enacted to help homeowners refinance when they owed more than the home was worth.

TELL ME MORE

HAMP is a loan modification. A loan modification replaces an existing mortgage with a new one that is more in line with the borrower's current financial situation. A HAMP is not a refinance, but a modification. A HAMP lender will document your current monthly income and attempt to adjust the mortgage until your mortgage payment is below 31 percent of your gross monthly income. A lender using HAMP guidelines can lower the interest rate on the loan, extending the loan term or issuing a payment forbearance, which writes off delinquent mortgage payments and begins anew. This program was expected to expire in 2016 but was extended yet again by Congress.

HARP is a refinance program introduced to help so-called underwater borrowers refinance an existing mortgage. HARP requires the mortgage loan be owned by either Fannie Mae or Freddie Mac. Typical refinancing of a conventional loan requires at least a 10 percent equity position. If someone owed $200,000 on a mortgage and the property was appraised at just $150,000, the borrower couldn't refinance to get a lower rate. With HARP, there is no appraisal needed and therefore no "underwater" status whatsoever. HARP is scheduled to expire in September of 2017.

Loans for Good to Great Credit

If your credit scores are above 680 and you've gotten your automated loan approval, you mostly have your choice at a smorgasbord of loans. There are literally hundreds of mortgage types from which to choose, and you can get a headache trying to research them all. This chapter is your aspirin.

8.1 WHAT SHOULD I LOOK FOR IN A MORTGAGE LOAN?

Get a loan that you feel comfortable with, one you don't have to worry about and that is easy to get in terms of qualifying and cost. You can knock yourself out on that one. Fannie and Freddie make up about two-thirds of all mortgages generated; the others are government-backed and portfolio loans. But instead of trying to find the absolute best loan for your situation, first ask yourself if indeed you are very different from most other borrowers. Do you have good credit? Do you have a down payment? Do you have a job and can you afford the new mortgage payment? If so, there's no reason to get cute about your mortgage.

Forget perusing through your mortgage lender's loan book exploring all the possible alternatives. Get a fixed or get an ARM. Get a fixed if you're in it for the long term or are risk-averse. Get an ARM if you see this purchase as being short term, say, three to five years. Get a hybrid if you're in between. Why such narrow choices? Pricing.

Look at it this way: If the single most common item on the market today is available with most every lender on the planet, and if the loans are exactly alike, then what do you think that does to the price? It keeps it low. If more people are trying to sell the same product and it's available 24 hours a day, then you would think that such a commodity's determining factor would be price, right? If a conventional loan is everywhere, then the only thing you accomplish by trying to find something better is a wasted effort.

Yet beware, the lowest-priced loan does not necessarily mean an enjoyable borrowing experience. Get referrals from friends, associates, and your real estate agent and find a lender with competitive pricing as well as a solid reputation.

8.2 SO EVERYONE SHOULD FIRST TRY FOR A CONVENTIONAL LOAN?

Yes, in most cases, you should try for a conventional loan first. There are more conventional loans and conventional lenders than any other type, which serves to keep the costs of these loans down. That's if everyone were exactly the same. But the differences in loans for people with good credit lie in special circumstances. Special circumstances may mean not having any down payment money. Special circumstances may mean having a cosigner on a loan. Special circumstances may mean having difficult-to-prove income.

8.3 WHAT IF MY LOAN ISN'T A FANNIE LOAN? WHAT IF IT'S A JUMBO OR A PORTFOLIO?

Most loans still will accept a Fannie or Freddie approval using an AUS, and simply ask that the loan officer document the file just as if he were sending a loan to Freddie Mac. Why reinvent the wheel, right? Most jumbo and portfolio loans may actually require that the loan be submitted through Fannie's automated system even though the loan isn't eligible to be a Fannie loan because the loan amount is too high.

Another loan program that doesn't fit Freddie limits will still require that the loan be submitted to Freddie Mac's automated underwriting system and follow the guidelines from there. In many instances, a nonconforming approval will look identical to a conforming approval in that the loan was underwritten and documented the very same way.

8.4 THEN HOW DO I MANAGE TO FIND THE LOAN THAT'S RIGHT FOR ME?

The first and perhaps foremost consideration is how much you intend to put down. Loans with no money down have higher interest rates and can be more difficult to qualify for than loans with 20 percent down or more. The more down you have, the wider the selection of loans that are available to you.

TELL ME MORE

There aren't many zero-down loans. If you don't want to put anything down on a home, then you have a couple of choices: government or nongovernment. If you want to put zero money down, the absolute best loan program is a VA loan. If you have VA eligibility, you need look no further. The veteran gets competitive interest rates and a choice between a fixed or an adjustable rate. Hands down, this is the best deal, if you qualify.

Not a qualifying veteran? Then take a look at the USDA program to see if it's a fit. If you're a first-time buyer, check with local and state agencies to see about a grant that can be used to offset the cost of a down payment and closing fees.

8.5 SHOULD I ALWAYS TRY TO PUT AS MUCH DOWN AS I CAN?

Sometimes, but not always. If you can put a minimum of 20 percent down, that might be ideal, provided you have the funds available. It gives you both a strong equity position to offset any near-term price depreciations while avoiding any PMI requirements. Putting more than 20 percent down is a personal preference, but putting much more than that down might be too much if you have other things you'd like to do with your money. In fact, some mortgage loan officers might think it is better to put as little down as possible and invest the difference in other vehicles. Having some money in the transaction, though, keeps your payments lower and you have immediate equity in your home.

8.6 DO I HAVE A CHOICE IN MY LOAN TERM?

Of course you do, as long as the lender offers it. Most loans start as low as 10 years, but terms can be anything between 10 and 50 years as long as the lender offers the product. Most advertisements on fixed-rate loans are for 30-year loans and sometimes for 15-year fixed loans.

The difference in term lies in the monthly payment and how much interest you can save over the long term. Even though the interest rate on a shorter term is usually lower, the monthly payments will be higher. For instance, for a 4 percent 30-year fixed rate on a $300,000 loan, the monthly payments are $1,654. For a similarly priced 15-year fixed loan at 3.75 percent, the payments inflate to $2,820. An increase of nearly 30 percent! Often this increase in monthly payment stops people from choosing a 15-year loan and they take the standard 30-year product instead. A benefit of choosing a shorter-term loan is that you're building equity so much faster and your home is paid off sooner.

Another factor in choosing your payback period is how much interest you're going to pay on that loan. Using the same example and taking both loans to term, you pay over $400,000 in interest with a 30-year loan and just over $175,000 with a 15-year note. That's a huge difference. Yeah, I know that few people take loans to full term, but even then the math works because the bulk of mortgage interest is paid at the beginning of the loan, not toward the end. Again using this scenario, after 10 years the loan balance on a 30-year note is $251,312, while after 10 years the loan balance on a 15-year loan is already down to $111,400. That's another reason to consider a shorter term for your mortgage.

8.7 WHY ARE PAYMENTS HIGHER ON A 15-YEAR LOAN EVEN THOUGH THE RATE IS LOWER?

Because the amortization term is squished in half. With a 30-year mortgage there's plenty of time to spread out interest payments, but when you cut the term in half, then payments must increase to both meet the term and accommodate the interest over 180 months.

TELL ME MORE

While paying less interest makes a 15-year loan attractive, the higher monthly payments can make it less so. In fact, someone who can qualify on a 30-year loan may not even qualify for a 15-year mortgage—there's that much difference. But guess what? There are other choices. One that might fit better is a 20-year mortgage. Or even a 25-year note. Many lenders simply keep the rate the same as a 30-year fixed mortgage but shorten the payback period. Using our example, payment on a 25-year loan at 7 percent would be $2,120 per month. It's slightly higher than a 30-year loan but still a saving of over $63,000 in interest. A 20-year loan would save you $141,700 in interest yet only raise your monthly payment by a couple of hundred dollars instead of more than $500 with the 15-year note.

Most lenders will offer amortization periods other than a 30-year or 15-year fixed, although most of them limit the choices to five-year increments, with a 10-year minimum. Instead of just 30-year or 15-year loans, you now can choose 10, 15, 20, 25, or even 40 years.

Some lenders will even amortize your loan over goofy terms, like 18 or 23 years. It's not common, but it's usually used when someone is refinancing a current mortgage with a lender and only wants to amortize over the remaining term of the current loan. But you usually have to ask for different terms. Don't assume that just because you only see 30-year and 15-year rate quotes that there's nothing else available. If your loan officer stammers and states that you can't set your own loan term, then find someone who can offer those terms. You just have to ask.

8.8 WON'T MY LOAN OFFICER HELP ME FIND THE RIGHT MORTGAGE?

Hopefully, yes. That's one of their jobs. Good loan officers, especially good mortgage broker loan officers, always keep a keen eye out for the newest loan product on the market. But it's not uncommon for a loan officer to get used to doing only one or two types of loans. Most every loan officer will do a conventional Fannie or Freddie loan. They're easy, and the way technology is today with AUS, they're fall-down easy. That can make some loan officers lazy, so they might try to pigeonhole you into a particular loan program simply because they know how to work that loan better than others. There's really no way to tell if a loan officer is trying to make you take one program over another until you interview that person (see Chapter 12), but just know that human nature sometimes allows for the easiest path to be chosen.

Government loans like FHA, USDA, and VA programs are documented differently. Because they have different paperwork from conventional mortgages, they're foreign to many loan officers. If you think that a VA loan might be a better deal for you, but the loan officer doesn't offer that program or tries to push you away from it, then you need to hear a good reason why. Furthermore, some mortgage companies aren't allowed or qualified to work with FHA loans. If you're in a loan meeting and you have 3 percent down and FHA never comes up in the conversation, then you need to find out why.

In general terms, however, loan officers can help borrowers find a good mortgage fit, if they do their job right. Remember, though, that one of the first things you need to do is submit your loan application for an AUS approval to see what you might be qualified for and what loan documentation you'll need for which particular product.

8.9 WHERE ARE THE "STATED" INCOME AND "NO DOCUMENTATION" LOANS?

They're history, along with many of the lenders who made them. The CFPB essentially eliminated such programs with the introduction of QM loans. There are still portfolio programs that have some characteristics of a stated income loan. A true "stated" loan means the lender uses the income listed on the application without using income tax returns or pay stubs. However, there are a few programs that review bank statements in lieu of income verification.

These "bank statement" programs look at the most recent 12 months of bank statements and use the deposits shown on the statements as income. Such loans require excellent credit and anywhere from a 20 to 30 percent down payment.

8.10 DOES THE TYPE OF PROPERTY AFFECT THE KIND OF LOAN I CAN HAVE?

Most definitely. Conventional mortgages finance a maximum of four units, including duplex, three-unit, and fourplex buildings. More than four units attached and you're looking at a commercial loan or apartment building loan. But if your property is simply a single-family dwelling, then you have access to most every loan there is.

TELL ME MORE

Other properties that might take special consideration are condominiums. Condos offer individual ownership in the living unit while all common areas, such as sidewalks and recreational areas, are shared. Condos also carry their own hazard insurance, so you won't have to take out an insurance policy for structural damage; on the other hand, you'll have to pay homeowners association dues. Condos have a few special requirements, but if your condo meets them, then almost every loan available also works for a condo. Special requirements for condos can be guidelines that restrict the number of units in a condominium project that can be rented out or limit the number of condos one person can own.

Lenders have to approve your condominium project, and they do so by evaluating how many units are in the complex, how many condos are rented out, and if the project is completed or not.

Lenders like to see a condominium project that is "owner occupied" rather than having most of the complex rented out. Generally, the "owner occupancy" percentage is 60 percent, and no one person or entity can own more than 10 percent of the project. The project must also be 100 percent complete, including all of the common areas, and the control of the project must have been turned over by the developer to the homeowners association. Once the control of the project is turned over to the homeowners association, that signals that construction is 100 percent complete and the builder has no more legal interest in the property. These classification requirements can be waived or relaxed with a higher down payment. Some loans may have additional requirements based on the height of the structure. For example, loans may require more money down if the building is more than four or eight stories tall.

There are two types of condominium classifications as defined by lenders: "warrantable" and "nonwarrantable." Warrantable condos meet the specifications I've just described with regard to owner occupancy, completion of common areas, and such. But what if the condos are brand new and still being built? Then they are nonwarrantable, and they have higher rates than warrantable condos.

What makes for a nonwarrantable condo? Typically the differences lie in phase completion. Most condominium projects are constructed in phases. Phase I is completed and buyers move in, while phase II and perhaps phases III and IV are still being built. Warrantable condos need to have all phases completed, while nonwarrantable just means that the subject phase is done.

8.11 WHAT TYPES OF PROPERTY CAN I EXPECT PROBLEMS WITH?

Units that are bought under a time-share agreement, condotels, mobile homes, and properties that are particularly unusual.

Time-Shares

A time-share is a property that you have partial ownership in, and you live there periodically throughout the year. A common time-share is a condominium or beach house in a vacation spot, so various owners share time to vacation there. Time-shares present a problem, regardless of whether the unit is part of a condominium. Lenders can't make a loan to someone who doesn't own the property 100 percent. Should the borrower default on a time-share loan, the lender can't foreclose, since the property has other owners.

Condotels

A similar situation arises with condotels, which are condominiums that are owned individually but function more like a hotel than a home. Someone will buy a condotel and let a management company rent out the unit just as if it were a hotel room. There's a check-in desk, just like in a motel, and the management rents out the unit weekly or monthly. The owner gets the rent, paying a portion to the management company. Lenders view such properties not as a house but as a commercial deal, more like a motel loan.

Mobile Homes

Are you considering buying a manufactured house or mobile home? A main requirement for a mobile home loan is that the property being bought has to be considered real estate and not personal property. With personal property, financing is more akin to an automobile or boat loan.

When is a mobile home personal property? When it's not permanently attached to the ground using specific methods or when the owner doesn't own the land the mobile home sits on.

There are fewer sources for manufactured housing mortgages than there are for "stick-built" homes. Conventional lenders may not be your first resource for financing although conventional and government-backed programs do allow for mobile homes under proper conditions. Your best bet is to find a lender that specializes in mobile homes.

Unusual Properties

You can also expect problems getting loans when there are no similar properties, or comparable sales, in the area. The lender needs to see three similar properties that have sold within the preceding 12 months and compare those sales with your new home. If you've got a 2,500-square-foot three-bedroom home in an established community, it's likely that similar three-bedroom homes will be found. If not, you'll have a hard time getting a good appraisal. No appraisal, no loan.

Many times this happens with rural property on acreage. If your house is in the country and sits on 10 acres, you'll probably be okay, as long as there are similar homes throughout the area that show up as sales. But what if you have a home that sits on 100 acres? What if your house is the only home in a 10-mile radius that sits on 200 acres? If you can't find properties that are like yours, with homes on large acreage, be prepared for some trouble. Lenders are less inclined to make loans when there are no comparable sales to be found.

C H A P T E R   9

Refinancing and Home Equity Loans

A *refinance* is just that, "redoing" the original mortgage. There are different reasons to refinance, including to get a different rate or different term, or to replace a current loan with a new one and pull money out at the same time to do with whatever you wish.

9.1 WHY WOULD I WANT TO REFINANCE MY MORTGAGE?

There are many reasons, but the primary one is to reduce the interest rate on your current mortgage loan. If your rate is at 8 percent and current rates are at 7 percent, then you might consider refinancing to get a lower payment. It really doesn't make much sense to refinance if rates go up, right? But lowering a monthly payment may make sense to you if you can save money on mortgage interest. Refinancing to get a new rate is called a *rate-and-term refinance*. You're changing the interest rate, and changing the term, or length, of the new note.

TELL ME MORE

Let's say you bought a home a few years ago and borrowed $200,000 when the interest rates were 5.5 percent. With a 30-year fixed-rate mortgage, that payment would be $1,304. Later, mortgage rates dropped to 4.375 percent, which would give you a new monthly payment of $1,206, saving you $98 per month. That's a fairly hefty difference. Taken out to full term, that's a savings of over $35,280 in mortgage interest, while at the same time freeing up $98 each and every month.

Another reason to refinance might be to go from an adjustable-rate mortgage to a fixed-rate mortgage to remove the uncertainty that adjustable-rate mortgages carry. Yet another reason might be to get a hybrid loan or an ARM when fixed rates are relatively high. If mortgage rates seem to be at a peak and there's not a whole lot out there under 8 percent, some borrowers take an ARM that has a lower start rate. Instead of an 8 percent fixed, say a borrower elects to take a 6 percent 3/1 ARM. A couple years later, rates begin to move down and fixed rates hit 6 percent, the same rate as the hybrid. At that point, it would be wise for the borrower to try to get out of an adjustable rate and move into a fixed one.

That strategy can also work in reverse. Some people want to get the lowest payment possible on their loan, regardless of whether it's fixed or adjustable. You can always move from a fixed to an ARM. Still another reason to refinance might be to pull some equity out of your home in the form of cash while at the same time bringing down your overall interest rate.

9.2 SHOULD I WAIT UNTIL THE INTEREST RATE IS 2 PERCENT LOWER THAN MY CURRENT ONE TO REFINANCE?

No, and I'll explain why. The real test is how long it takes to recover your closing costs using your new lower payment, compared to how long you anticipate keeping the house. Forget all the so-called rules of thumb.

TELL ME MORE

Subtract the new lower monthly payment from your old payment, then divide the closing costs of your new loan by that difference. The result is the number of months required to "recover" the closing costs paid. For instance, if your savings are $150 per month and your closing costs add up to $1,500, then it would take 10 months to recover the fees associated with the new loan. If you plan on owning the home more than 10 months, then you might want to consider a refinance. That's about it. It's not rocket science.

If you decide to wait until rates drop another 1/2 percent to get to the magic "two years" date, you may be waiting for two more things: lost interest savings because you didn't refinance sooner and the possibility that rates will turn back up!

On the flip side, say you refinanced and saved $150 per month. However, you immediately got transferred and had to sell your home, which means that you would never recover those closing costs, much less enjoy lower payments on that house. The key to a refinance is saving mortgage interest while keeping an eye on closing costs, and at the same time anticipating how long you'll own the house.

9.3 WHAT IS MY RESCISSION PERIOD?

A *rescission period* is a unique feature of refinanced mortgages and only applies to your primary residence. It's a three-day grace period that lets you out of your mortgage agreement with no strings attached.

TELL ME MORE

When you first bought your home and closed your loan, your lender funded that loan the very same day. There was no "buyer's remorse" period. If, however, you later refinanced that home, your primary residence, the loan didn't fund that day. Instead, there was a mandatory three-day "cooling off" period to allow you time to reconsider your actions. Those three days start the following day and end the third day. Your loan would fund after the third day. Please note that those three days must fall between Monday and Saturday. Note that Sundays and holidays don't count. Why is there a rescission period? It gives you time to evaluate your loan and review your papers and closing fees. If there is a problem, you simply sign your rescission papers and the whole deal's off.

If you refinance your mortgage, go to closing, and find that the interest rate wasn't what you were quoted and the loan officer won't change the papers, then you have three days after that to decide whether you want the loan. Are closing costs much more than you anticipated? You have three days to decide if you still want the deal.

For that matter, you can change your mind for absolutely any reason, or for no reason at all. You can rescind simply because the wind changed direction. Be warned, however, that if you decide to rescind, you're not going to get some of your fees back that you already paid. The deal simply falls through and everybody goes home.

9.4 HOW LONG SHOULD I WAIT TO RECOVER CLOSING COSTS?

That's a fair question. If you applied the refinance test solely to owning the home longer than it takes to recover the fees, then it might get a little stupid if your recovery time is 10 years. So what's a good period? I think anything less than two years to recover fees is a good test, but your personal mileage may vary. Anything longer than two years and you could have done better by investing a couple of thousand dollars somewhere or simply paying down your principal balance. We'll look at ways to save on your closing costs in Chapter 14.

Several states, in response to predatory lending legislation, have set certain standards whereby a person can refinance a mortgage without having it labeled a "predatory loan." Some states employ a test called Reasonable and Tangible Net Benefit (RTNB). This is a requirement that the consumer understands that there will be a real benefit to refinancing a mortgage loan. There is a form to be completed by you that asks several questions, such as, "Are you reducing your interest rate by 2 percent?" or "Are you reducing your loan term?"

When legislators make a law, lenders have to devise their own strategy as to how to comply with that law. Some lenders will use different methods to make sure they're making legal loans, but most require that the borrower and the loan officer sign a piece of paper stating, "Yes, I have a good reason to refinance," and explaining why, and then they move on. I realize it sounds a little strange to have to explain why you're refinancing, but there are some bad people in the world, and it's those bad people who mess things up for everybody.

9.5 DO I HAVE TO CLOSE MY LOAN WITHIN 30 DAYS, OR CAN I WAIT TO SEE IF RATES DROP FURTHER?

No, you can close a refinance anytime you want. I've had clients in process for months before they decided to take the plunge and refinance to a lower rate. When rates begin to drop, it's tempting to squeeze out one more week to see if rates drop further. It can be disappointing to close your loan at 5 percent when three weeks later, rates drop to 4.75 percent. But no one can tell the future, and sometimes waiting too long can actually damage your effort.

TELL ME MORE

Let's say that your payment on an 8 percent 30-year $200,000 mortgage is $1,467. Of this amount, only about $140 goes to principal reduction while the rest is all mortgage interest. Meanwhile, rates are at 7 percent and you're deciding whether to refinance now or wait and see if rates drop even more. A 7 percent rate drops your payment to $1,330, or a savings of $137. But you're waiting to see if you can get below 7 percent—say, 6.875 percent, which would drop your payment down by another $17 to $1,313. So instead of taking the 7 percent and the $137 reduction, you wait another month for rates to drop further still.

And you wait a little longer. And a little longer. So far, three months have passed and rates still haven't gone below 7 percent. If you had refinanced to 7 percent, you would have saved $411 already, but by waiting you essentially lost that savings, costing you $408. And what about that $17 per month savings at 6.875 percent? Divide that $17 into $411 and that's how long it will take to recover what you lost by waiting. That's 24 months.

9.6 WHY ARE THERE FEES ON A REFINANCE?

A refinance is a brand-new mortgage, that's why. You will have new title insurance, a new note, a new lien, a new everything, mostly. Yes, you might have an appraisal that's three years old, but lenders want to see an appraisal showing more recent sales. You'll also need a new credit report for the same reason. Lots can happen to a credit report over just a few months' time. But to make a mortgage loan eligible to be sold in the secondary markets, it will have to be handled the same as if it were a brand-new purchase loan.

One welcome difference in a refinance is that you can roll your closing costs into your loan balance instead of paying for them out of pocket as you did when you bought the house. But there are ways to reduce those fees or eliminate them altogether when you refinance.

TELL ME MORE

One way is to let your lender pay those closing costs for you. This is called a *no-fee loan*. If you agree to a slightly higher interest rate, then the lender might pay your closing costs for you. Usually you'll get a 1/4 percent change in rate for each one discount point. One discount point is equal to 1 percent of your loan amount; so by increasing an interest rate from 4 percent to 4.25 percent, you could save $2,000 in closing costs on a $200,000 mortgage. Your lender will happily offer a higher interest rate and you will happily reduce your monthly payment essentially free of charge. The difference in a quarter of a percent on a $200,000 30-year fixed-rate loan? About 22 bucks. Your monthly payment will be a little higher on a no-fee loan, but the difference is marginal compared to the amount of closing costs associated with the lower rate.

Note that there is really no such thing as no-closing, or no-fee, or zero-closing-cost loans. In fact, that's really a dubious claim, and with good reason: There *are* closing costs! Instead of your paying them at closing, they're buried in your new, higher rate. You pay every month.

9.7 SHOULD I PAY POINTS FOR A REFINANCE?

I've never been a big fan of paying discount points and origination charges on any loan, purchase or otherwise. If you paid a discount point one year ago to get a better rate and now rates are even lower, that discount point is essentially lost, isn't it? Yes, you may have gotten an income tax deduction from the point, but it didn't really help you out in the long run, did it? Especially in light of what interest rate cycles look like at the time you buy your home. When you bought your house, there were closing fees involved, and if you refinance, there will also be closing fees involved unless you choose a no-fee loan. However, it pays to look at recent interest rate trends to see if you're at the top of an interest rate market or at the bottom of one.

If rates are at historic or near-historic lows and you intend to keep the property for several years, then you might want to pay a point or two to get the absolute lowest rate on the planet. If interest rates are not at historic lows, you may be hard pressed to make a case to pay extra fees just for a lower rate you might not have for very long. If you paid one point to get a 7 percent rate instead of a no-point 7.25 percent rate, on a 30-year fixed-rate mortgage for $100,000, the difference in payment is $16 per month. Over the life of a 30-year loan, that's over $5,700 in interest. But if interest rates drop over the next couple of years to 6 percent, then you won't see the long-term benefit of paying the additional point in exchange for the lower rate. What if you took that same thousand dollars and invested it in a guaranteed instrument, like a tax-free bond or note? Better yet, if instead of using the $1,000 for a discount point you used it to pay down your principal at closing, you'd save over $7,000 in interest over the life of the loan.

Interest rates go in cycles, and they'll typically cover a three-to five-year period. If you buy a home or refinance one at or near high interest rates, choose a no-fee loan. This way, if rates do indeed drop in two or three years, it's less costly in the long term. So forget about the "rules of thumb." Look at your particular situation to see if it makes sense.

9.8 WHAT ABOUT REDUCING MY INTEREST RATE AND ALSO REDUCING MY LOAN TERM?

Changing your loan term along with your rate may also be a good reason to refinance your mortgage from a 30-year to a 15-year loan. In fact, this is one of the most common reasons people decide to refinance in the first place. For instance, let's say you have a 30-year mortgage at 8 percent with a $125,000 loan and you've been paying on it for a couple of years. Soon, interest rates drop to 6.5 percent for the same 30-year fixed rate loan, but you also see that 15-year loan rates are in the 5.75 percent range. While the monthly payment for a 15-year loan will actually increase from $917 to $1,038 per month, it's not a huge difference, especially when compared to how much interest is being saved by switching loan terms. That 30-year rate of 8 percent costs $205,000 in interest over the life of the loan while the 15-year rate has just $61,800 in interest charges. That's a heckuva difference and something to consider instead of just thinking about lowering your monthly payment.

Another advantage of loans with shorter terms is that they let borrowers get rid of their debt quicker. Are you retiring in 20 years? Fifteen years? Do you still want to be making house payments in your golden years, or do you want to own your home free and clear? Choosing your loan term is something that should be an integral part of your retirement plans.

9.9 WHY NOT JUST PAY EXTRA EACH MONTH INSTEAD OF REFINANCING?

You can. For some people, paying the same amount each month, every month, is a little more "automatic." Payment by payment, more money goes to principal rather than to interest. I had a client who refinanced his mortgage from a 30-year to a 15-year for a very specific reason: his daughter. Why? He knew his daughter was going to be starting college in 15 years and he didn't want any house payments at that time. He also knew that while he sometimes paid a little extra on his note each month, he didn't have the discipline to make those additional payments month in and month out. So instead he chose a 15-year loan, and when his daughter goes to school he'll be mortgage-free.

9.10 WHAT'S A CASH-OUT MORTGAGE?

A *cash-out refinance* is the exact same process as a refinance, only this time you come away from the closing table with a check in your hand, taken from the equity in your home. For instance, you refinance your 8 percent rate on a $125,000 loan to 6.75 percent. But instead of refinancing $125,000 you obtain a new loan of $150,000, giving you $25,000 extra to do with what you please. Not a bad deal, right? Yes, it's not bad, but there are some things you must pay attention to, otherwise you might make some critical mistakes. The first mistake often made is the amount requested compared to the value of your home.

TELL ME MORE

If you recall, your first mortgage needs to be at 80 percent of the appraised value of the home or you'll need private mortgage insurance. This requirement doesn't change when it comes to refinancing your note, either. While you can finance more than 80 percent of the value of the home—up to 90 percent, in most cases, while taking cash out—you'll have more than just a PMI premium. Your interest rate will increase slightly as well. In fact, if you take cash out while refinancing and your loan accounts for more than 75 percent of the home's value, you might also find you have to pay a 1/4 point fee to do so. No PMI, but a 1/4 point fee.

It sounds like a no-brainer, but I'll mention it anyway: If your home is valued at $100,000 and you're taking cash out, a $76,000 loan (76 percent loan-to-value, or LTV) will cost you an additional $250 compared to a 75 percent LTV loan that carries no additional fee for cash-out. Why this "bump" for cash-out loans? Lenders have found that home loans with cash-out have a higher default rate.

Be careful about pulling out cash. Some loan officers can look up old loan files that they've closed before, call you up, and tell you how much money you'd save each month if you paid off your two car payments and credit cards. The math always works, but don't refinance just to pay off other debt besides your mortgage. Why?

Let's say you have two car payments of $400 each, with a $10,000 balance on each auto loan. Now add some credit card balances you want to pay off totaling $10,000. So you'll need to add $30,000 to your new loan. If you add $30,000 to your loan under the new lower mortgage rate of 7 percent, suddenly that $1,000 in automobile and credit card payments is reduced to $199. A loan officer can make a pretty good case for this transaction. Who wouldn't want to save $800 per month?

Remember, though, that you're now amortizing that $30,000 over 30 years, and at 7 percent you'd pay over $41,000 in interest, much of it in the early stages of your newly refinanced mortgage.

Refinancing and pulling cash out can be advantageous to your cash flow and can make lots of sense, but don't do a cash-out unless it really makes sense to you and not just to your loan officer.

9.11 HOW DO I GET MONEY OUT OF MY PROPERTY WITHOUT REFINANCING?

You can do a couple of things, actually. And they're fairly easy. The first is to get an equity second mortgage on your house for almost any amount you'd like, up to the standard loan-to-value guidelines. The second is to get a home equity line of credit.

TELL ME MORE

Most cash-out second mortgages let you borrow up to 90 percent of the total loan-to-value (TLTV) and carry little, if any, closing fees. Some direct lenders don't charge anything for a second mortgage, while others do. Still other title agencies and settlement companies charge a fee for a second mortgage, but they're marginal when compared to fees associated with refinancing a first mortgage loan. Expect no more than a couple hundred dollars in fees, if that.

Most equity seconds (i.e., home equity second mortgages) are in fixed-rate terms, with the most common being the 15-year fixed-rate note. There are other options, such as a 20-year note, and you might even find a 30-year loan out there, although they're not as common. In fact, most of the equity seconds that allow for a 30-year amortization (which reduces the payment) balloon after 15 years. These loans are called 30 due in 15, or 30/15. You make payments amortized over 30 years but the loan will come due in year 15.

Another popular option is called a *home equity line of credit* (HELOC). A HELOC is similar to a credit card in that you're given a limit on how much you can borrow. Whether you borrow the full amount right away is up to you. Typically you're simply given a credit line and you write a check against it when you need it. Usually HELOCs are adjustable-rate loans; in fact, I'm not sure if I've ever seen a fixed-rate HELOC, because the interest rate is set when a balance is actually drawn. And the most common index for HELOCs is the prime rate plus a margin, with margins being anywhere from 0 to 3, depending upon the credit grade of the borrower.

Want a neat trick on using a HELOC to help buy a home? Actually it's not to help you buy the home, it's to help what you do immediately after you buy your home. Let's say you find a house that's selling for $200,000 and you want to put 20 percent down to avoid PMI and to keep your mortgage payment low. But you also are a little skittish about putting all your hard-earned money into a house, leaving your financial cupboards bare, so to speak. Banks can issue a HELOC right after closing, giving you access to a new line of credit on your house, and if you want to replace some of your down payment money you can make a withdrawal on your HELOC. Deposit institutions such as banks, savings and loans (S&Ls), and credit unions typically issue HELOCs, so you won't find this option at a mortgage banker or mortgage broker.

But you also don't have to get your mortgage from a bank or credit union to get a HELOC; you can get your mortgage anywhere and still get one of these loan programs. Certain lenders and certain states may regulate how big your credit line may be or how much you can borrow, so check with your local lending laws and guidelines. But all in all, HELOCs can be a handy financial tool.

9.12 HOW DO I REFINANCE IF I HAVE BOTH A FIRST AND A SECOND MORTGAGE?

Good question. There are some very important considerations here when refinancing a mortgage that has subordinate (second) money behind it. First, given enough equity, many people are simply rolling their first and second mortgage into one. Most second mortgage interest rates are higher than those for first mortgages, which lowers the overall monthly payment.

But the surprise for those who carry second mortgage balances is caused by recent changes in lending guidelines. If you had just one mortgage when you bought your property but later on got another loan—be it a home improvement loan or a HELOC—lenders assign this second loan "cash-out status." Because cash-out loans carry a higher default rate than non-cash-out loans, you could be in for a surprise. If both your loans together total more than 75 percent of the appraised value of the home, you might very well see a slightly higher rate or a fee.

9.13 WHICH IS BETTER, A CASH-OUT REFINANCE OR A HELOC?

If all you're wanting is to have access to some of the equity in your home, then take the HELOC. They're inexpensive (sometimes free) and quicker to get. A refinance cash-out loan carries closing costs just as a standard refinance does, so only do a cash-out if you're simultaneously refinancing for other legitimate purposes such as lowering your current interest rate, going from an ARM to a fixed, or changing loan terms.

9.14 WHY IS MY LOAN PAYOFF HIGHER THAN MY PRINCIPAL BALANCE?

Because the lender is adding mortgage interest that you've yet to pay your current lender. When you refinance your mortgage, your new loan officer will order a final payoff from your old lender. This is your current principal balance, which will be showing up on your credit report, plus unpaid interest.

Mortgage interest is paid in arrears, or backward. Unlike rent, where you pay for the upcoming month, mortgage interest accrues daily until you finally make your payment on the first of the following month. Your July 1 payment is for interest that added up every day in June. When your lender gets a payoff and you're scheduled to close on the 20th of the month, your payoff will be your principal balance, plus accrued interest to the 20th, plus interest for your three-day rescission period.

You will also see another interest charge: prepaid interest. This is the daily interest rate that takes you up to the first of the following month. In this example, you would have seven days of prepaid interest added to your loan. Because you make a prepaid interest payment when you go to a loan closing, you will "skip" your first month's house payment. Well, not really skip it altogether; it's just that you paid it ahead of time in the form of prepaid interest at closing. It just feels like you're skipping it. Some lenders advertise that you can refinance a mortgage loan and "skip" two or three payments. Don't fall for it. Lenders don't let you skip payments; instead the interest is rolled into your new loan balance.

9.15 MY CREDIT HAS BEEN DAMAGED SINCE I BOUGHT THE HOUSE. WILL THAT HURT ME?

Maybe. You'll have to qualify all over again, just as when you bought the home, so if you've experienced some credit problems, such as collections, late payments, or even bankruptcy, you may not be able to refinance your mortgage due to the bad credit. If you have a healthy equity position due to values increasing in your area, or perhaps you've paid extra on your mortgage many times, your better equity can offset negative credit. Again, just because you think you won't qualify due to bad credit, don't let it stop you from going ahead and applying. If you don't apply you'll have no opportunity at all to get a lower rate, right? But just because you qualified when you first got the mortgage doesn't necessarily mean you'll qualify with a refinance.

TELL ME MORE

Let's say that you applied for a refinance and got turned down. Something happened since you got your first mortgage, and the new lower payment you're applying for has nothing to do with what you're paying now. It has everything to do with looking at your application as a brand-new loan. Which it is, right? If this is your case, then you may not have much of a choice and instead must simply sit this one out. That is, if you have a conventional mortgage. If you've had bad credit but have a government mortgage, such as a VA or FHA loan, you're in luck.

FHA and VA loans both have a refinance feature that basically doesn't care what the credit looks like as long as you've made your house payments on time and you're reducing your mortgage interest rate. FHA calls it a streamline loan and VA calls it an interest rate reduction loan (IRRL). Leave it to the government to come up with the weird acronyms. Both programs operate in a similar way when it comes to refinancing and credit issues.

One important thing to remember with an FHA loan when refinancing is to always close at the end of the month. Why? When a lender pays off your old FHA mortgage, interest is automatically added to your outstanding loan balance up to the first of the following month. If you close your refinance on the fifth of the month, your new loan will contain additional interest all the way up to the first of the next month, even though you didn't have the loan to the end of the month. You have to pay a full month's mortgage interest regardless of when you close an FHA refinance, so to avoid unnecessary interest, close at the end of the month.

9.16 HOW DO I GET A NOTE MODIFICATION?

A *note modification* is taking the original terms of the note and reducing the interest for the remaining term of the loan, without changing any other part of the obligation or title. A note modification therefore means you can't "shop around" for the best rate to reduce your payment; instead, you must work with your original lender who still services your mortgage. In a modification, nothing can change except the rate. How do you get your note modified? You ask.

You won't go directly to your old loan officer, but you'll most likely end up with the lender's servicing department. Plus, you won't get the best rate on the planet, either. Your lender knows that it will cost you to get another mortgage in terms of fees, but even though you may not get the best interest rate available, you'll get one that's in the same ballpark. Not all lenders modify their notes. They don't have to if they don't want to, and some simply don't want to. But before you begin the sometimes-arduous task of refinancing your loan, contact your lender and see if they will modify your note and, if so, at what rate.

Loan modifications have become more common since 2008 with various programs introduced such as the HAMP loan described in Chapter 7.

9.17 WHAT IS A "RECAST" OF MY MORTGAGE?

A *recast* applies to ARMs and is used when extra payments are made to the principal balance. When you make a regular payment on your adjustable-rate mortgage, the payment is calculated each time your adjustment period arrives. Your remaining principal balance is calculated along with your remaining term and new interest rate. This happens naturally as fully amortized ARMs come up for their annual recalculation. Your note is "recast" and your monthly payment is calculated for you.

Let's say that you get a windfall one month and win $10,000 in the lottery. I know, you're thinking, "Yeah, right," but hang with me here. Instead of buying 10,000 more lotto tickets you decide to pay down your mortgage balance. Now, your new payment will be calculated using your new loan balance and mortgage terms. When you recast with an ARM, your payments will drop, assuming your interest rate doesn't go up to offset the decrease in loan amount. Prepaying an ARM works differently from prepaying a fixed-rate mortgage. When you prepay a fixed-rate mortgage, your payment doesn't change, it just reduces the term. When you pay extra on an ARM, your payment drops.

9.18 WHAT HAPPENS WHEN MY LOAN IS SOLD?

Nothing, really, except that you'll be sending your mortgage payment to another lender. Lenders can make money by collecting monthly interest payments, or they can sell your loan to another lender. If you have a $100,000 mortgage and a monthly payment of $650, then your lender makes about $600 every month for the first year or two of the loan. That's not bad, but a loan taken to a term of 30 years also packs about $224,000 in interest. Sometimes, instead of waiting for a loan to come to term to collect all that money, a lender might decide to sell that loan.

Why do lenders sell loans? That depends upon what their current financial strategy is. If lenders want to make more mortgage loans, they need to go find more money. They can do that by selling their loans. Sometimes they sell them one by one, called "flow," and other times they package them all together and sell them as a group, called "bulk." What's the sense in selling a mortgage just to make another one? Good question.

Mortgage rates change. And some loans that lenders have lying around in their vaults might have lower interest rates than what's currently available on the market. If the lender has a bunch of loans yielding 5 percent and rates are at 7 percent, they're losing money by not making new loans. But they need new money to make new loans, so they sell the old ones. Now, why would a lender buy loans at interest rates that are lower than the market?

Again, lenders can have different strategies. There's a lot to be said for having guaranteed rates of return at 5 percent rather than risking some or all of that to try to make more loans to more people. Selling loans to make more loans carries some risk. At other times, lenders make agreements to buy and sell from one another at preset prices, way before a loan is closed.

More important than the question of "why" lenders buy and sell loans is the impact it has on a consumer. Your note and the terms of your agreement will never change. When your loan is sold, your new lender can't call you up and tell you they're raising your interest rate or they want to call in your loan. Mortgages can't be changed when the loan is sold. For the consumer, there is only a temporary inconvenience. You may find that it's a slight pain to have to write a check to the new lender, or you may worry whether your last payment got credited or your new payment made it on time.

Lenders send out "hello" and "goodbye" letters, typically 45 to 60 days in advance of your loan sale. The goodbye letter is from your soon-to-be-old lender, telling you who the new lender is and explaining your rights as a consumer. The hello letter is from your new lender, giving you your new coupon book or mortgage statement. But other than a little paperwork, selling your note changes nothing.

9.19 WHAT'S A REVERSE MORTGAGE?

A *reverse mortgage* is designed to help older Americans who own their homes by paying the homeowner cash in exchange for the equity in their home. Many times the elderly are "house rich" but "cash poor," and they need a way to tap into the equity in their home to help pay the bills or pay for a trip or practically anything their heart desires. When the homeowner no longer owns the home by selling or moving out or dying, then the reverse mortgage lender is paid back all the money borrowed plus interest.

9.20 WHO QUALIFIES FOR A REVERSE MORTGAGE?

Anyone who owns their home, lives in it, and is age 62 or older can qualify. There are no credit or income qualifications for a reverse mortgage, but the lender must determine you have the ability to pay the property taxes, insurance, and maintenance. You don't sell the property to the reverse mortgage lender, either. Ownership never changes hands and you always retain title. The reverse mortgage lender simply does not own the home, a prospect that could scare some people into thinking that a reverse mortgage would be a last resort when trying to figure out how to pay for retirement or other financial needs in their golden years. Simply put, the lender can never "foreclose" on the property.

9.21 HOW MUCH CAN I GET WITH A REVERSE MORTGAGE?

That depends upon a few things, but reverse mortgages are primarily calculated based on the age of the borrower (loan-to-value numbers are triggered by life expectancy), the market value of your home as determined by an appraisal, and any other liens on the property. Typically, the bottom line is that the more equity you have in your home, the larger amount you'll be eligible for. For a home that has $200,000 available equity and where the borrower is 75 years old, the approximate loan amount would be just over $100,000.

One of the biggest differences between a reverse mortgage and a cash-out refinance is that it's a safer vehicle in which to borrow money. With a cash-out refinance, when the payments aren't made, the lender can foreclose and grandma loses her house. With a reverse mortgage, that can never happen. Reverse mortgages require some counseling, so find a loan officer to help you sort out the details and decide how and when you'd like to have your funds sent to you.

9.22 WHY NOT DO A CASH-OUT REFINANCE INSTEAD OF A REVERSE MORTGAGE?

Because a cash-out refinance requires the homeowner to make monthly payments back to the lender, which sort of defeats the purpose. Furthermore, reverse mortgage funds are tax-free. With a reverse mortgage, the lender agrees to pay the homeowner a certain amount of money either in a lump sum or in installment payments in exchange for equity in their home. The homeowner doesn't have to qualify for the mortgage from a credit or income perspective, but does need to be at least 62 years of age. The homeowner never has to pay it back and doesn't "sell" the home to the reverse mortgage lender. The lender gets their loan back when the property is sold after the homeowner dies or when the homeowner moves to a different house. All loan proceeds due the lender get satisfied at that time, not before.

That's what makes reverse mortgage lending "odd"—it's certainly a mortgage but doesn't act like one. Since there are no payments made from the homeowner, there's no such thing as a foreclosure or delinquency, and title doesn't change hands. The homeowner doesn't sell the property to the lender; it's simply an advance on the equity of the home, plus interest. There are closing costs involved, and those costs are going to be somewhat higher than for a conventional loan, primarily due to the mortgage insurance premium required for all reverse mortgages. But just as with a conventional refinance, you can include those with your mortgage. You need to sit down with a reverse mortgage loan officer who will detail the plans available to you and answer any questions you may have.

9.23 ARE THE CLOSING COSTS FOR A REVERSE MORTGAGE THE SAME AS WITH A REGULAR MORTGAGE?

Many of the closing costs for a reverse mortgage are similar to a refinance, and you'll need title insurance and a survey and escrow charges and so on. The difference is that closing costs are deducted from reverse mortgage proceeds instead of your writing a check for them. The only thing you might pay for out of pocket is your appraisal, which runs around $350 or so. But closing costs on reverse mortgages can be expensive. There is also a monthly servicing fee for reverse mortgages, called a "set aside," which is used to help cover monthly servicing. It usually costs about $30 a month or so and is deducted from your loan proceeds, based upon how long the lender assumes the reverse mortgage loan will be in place.

The primary reverse mortgage today is one from FHA called the Home Equity Conversion Mortgage, or HECM (pronounced "heckum"). FHA also has a mortgage insurance premium equal to 2 percent of the reverse loan amount plus a monthly or annual fee equal to 1/2 percent of the reverse mortgage balance, similar to any other FHA loan. Mortgage insurance is probably the single biggest closing cost with a reverse mortgage. It is not the type of mortgage insurance that pays off a lender if someone dies, but in this case it is used to guarantee that you will always have access to your funds if your reverse mortgage lender goes out of business.

9.24 WHAT ARE THE RATES FOR REVERSE MORTGAGES?

Lenders can set their own rate programs, but most reverse mortgage loans are ARMs based upon a common index, such as a treasury or LIBOR note, plus a standard margin. If you take one big lump sum, interest at those rates begin to accrue immediately. If you take out funds bit by bit from a reverse mortgage HELOC, then interest only accrues on the money withdrawn and not on your available funds.

9.25 I HAVE A CURRENT MORTGAGE ON MY HOUSE. DO I GET TO KEEP THAT?

No, a reverse mortgage will first pay off any current mortgages on the property, and then you'll be left with your reverse mortgage funds. If you have a large mortgage compared to your appraised value—say, something approaching 70 percent of the value of your home—you may not qualify for a reverse mortgage purely because you lack sufficient equity.

9.26 HOW DO I KNOW IF A REVERSE MORTGAGE IS RIGHT FOR ME?

Reverse mortgages require counseling that has been prescreened and presented to you in a formal manner. Reverse mortgage loan officers must also go through training and screening to make sure they're giving you the proper information.

One of the best resources for reverse mortgage information is at the website of the American Association of Retired People, *www.aarp. org.* Ask plenty of questions and make sure you know exactly what you're getting into, but if you need or want to access your home's equity without incurring a brand-new debt along with its monthly payment, then explore a reverse.

Construction and Home Improvement Loans

Construction loans and home improvement loans are short-term funds designed to pay for hammers, nails, and labor. After the construction or remodel is completed, you'll get a permanent mortgage to replace your construction loan.

10.1 WHY WOULD I WANT TO BUILD A HOME? WHY CAN'T I JUST GO OUT AND BUY ONE?

Great questions, but it's simply a matter of preference. For example, I know a guy who will shave his head before he will ever buy a brand-new car. "Why pay the dealer the 20 percent depreciation on a new car just when you drive it off the lot?" he says. Instead, he'll buy a car that's a couple of years old that has all the "kinks" worked out. But I also know a woman who will never buy a car that "someone else has already driven, spilled food in, or had some kid throw up in." She wants that brand-new car with the brand-new smell with the brand-new warranty, and she prefers to pay the new car premium rather than buying "somebody else's problems."

Both are right in their own way. There is no right or wrong reason to buy a new house. There's a lot to be said for buying brand new. The fixtures are new, the roof is new, the floor is new, the cabinets are, well, new. And you're the only one to have ever owned it. If there are problems, there are new home warranties and guarantees offered by the builder that take care of them. Buying new is a very different experience from buying an existing home.

10.2 HOW DO CONSTRUCTION LOANS WORK?

Construction loans differ from regular mortgages, but typically, when you get a construction loan you'll also need to get a mortgage at the end.

Construction loans are short-term loans issued to borrowers who want to build their very own, brand-new house. When the construction loan is up, the construction lender wants the money back, which happens through a permanent mortgage. A permanent mortgage in construction parlance is simply a regular mortgage, as discussed in other chapters. So how do construction loans work?

Borrowers who wish to build begin by getting some building plans and specifications, and then they contact an architect to design the house. After the design work is done, the borrowers contact several builders to get a quote on how much they will charge to build the house and how long it will take. Often this is the longest part of the entire home-building process. When the bid to build comes in way too high, the borrowers go back to the drawing board and scale back their plans. Or when borrowers find out that they can actually build much more house than they had budgeted for, they start adding another room, another story, or a swimming pool.

A key consideration is where to actually build the home. Do you have to find a lot somewhere and buy it first, or do you already own your vacant land? Does your design meet local building codes? Does the house sit far enough away from the street? Is your house too big for your lot? These matters can take a long time to resolve if you're acting on your own. Even with an architect and a builder by your side, you'll need some patience.

10.3 DO I BUY A HOME FROM A DEVELOPER, OR IS IT BETTER TO START FROM SCRATCH?

Starting from scratch allows you to build your own home exactly the way you want. Down to the linen closets. When you buy from a builder in a new development, you'll typically choose from different home styles on several lot sizes. You'll then pick out carpeting, tile, wallpaper, or whatever else from the builder's database of offerings. Obviously the design styles are more limited than when you're building your very own home from scratch, but not so much as to be a bad thing. After all, if a builder didn't offer nice stuff in all the latest styles and with all the latest home innovations, that builder might have trouble selling new homes.

Building from scratch will take a little longer. You'll also need to make sure you have land ready to build on. That means putting in utilities if there aren't any, making sure you're in compliance with any local regulations or building codes, and ascertaining that you're not building on top of some heretofore unknown habitat of a Tasmanian lizard that's on the endangered species list.

When you buy a new home from a builder in a new neighborhood, all those zoning, utilities, and endangered species problems are taken care of. Here you're not building on land you own, but you are buying both the house and the land at the same time.

10.4 HOW DO I GET APPROVED FOR A CONSTRUCTION LOAN?

Mostly the same way you get approved for any other mortgage. You need good credit and all that goes with it, but the most important thing you'll need for a construction loan is a commitment letter. This letter comes from your future mortgage lender and promises to pay off the construction loan at the end of construction. Construction loans are for a very short term—just long enough to build the house. They usually only require interest payments during construction, although some construction lenders will let you slide on that as well and have the mortgage pay the construction loan plus interest.

10.5 HOW MUCH DO I NEED FOR A CONSTRUCTION LOAN?

Construction costs are divided between "hard" and "soft" costs. *Hard costs* cover things like hammers and nails, wood, labor, and anything physical needed to build the home, including the land. *Soft costs* are closing fees on the property, such as appraisals and title work, along with all the necessary permits and taxes.

Construction loans will also require a *hold-back* or contingency fund of anywhere from 5 percent to 10 percent. This hold-back is there for any change orders that might occur during the process. A *change order* is what happens when you change your mind. When changing your mind costs more than the original estimate, the hold-back will help pay for the change. An example of a change order might be if you decide you'd rather have hardwood floors in the baby's room instead of carpeting, or you want to add a deck that originally wasn't part of the plan.

TELL ME MORE

To figure how much money you'll need, simply add your costs together. Let's say your land cost you $50,000; your plans, specifications, and permits cost you $20,000; the builder needs $200,000 for materials and labor; and your closing costs are $10,000. Your total cost to build would then be $280,000. Add a 10 percent hold-back of $28,000 and your total cost would be $308,000.

Another type of hold-back is used for a specific upgrade or remodel and not held in case there were surprises or cost adjustments during the course of construction. An escrow hold-back in this instance would describe the improvements to be made; the borrower hires a contractor to complete the project while the funds for the improvements are held in escrow by a third party. Escrow hold-backs for specific improvements vary by lender; some won't allow them while other lenders are more accommodating. Once the improvements have been completed, the escrow company releases the funds to the contractor after a property inspector confirms the job has been successfully completed.

10.6 DOES THE LENDER APPROVE MY BUILDER?

Your builder will need to pass muster, both from an experience as well as a financial perspective. Lenders will review the net worth of your builder, including obtaining a credit report and getting at least three references from other construction lenders. Don't think that just getting a mortgage approval is all that's needed. Your builder will need to be reputable and have a record of building good homes. You wouldn't want it any other way, right? Neither does your lender.

10.7 HOW DOES THE MORTGAGE LENDER KNOW WHAT THE HOUSE IS WORTH BEFORE IT'S BUILT?

The lender will take your building plans and give them to a licensed appraiser, who will determine a future market value of the completed home. The appraiser will look at similar existing homes in the area and pretend that your home is finished and you're living in it. This appraised value is based upon "subject-to" conditions.

In this instance, the value is assigned to your to-be-built home "subject to" the house being completed and your signing an occupancy certificate. The appraiser will also gauge progress during the construction process and assist the lender in determining how much and when your builder will get paid.

TELL ME MORE

Once you get your permanent mortgage approval, you take that to your construction lender if they're different institutions. At that point, building begins. But the builder isn't given your entire $308,000. It's not a very prudent policy to start handing out lump-sum checks to builders when any collateral is still to be built. Instead, builders are given percentages of the total loan amount during the process until completion.

This is where the appraiser steps in. Let's say the builder has been working for six weeks and wants more money to either help build more of the house or to be reimbursed for building costs already incurred. The appraiser then inspects the property and determines that "yes, the foundation has been poured and the framing is completed." Now the builder gets more money, based on the percentage of completion at that stage. For example, if pouring the foundation and framing the house means that the home is 20 percent completed, then the builder gets 20 percent of $308,000, or $61,600. Inspections are made and more money is given to the builder either at predetermined intervals or as the builder requests funds. The way your construction loan is structured will determine what you'll pay during the construction process.

You won't make any loan payments at all until funds are given to the builder, and even then you'll pay only the interest on the amount of funds disbursed, not on the total construction loan amount.

If your construction loan rate is 6 percent and the builder has only received $50,000, then your interest payment would be calculated on only the $50,000. You can make that payment now or let it add up and pay at the end.

10.8 WHAT IF I ALREADY OWN THE LAND? DO I STILL INCLUDE THAT AMOUNT IN THE CONSTRUCTION LOAN?

No. If you already own the land, then instead of coming to the closing table at the end of construction with a down payment, you'll be able to use the value of the land as your down payment. This arrangement usually only works if you've owned the land for 12 months or more. Again, using our previous example, with your land being valued at $50,000 and representing just over 16 percent of the construction cost, you won't need a down payment. The land equity will do that for you.

There's another benefit of owning your own land for more than a year before the home is completed: The mortgage lender will treat the permanent mortgage like a refinance instead of a purchase transaction. The benefit here is that the lender will use the appraised value of the home and not the construction cost when determining minimum required down payments and loan amounts. If the construction costs are $258,000 ($308,000 less $50,000 land value) but the appraiser determines that the property is worth $400,000, then you'll simply "refinance" the $258,000 construction loan, which represents 64 percent of the value of the home. Forget the down payment part.

10.9 WHAT IF I DON'T WANT A PERMANENT MORTGAGE, BUT JUST A CONSTRUCTION LOAN?

There is no requirement that you take a permanent mortgage at the end of construction as long as the construction note is retired. But you'll have to replace that money somehow, and it can come from any source available to you. You could pay cash to replace the construction note, but this would be a rare occurrence. People who can afford to pay cash to replace a construction loan will usually have paid for the construction out of pocket as the home is being built.

10.10 WHAT CHOICES DO I HAVE FOR CONSTRUCTION LOANS?

There are two common options: a one-time close and a two-time close. A *one-time close* loan means you obtain construction financing and a permanent mortgage at the same time. A *two-time close* loan means you first get a construction loan and then get another mortgage at the end of construction. You'll go to two different closings for a two-time close loan.

A one-time close loan locks in your permanent mortgage rate, which is decided by your original loan. And you pay closing fees just once.

10.11 IS A ONE-TIME CLOSE BETTER THAN A TWO-TIME CLOSE?

You need to compare your choices, but neither will ever be hands-down better each and every time. Yes, with a two-time close you'll have two different closings, but don't be misled that your closing costs will double. You'll have two sets of closing costs, but the costs aren't duplicated at each closing. You won't have two full title policies or two different appraisals, for example. Two-time closing costs add up to slightly more than one-time closing costs. The fees are higher, but not dramatically "slap you in the face" higher. The advantage of a two-time close is that if mortgage rates are lower at the end of construction, you'll get the new lower rates.

The one-time close loan tells you what your permanent mortgage rate and term will be at the end of construction. You won't need to go through all the paperwork again, other than signing a piece of paper declaring that you've moved in. The benefit of a one-time close may also be a disadvantage. Because a one-time close loan guarantees your interest rate at the end of construction, you need to consider what interest rates might do six to twelve months down the road. If interest rates are at or near historic lows, you would want to opt for a one-time loan. If rates are at their peak or at higher than normal levels, you might want to consider a two-time loan.

There is also a twist with a one-time close loan that comes with a *float-down* feature. A float-down means that whatever your predetermined rate will be, you will have the option of taking the then-current interest rates. This means that if your predetermined rate for a one-time close loan is at 8 percent and rates have dropped during your construction period to 7 percent, you can lock those new, lower rates in as you're about to move into your new home.

If your one-time close loan offers this feature, it's hard to beat.

Not every lender offers both one-time close and two-time close loans. All mortgage lenders offer a permanent mortgage. That's their business. Fewer mortgage lenders offer construction loans. Fewer still offer a choice between a one-time close and two-time close construction loan. That means you can bet that someone who doesn't offer a one-time close loan will talk it down and make you afraid of it or tell you that there's no benefit. Take their advice with a grain of salt. Why would they promote a one-time close loan when they don't offer one? Doesn't make much sense, does it?

10.12 WHAT IF RATES DROP DURING MY ONE-TIME CLOSE LOAN?

If you don't have a float-down feature, you can always refinance or modify. No one can predict the future, so you're not the only one asking that question. You're right, rates might be higher. Or lower. You don't know. The one-time loan, while offering a slightly higher permanent rate, also offers the sense of tranquility and well-being that comes from knowing exactly what your rate will be. It takes the guesswork and sleepless nights out of the equation. That offers a lot by itself. But there are a couple of ways to help offset the potentially higher rates inherent in some one-time close loans.

One way is converting to a hybrid loan instead of a fixed loan when you convert from the construction to a permanent loan. A hybrid will offer a lower start rate for a fixed period than what might be available for fixed-rate mortgages. Comparing a one-time loan with a two-time loan can be difficult and confusing, but remember that absolutely no one knows what's down the road. Should you choose wrong, hey, you could always refinance, right?

10.13 WHAT IF MY BUILDER IS FINANCING THE CONSTRUCTION?

Just get approved for a regular mortgage loan and wait for the house to be built. When you buy a new home in a brand-new development, usually the builder just tells you how much your home will cost, as long as you can provide a commitment letter. No need to worry about comparing a one-time close to a two-time close loan, since you won't need construction funds. You just need to fret about the interest rate on your permanent loan, which could be six months or more after you've signed the contract.

There are also builders who own their own mortgage companies. They will give you a better deal if you go through their mortgage company. Or at least so they claim. Builders who don't own a mortgage company may have an official business relationship with one, which they'll encourage you to use. If there is an official relationship between a builder and a mortgage company, that fact must be made known to you up front. Does the builder get a referral fee by sending business to a particular mortgage operation? Such arrangements must be disclosed to you, and you'll need to sign a piece of paper declaring your awareness of the situation.

TELL ME MORE

Sometimes you get incentives to use a builder's mortgage company. For example, the builder's salesperson may offer upgrades worth $10,000 by using the builder's mortgage company. Not a bad deal, right? Do you think the builder might include the $10,000 in the final negotiated price of the home, or do you think the builder likes you so much you're getting $10,000 in free stuff? If you're not sure how to answer that question, simply ask that any upgrade offers be independent of the home's contract price.

Your great big national-brand builders all have their own mortgage companies, and there may well be some financial incentives to using their mortgage operations. Smaller regional or independent builders usually won't own their own company, but they'll use a mortgage broker or banker to refer buyers to. The kicker is that since all lenders get their mortgage money from mostly the same places, you'll be really hard pressed to find a builder's mortgage that is a full percentage point lower than anything you can find on the street. Or even a half percentage point.

Builders may also offer to cover some of your closing fees if you use their lender or select from a list of "preferred" lenders. Don't take this preferred list at face value. You still need to compare rate quotes and fees from nonpreferred lenders as well. Most any lender or mortgage broker can quote you a loan program that pays for some or all of your closing costs.

By increasing your interest rate, a lender can make enough money selling the loan to another lender to pay $2,000 of your closing costs. Any lender or mortgage broker can do that. If the builder's rates are higher than what you've been quoted, you can guess how they're able to offer you such a deal on closing costs or upgrades.

Another problem is that most interest rate quotes are for a 30-day period, while your construction period may last much longer. When you're comparing interest rates, it's important to get a rate quote for the same time period. But if your home won't be finished for another eight months, it doesn't matter what rates are today, right? We'll discuss rate lock periods in more detail in Chapter 13, but look out for lenders who quote artificially low rates knowing they won't have to honor those rates because the rate is not good enough to cover your construction period. "Mr. Borrower, I could offer you a 4 percent interest rate if you were closing today, but you're not. Call me when you get a month or two away from your closing and we'll talk."

When calling different lenders for a rate quote, don't tell them it's for a home that won't be finished for eight months. Just ask them for their best 30-year rate for a loan that will close in one month. Keep lenders honest by having them quote on the same product.

10.14 DO I HAVE TO USE THE BUILDER'S MORTGAGE COMPANY?

No, but it's critical to examine the sales contract. There may be a provision that you make a loan application with the builder's mortgage company, but it's illegal to force you to use their mortgage company. Most mortgage companies are honest, but it's the dishonest companies that you need to be prepared for.

Sometimes, in the sales agreement to buy a new home, the contract not only states that the buyer must make a loan application at the builder's mortgage company, but that if the builder's mortgage company gets an approval and if the buyer can't get an approval anywhere else, she is forced to take the mortgage. At first glance, this doesn't seem to be a bad deal, does it? If all else fails, the buyer can always get approved at the builder's mortgage company! What if all else did in fact fail, and what if the loan offered by the builder's mortgage company was terrible?

I recall a buyer who was in that situation. He made an offer on a $700,000 home to be built, signed a contract, and subsequently listed the house he was currently living in. And he put 10 percent down as earnest money, as the contract required. He also needed to sell his current home in order to buy the new home. He couldn't afford both mortgages.

As the new home was being built, his current house began to languish. He didn't get any serious offers and he was becoming nervous. He didn't use the builder's mortgage company; he used his own mortgage broker, but his loan approval was contingent upon selling his current house. After all, he couldn't afford two mortgages, so one of the main conditions for the new loan was that his old mortgage must be retired.

Soon, the new home was completed; but his current house hadn't sold. The builder called and wanted him to fulfill the contract and the buyer said, "Hey, I can't qualify because I can't afford two loans. My approval is contingent upon my current house being sold and it's still not sold. I'm afraid I can't buy the house after all, or else give me more time."

"I'm sorry," said the builder, "but your contract states that if our mortgage company has an approval for you, then you must take it or else lose your deposit of $70,000."

"Fine," said the buyer. But when he saw the loan approval, he was stunned: The interest rate was about 2 percent above current market rates. He couldn't accept that loan, could he? In fact, he was forced to, or else he'd lose his earnest money. The builder's mortgage company did in fact have an approval. How could they have an approval while the buyer's mortgage broker did not?

The builder's mortgage company issued a loan approval. He was stuck. There was no way in the world he could even think of paying both mortgages. He would soon be foreclosed on whichever house he didn't live in. But his contract did state clearly that "if we get you approved, then you must use us or lose your earnest money."

If this buyer in fact did take the new loan from the builder's mortgage company—which he agreed to do in the sales contract— he would have two mortgages that added up to over what he made every month. If he took the new loan, he would be foreclosed on, and quickly, because he couldn't afford both homes and he was looking at losing his sizable earnest money. He was forced into making a bad decision.

Ultimately he dropped the price on his current home so that it would sell faster, and kept the new home and his new deposit. He got his new home, but he didn't like how it worked. Nonetheless, the details were right in front of him the whole time.

10.15 WHAT ARE MY OPTIONS IF I JUST WANT TO BUILD ONTO MY CURRENT HOUSE?

That depends on how much you want to borrow. If you just want to borrow $20,000 for a new deck or to redo the master bathroom, then you'd probably want to simply take out a home improvement loan. These loans are second mortgages and carry few fees, although their interest rates will always be slightly higher than first mortgage rates. Some home improvement lenders require detailed plans and specifications as to what you're building and how much it's going to cost, which will be compared to your home's value and any other liens that might be against the property. If you don't want to go through the hassle of getting building plans and specifications and just want the money to go at your own pace, then simply get an equity second mortgage, or HELOC.

10.16 HOW CAN I BORROW ENOUGH TO MAKE MAJOR IMPROVEMENTS ON MY HOME?

You'll run into some equity problems if you don't watch out. Your lender can use the "subject to" value of the improvement when your current equity position in the home isn't enough to cover a new lien. You have a couple of choices here: One, get a home improvement loan for the second mortgage—usually at a higher rate than a first mortgage—or two, find a *renovation loan*.

There are various marketing names for these new products, but there are mortgage loans where you can refinance your first mortgage while at the same time obtaining new funds to make improvements. This makes obvious sense only if current market rates are lower than what you might have on your first mortgage. But if rates are lower, you can kill two big birds with one stone. These loans are sometimes hard to find, but when you do find one, it is a very cool deal.

TELL ME MORE

Let's say you want to refinance your current mortgage of $100,000 and do $45,000 worth of home repairs. You get your plans and specs from a contractor who gives you a bid on the work to be done. Your lender will get an appraiser to assess your property based upon the "subject to" value, just as with any construction loan. Your costs of repairs have a limit compared to the "subject to" value; usually this value is 30 percent. This means that if your improvements cost $45,000, your value can't be less than $150,000 (30 percent).

Your construction funds are held back by the lender and doled out to the contractor as work progresses. When work is completed, a final inspection is ordered and you're done. You've done some much-needed home improvements and paid for them at the lowest rates available.

Another bonus? These loans don't have to be for a refinance. Let's say you find a real fixer-upper but don't have enough money to fix it up. Use the same loan to purchase the house and to borrow funds to improve the home at the same closing. The same general guidelines for qualifying and the same loan requirements apply both when you buy a home and when you refinance.

10.17 WHAT IS AN FHA 203(K) LOAN?

An FHA 203(k) is a little different from a renovation loan and doesn't cost as much as a conventional renovation loan in terms of equity required. In fact, the FHA will still allow you to do a rehabilitation loan, or 203(k), with as little as 3 percent down, just like any other FHA loan. Why are they called something weird like 203(k)? That's the name of the HUD section that sets the loan parameters and guidelines for this product. Again, this is a government deal, so you should expect a name like that.

TELL ME MORE

FHA 203(k) loans have a few more steps that you must complete. Basically those steps are:

❏ Finding your property. No big difference here, but note that the entire acquisition cost, along with improvements, can't exceed allowable FHA loan limits for your area.

❏ Getting the property inspected by a qualified 203(k) consultant. These folks aren't exactly falling out of trees, but your 203(k) lender has a list for you.

❏ Getting a bid on how much your renovations will cost. Your consultant will again help you with this step and can assist in finding contractors who can bid on your project.

❏ Having your property appraised "subject to" the work being completed.

Your loan gets closed just like any other loan. It goes to underwriting for approval, you go to closing, and your loan gets funded. A neat benefit of these loans is that not only can you roll your closing costs into your loan, but you may also roll up to six months' worth of house payments into the note. Not a bad deal. Of course, you might need that money to pay the rent or mortgage on your current home while the renovation work is being done.

There aren't as many 203(k) lenders as perhaps there need to be. The loan program is sometimes assigned to a special 203(k) loan officer who does little else but these types of loans. A 203(k) loan takes a little longer than a conventional mortgage to process and underwrite, mainly because of the government rules that need to be adhered to throughout the process. All in all, though, the 203(k) option is an excellent loan program designed to help people buy and renovate owner-occupied property.

10.18 I WANT A VA LOAN. CAN I ADD IN MONEY FOR IMPROVEMENTS WITH A VA LOAN?

Yes, the VA has a program called the Energy Efficient Mortgage, which allows the veteran to add up to another $6,000 into the loan amount to be used for energy efficiency improvements. The first step is to have an energy audit performed, typically at the cost of the borrower. The audit will be used to identify which types of improvements could be made as well as document to the lender what the additional funds will be used for. Allowable improvements include:

- ❏ Thermal windows and doors
- ❏ Insulation for walls, ceilings, attics, floors, and water heaters
- ❏ Solar heating and cooling systems
- ❏ Furnace modifications (but not an entirely new furnace)
- ❏ Heat pumps
- ❏ Vapor barriers

The lender will consider the costs of the improvements to be made as well as make a determination that the improvements will lower the utility bills to the point where the utility savings are greater than the cost of the original improvement. Veterans have six months in order for the improvements to be completed, at which point the lender will send an inspector to the property verifying the improvements have been made.

The Right Lender and Rate

CHAPTER 11

Finding the Best Lender

After you've determined which loan you want, then you should begin shopping for lenders. Lenders can come in all different shapes and sizes. Certain lenders specialize in certain types of loans, while other lenders try to offer every program imaginable.

11.1 I'VE DECIDED ON MY LOAN. NOW WHAT?

You now find the lender that offers your chosen loan. If your mortgage is more commonplace, such as a conventional Fannie or Freddie loan, then most everyone can help. But sometimes small changes in the loan type can throw some lenders for a loop. What changes? When you switch from a conventional loan to a government loan, such as FHA or VA.

TELL ME MORE

Government loans, while still automated, have their own guidelines, paperwork, and verbiage. That takes some getting used to. Granted, it's not a big deal, but if a mortgage company only does conventional loans, then you can bet they won't handle your deal as efficiently (if at all) as a company that specializes in government loans. The FHA allows certain mortgage bankers to underwrite and approve FHA loans, granting them a special status that is called *direct endorsement*

(DE). If you determine that you need an FHA loan, the very first thing you need to ask the lender is if they have DE approval from HUD. If they don't, go elsewhere. If they have no idea what you're talking about, go elsewhere. FHA lending is just a tad different from conventional lending; not a lot, but enough to slow things down when you don't need them slowed down. Want an FHA loan? Get an FHA lender.

Are you a veteran or do you otherwise qualify for a VA loan? Just as HUD grants special DE status to certain FHA lenders, the VA grants special status for VA loans. If a lender is VA approved, then the process is streamlined. All approvals are done in-house. For example, having a lenders appraisal processing program (LAPP) allows the lender to do the appraisal without all the paperwork involved when ordering one through the Department of Veterans Affairs. If you want a VA loan, ask your lender if they're LAPP approved. If not, again, move on.

Once you've decided which type of loan you're going to get, stand firm in your decision. Sometimes, if a banker or broker can't offer the loan you've decided on, they'll try to talk you into switching to something they prefer. For example, say you call a lender and ask for a 3-percent-down FHA loan and they try and talk you into a conventional 3-percent-down loan instead. They'll run the numbers, quote some rates, and try to convince you to go conventional instead of government. If this happens, simply ask them if they've got their DE approval from HUD. If they don't, I'd be a little suspicious as to why they're trying to talk you out of a government loan.

If you see that a lender or broker specializes in your type of loan request, then certainly include them on your list of prospective lenders. Lenders who specialize in government loans tend to do a lot of them, which will mean an easier approval process for you. Be careful, though. Make sure that the lender who claims to specialize in VA loans also doesn't claim to specialize in FHA, conventional, jumbo, first-time buyer, construction, bad credit, excellent credit, and so on. It removes some of the credibility in the claim when the lender specializes in every single loan on the planet. Specializes in everything? Please. I'm not saying they're not any good at a VA loan, but wouldn't you feel better about a lender who can say, "We specialize in VA loans," without also claiming to specialize in everything else? Makes some sense, doesn't it?

11.2 HOW DO I FIND THE BEST LENDER?

If you only looked at newspapers, television ads, or websites, it would seem that all lenders are your best lender. No one's bad. In fact, many tout themselves as not only being the best lender, but also guaranteeing the best rate with the best closing costs and the best service, blah, blah, blah. Your best lender will be the one that offers the loan program you've chosen, at a competitive rate, and can deliver your loan when you need it. You begin your search with referrals. One of the keys to finding your best lender is to identify the various mortgage sources.

11.3 BUT WHERE DO I GET THE NAMES OF ALL THESE LENDERS IN THE FIRST PLACE?

If you're using a real estate agent, get referrals from him first. Most real estate companies get solicited all day long from lenders wanting referrals. So that would be a great place to start. Then ask some friends or acquaintances who they would recommend. Personal referrals can always help narrow the field, so talk to your agent and your buddies as well. You can also look in the newspaper or online for a list of lenders in your area, and certainly feel free to call a few. We'll talk about finding the best loan officer in the next chapter, but just remember that "dialing for dollars" can be a dangerous thing.

So make a plan to start with your current bank or credit union, then get referrals from real estate agents and from friends, family, and coworkers.

11.4 HOW DO I KNOW IF I CAN TRUST THESE LENDERS?

Begin by using the Better Business Bureau to check for any record of consumer complaints. In addition, check with the state agencies that regulate lenders, and see if your potential lender has any violations or records of misbehavior.

There are many reasons to do business with any particular mortgage company. One of the best ones is "trust." Who cares if the loan company "guarantees" the absolute lowest rate if you can't trust them? That's why many people do business with people they know and who care a lot about who gets their loan. XYZ Bank might be 1/8 percent higher than what's advertised, but it might also be the bank that issued your credit card and where you have your checking and savings and retirement accounts.

Why go somewhere else if there's a doubt in your mind about any new lender? Different people have different reasons for choosing any product, and loyalty and trust are certainly solid reasons to choose your mortgage loan. If you feel comfortable with the lender you're with, then what's the point of shopping around, right?

11.5 SHOULD I USE MY REAL ESTATE AGENT'S MORTGAGE COMPANY?

You can certainly start there, but you may not end up there. A growing trend in the real estate industry is for real estate brokers to either own their own mortgage company or establish a "preferred" relationship with a mortgage operation. Get quotes from the real estate agent's mortgage company just like anyone else.

Be a bit cautious, though. Sometimes these relationships get a little too cozy. Just because your agent referred you to her lender by no means gives that agent the right to know about your credit or your income or anything else personal you'd rather not share. In fact, unless you give express consent to a third party that's not your lender and is not involved in your loan approval, it is against the law to divulge anything about you or your credit or your job.

An agent might call her affiliated lender and say something like, "So, tell me about David Reed. What are his credit scores?" Some people might not want this information shared with others. If the agent found out you had bad credit she might decide not to work with you, or she may try to steer you in a direction you may not want to go when, in fact, it could just be that the loan officer at the agent's office wasn't any good. Many loan officers who work in agent offices don't get the best commissions splits, because the business is brought to them by the agents instead of the loan officer going out on his own to find new loan business.

11.6 I THOUGHT ALL MORTGAGE MONEY CAME FROM THE BANK. DOESN'T IT?

Eventually mortgage money comes from a bank. Or at least from a banker. But getting a mortgage now is very different from what happened in the movie *It's a Wonderful Life*, where home loans were made directly from other people's deposit accounts. The two main sources of mortgage money these days are mortgage bankers and mortgage brokers.

TELL ME MORE

Mortgage bankers lend their own money. Mortgage brokers do not. Actually, mortgage bankers don't use their own money; they borrow from a line of credit to place mortgage loans, but even if a mortgage banker borrows money to lend to someone else, then the money still comes from the mortgage banker. Mortgage bankers are direct lenders. They lend money directly to the borrower. Mortgage bankers can be a retail bank, a mortgage banker (exclusively), a credit union, a correspondent banker, or a "net" branch.

Retail Banks

Retail banks are surely the most common. They're where you keep your checking or savings account, deposit your paycheck, cash checks, and maybe get an auto loan. They're on every street corner, it seems. And they offer mortgages as part of their business, along with credit cards, student loans, ATM cards, personal loans, and a bevy of financial services. Yet retail mortgage lending by banks is fading with some national brands getting out of the mortgage business altogether.

Mortgage Bankers

Mortgage bankers do one thing: make mortgages. They do not issue credit cards, nor do they offer other consumer services such as checking accounts or debit cards. Mortgage bankers might "sell" your loan to someone else or they may "service" the loan themselves.

Credit Unions

Credit unions are similar to a retail bank, except that one has to be a member of the credit union in order to receive its benefits. Credit unions offer checking accounts, savings accounts, auto loans, and more, just as many retail banks do. Smaller credit unions act more like a mortgage banker or broker by originating a mortgage loan, collecting the documentation from the borrower, and then forwarding the loan to the lender. National credit unions operate with a line of credit.

Correspondent Bankers

This is a special type of mortgage banker that operates much like a broker. They are sometimes smaller mortgage bankers and are referred to as *correspondent bankers* because they may have a regional presence but not a national one. They can shop various rates from other correspondent mortgage lenders that have set up an established relationship to buy and sell loans from one another. The benefit to the consumer is that they don't set their own interest rates per se; instead, they're able to shop around for you just as a mortgage broker would. These bankers don't advertise themselves as lenders who can "shop for the best rate"—which they attempt—but simply as "mortgage bankers." Usually they are small in scale and never service their own mortgage loans.

When you work with a regional mortgage banker that works with correspondent lenders, you're really getting the best of what a broker can offer and what a banker can provide. They control the process as to who gets approved and when papers can be drawn. They can offer special programs but are also able to shop mortgage rates.

"Net" Branches

A net branch is a mortgage banker, too, but typically a very small operation consisting of perhaps three or four loan officers, a manager, and a loan processor. A net branch is so called because it receives all the net income from originating a mortgage loan. Net income is income after overhead on an individual mortgage loan is deducted.

Net branches are dedicated to their parent mortgage banking company and sign an agreement that the branch will only fund loans from that parent company's credit line and not broker to other mortgage lenders. The trade-off is that the parent company provides a credit line that individual mortgage brokers couldn't afford, and offers in-house loan approvals and low fees for doing so.

Net branches keep most of the profit in the transaction and require a certain level of experience, personal net worth, and solid credit profile. Mortgage loan officers who typically split the income with their employers find that net branches pay them more. Good mortgage brokers can find or establish their own net branch with national and regional mortgage bankers that cater to this line of work.

There aren't many differences among any of these types of mortgage bankers. In fact, you'll be hard-pressed to find a retail bank that doesn't offer the same types of mortgages that a mortgage banker does, or a credit union that issues home loans that are specific to that particular credit union. Most mortgages are alike; it's just the businesses that offer them and how they operate that are different.

11.7 WHAT IS A MORTGAGE BROKER?

Mortgage brokers find mortgage money for the borrower from other mortgage bankers. Brokers don't make the loans themselves, but arrange mortgage financing at the request of the borrower.

11.8 ARE MORTGAGE BROKERS MORE EXPENSIVE?

No, not at all. Brokers get interest rates at discounts not available to the general public. As with most businesses in the United States that offer a product for sale, there is a wholesale side as well as a retail side to the mortgage business. Mortgage brokers get their loans on a wholesale basis, mark them up to retail, and get paid the difference. Brokers get their mortgage money from wholesale divisions of mortgage bankers. Mortgage bankers that work with mortgage brokers have operations within their company, called "wholesale" divisions, that offer reduced mortgage rates to mortgage brokers.

11.9 WHY DO MORTGAGE COMPANIES USE MORTGAGE BROKERS?

Most mortgage brokers are smaller operations than mortgage bankers. Mortgage bankers use brokers to be able to make more loans with less overhead. Instead of opening up a retail operation and hiring loan processors and loan officers and paying rent, utilities, insurance, and all the associated costs of running a mortgage operation, wholesale mortgage bankers use brokers to market their loans for them. In this case, the brokers use their own overhead, hire and manage their own staff, pay their own bills, and in turn get reduced mortgage pricing. There shouldn't be any higher rates or fees just because you choose a broker instead of a banker. In fact, mortgage brokers have helped keep mortgage rates low by adding increased competition in the mortgage industry.

11.10 HOW DO MORTGAGE BROKERS GET PAID?

You can pay them, or their wholesale lender will pay them, or some combination of the two. There is no rule requiring that mortgage brokers must make a certain percent of the transaction; they will try to make what they can make, but they must also stay competitive while doing so. When you pay the broker, usually it's in the form of an origination fee, junk fees, or mortgage broker fees. When the wholesale lender pays the broker, it's usually in the form of a yield spread premium (YSP). A YSP is expressed as a percentage of the loan amount and is also a function of prevailing interest rates. The higher the interest rate, the more the YSP. The lower the interest rate, the lower the YSP, and sometimes there is no YSP at all.

TELL ME MORE

Just as you can decide to pay more discount points to get a lower rate, you can also decide not to pay discount points and end up getting a slightly higher rate.

For example, on a $100,000 loan your broker quotes you 4 percent with one point and one origination fee, 4.25 percent with no points and one origination fee, or 4.5 percent with no points and no origination fee. Now remember that the lender gets the points and the broker gets the fee. If the broker wants to make $1,000 regardless of which rate you choose, at 4 percent and 4.25 percent it's you who's paying the broker's origination fee. At 4.5 percent you pay no discount points and no origination fee. Because you are taking a higher rate, the wholesale lender, in exchange, pays the $1,000 fee directly to the broker. There can be a combination of payment, where you pay an origination fee and the wholesale lender also pays $1,000.

These options are almost always allowed, and it's up to you to decide which one to take. Brokers, however, are required to disclose to you how much money they're going to make on the transaction and who's going to be paying them.

11.11 HOW MANY LENDERS DO MORTGAGE BROKERS USE?

You'll hear advertisements from brokers bragging about how many lenders they do business with, some claiming to work with a hundred or more. That may be true, but in reality they probably only work with a select few, say, two or three, on a regular basis. Think about that for a moment. If you apply at a mortgage brokerage company, do you really expect them to sit down and compare over 100 different companies? Of course not. Instead, the broker will most likely go with lenders they know and have done business with.

TELL ME MORE

What determines where a broker will send your loan? Most often that determining factor is price, or whoever can get them the lowest interest rate. If wholesale lender A offers a 30-year fixed rate at 5 percent, and lender B offers 5.25 percent, whom do you think the broker will send your loan to? Usually it's the lender with the best interest rate. If brokers advertise that they have access to over 100 lenders, then their prime motivation for having so many is to discover the best interest rate offering possible. In actuality, you'll never find a lender that offers the exact same loan at 1/2 percent less than anyone else. Lenders price their loans the same way others do, so don't expect a broker to find a mortgage rate that's too good to be true, because it most likely is.

Another reason brokers select certain wholesale lenders is to get good customer service. After all, if the wholesale lender treats the broker responsibly, then there's less chance of your loan being handled incorrectly. Brokers don't want to look bad any more than anyone else. In fact, brokers may need to rely on their reputation more than some of the larger lending institutions in town. What's losing a deal here or there to a megabank? Not much. What's losing a deal to a small mortgage shop? It could mean the difference between being

successful or closing their doors. Good customer service is essential
to being a good broker. I'll give you a true story that happens over
and over again.

At a wholesale division of a major mortgage banker, the mortgage
production was down. Way down. They decided to "buy" the market
by offering mortgage brokers better interest rates by nearly 1/4 percent. That's a lot of money to a broker. It's a lot of money to anyone,
for that matter. On a $200,000 loan, that 1/4 percent means another
$500 in profit to the mortgage broker. So the lender printed up some
new rate sheets offering the ultra-low rates and armed the sales force
with lots of slick advertising, directing them to get as much business
as they possibly could. They got their wish. Soon, mortgage applications came pouring through the lender's door and they were happy.
For about two weeks. Then they realized that they had so much volume they couldn't get to the loans fast enough. Closing dates were
not met. Rate guarantees were expiring. People were getting mad.
The mortgage applicants weren't mad at the lender—they were mad
at their mortgage brokers. So yeah, the brokers might have made an
extra $500 on each deal, but because the lender couldn't approve
their loan on time they didn't make anything at all.

To make matters worse for the lender, their reputation in the
brokers' community was shot. Word spread: "Don't send your deals
to XYZ Mortgage, they'll screw it up." Both good customer service
and balance of competitive mortgage rates make for a good wholesale lender.

Another reason to use a broker is that while most of their lenders
offer the same exact product, sometimes one of those lenders actually has a loan program that no one else can offer. And unless that
same mortgage banker can offer the same product to retail customers, the broker might be the only efficient avenue to get the special
loan program. For instance, you need a special mortgage that lets
you qualify using unverified income. Your bank may not offer it, but
a broker might have a lender who does. This is another job of the
wholesale lender's account executive—to market new loan programs
to the mortgage broker community.

One reminder: You're not getting a mortgage *from* a broker;
you're getting a mortgage *through* a broker. You may not know who
the lender will be, because the broker may not have decided. You
don't have a choice when you go to a broker; the broker does. Oh

sure, if you've had bad experiences with a particular mortgage banker you can tell the broker that "whatever you do, don't take me to them," and the broker will comply.

11.12 WILL THE BROKER KEEP MY LENDER A SECRET?

No. In fact, you'll know almost immediately when you submit a completed loan application. The broker puts your loan package together, sends it to the lender, and the lender takes it from there. Some wholesale lenders prefer to deal directly with the borrower once an application is submitted while others want the broker to continue to do the legwork while the loan is being processed. And once again, when your loan is transferred to the ultimate lender, you can expect another round of loan disclosures and authorization forms.

11.13 IS A MORTGAGE BROKER MY BEST CHOICE?

A broker might be your best choice, but then again, a mortgage banker may be able to help you more. There are advantages that mortgage bankers have that brokers do not.

TELL ME MORE

One distinct advantage is that your banker is in fact the lender. The mortgage banker takes your application, approves the loan, and issues your mortgage funds. Due to the efficiencies in working with a mortgage banker, you can sometimes cut significant time out of the process. If you're looking to close quickly, say, within a couple of weeks, you might be able to save some time in the process by going directly to a mortgage banker. Working directly with a banker also helps to cut through some of the red tape in applying for a mortgage loan. When brokers get their approvals from lenders, they have a list of things, called loan conditions, that the lender wants before they'll close the loan. The broker gets information from the lender, relays it to you, and you give it to the broker, who then gives it back to the lender. This may seem like such a small difference that it's hardly worth mentioning, but in the mortgage process it's the details that matter most.

What if you are at your closing and discover there's a problem with your note? When working with a mortgage banker, the banker corrects the mistake and redraws the closing papers. If you use a broker, the broker has to contact the lender to make the corrections, redraw the papers, and send them back to the closing. I've been both a banker and a broker, and I can say that the number-one advantage the banker has is control over the process.

A banker can also be a better choice if the banker has a loan program that isn't offered to mortgage brokers and is only available directly from the mortgage lender. A few years ago, a major national mortgage company offered a valuable and unique mortgage program previously unheard of. The program was geared toward doctors who had just graduated from medical school and were about to start practicing. This particular loan program for physicians offered zero money down, with very competitive mortgage rates and no mortgage insurance requirements. No competitor could touch those terms. Further still, no mortgage broker had access to that loan program, even when the mortgage broker was an approved broker. So just as brokers may have access to some loans that bankers don't have, sometimes the reverse is true. Just not nearly as often.

11.14 SHOULD I CHOOSE A BROKER OR A BANKER?

Perhaps neither one at first. The mortgage process can be confusing, especially if it's your first home. For starters, I would begin with the people at wherever you have your checking or savings account. One of the easiest ways to slide into the mortgage process is to speak with someone you know and trust. That means you start at your retail bank or credit union. You may not find your best interest rate there (but again, you just might), but it will give you a yardstick by which to judge other lenders. Make an appointment and sit down with your lender and let them explain the process to you. Some retail operations give certain discounts or waive certain fees to checking account customers. After you feel comfortable with the process and have a good idea of where you're going and how you'll get there, then you should begin considering other choices.

TELL ME MORE

A banker offers certain advantages over a broker, and vice versa. It's up to you to determine which one is right for you. I began my career as a mortgage broker and certainly closed my fair share of loans. We got all of our loan programs from wholesale divisions of mortgage companies. I forget how many lenders we were authorized to market for, but it was probably in the range of 50 or 60. I know that sounds like a lot, but let me explain a brokerage operation in a little more detail.

Wholesale lenders hire account executives whose sole job is to find mortgage brokers that will be willing to start sending loans to them. Brokers, while not approving the loans themselves, do most of the work up front before the wholesale lender ever gets to see the loan file. Brokers meet with customers and take the loan application with them. They help select the proper mortgage program, prequalify the customer, pull their credit, document the file, order the appraisal and title work, and essentially do whatever is needed to get the loan to an approval stage. It might take a couple of weeks before a loan is documented enough to send to a wholesale lender.

After a loan is submitted for approval, either electronically or manually, the broker helps with any loan conditions that might be outstanding, assists in arranging the closing, and makes certain the loan closes when it's supposed to close.

I've heard the banker vs. broker battle for years, and the bottom line is that there really is little difference. Bankers and brokers offer the same group of products, the rates are almost exactly the same, and the difference may only be in the fees.

Remember the example of the lender who had such good rates that it drove volume up and almost shut the business down? This shows that price shouldn't be your only concern. You need to gauge the lender's anticipated performance over the course of your loan application. Yeah, your rate might be great, but what good is it if you never can close your deal? Perhaps the most important reason to choose a lender is simply because you feel it's the right move.

After you've done your homework and compared different lenders, then perhaps your choice is the company that "just feels right." If you're at some sort of a crossroads about which lender to pick after you've done all you need to do to compare them, then you might ask yourself, "Do I feel comfortable with these people?" Have you ever stopped some big project or purchase for no other good reason than the feeling that "something's not right here"? Of course. Everyone has. And at this stage, if you're splitting hairs over lender A vs. lender B, then perhaps both are so close that it doesn't matter which one you choose.

11.15 WHAT HAPPENS IF I WANT TO CHANGE LENDERS IN THE MIDDLE OF MY LOAN PROCESS?

You need to be careful how and when you do this. If you're buying a home, closing within 30 days, and it's day 28, you won't have time to change. There's a lot that's happened since you signed your sales contract, and if you change lenders now you'll have to start some of those things all over again. Even though you can use the same documents or copies of those documents, you'll still have to get approved at another lender. Just because you got an approval with one company doesn't mean another company will accept that approval and just scratch out the old lender's name. Nope, you have to make a brand-new application and get your new approval.

But if you're only a week or two into the process and you want to change lenders, you certainly can. Note that if you've paid any application fees up front you might not get those back, but if you've paid for your appraisal, you can get that transferred to your new lender with the new lender's name on it. Sometimes there's a fee for this service, maybe $50, but if you transfer an appraisal from one lender to the next, you should anticipate this charge. Your title company, settlement agent, attorney, or whoever else has their hands on your file may also have to make some changes. Your new lender will be part of this legal transaction; the old lender's name must be erased from the old file and replaced with the new lender's name.

Finding the Best Loan Officer

Getting a good lender and a good loan program can mean little if your loan officer isn't up to par. In fact, the best loan program in the world isn't worth a damn if your loan officer can't close your deal.

12.1 HOW DO I FIND THE BEST LOAN OFFICER?

By interviewing them and asking the right questions. If you thought finding the best lender was a chore, you might think that finding the best loan officer will be even more work. Not true. In fact, the loan officer can help or hurt a lender's reputation. Finding a good loan officer means finding someone who will answer all your questions or find someone to answer them for you. It also means finding someone who is respected in the community, who has been in the business for several years, who offers a competitive mortgage package, and who comes from a trusted referral source.

Good loan officers return phone calls promptly. Good loan officers treat the small loans with as much care as the big ones. Good loan officers are able to explain the sometimes-complex mortgage process in everyday, understandable language. Good loan officers have your best interest at heart rather than their own.

A bank or mortgage company can spend all the money in the world promoting their mortgage offerings, but it takes only one lousy loan officer to screw it up for them. The trouble is, the mortgage company probably won't find out about bad loan officers until they have already messed up several deals. If you're using a real estate agent, start by asking your agent for a referral.

TELL ME MORE

When you're looking for a home, one of the first things an agent is going to ask is whether you have obtained financing for it. If you haven't, you can bet they'll wait until they see your preapproval letter before they spend too much time on you. If you ask, that agent will give you the names and phone numbers of a couple of loan officers in the area with whom they've worked in the past. It's safe to assume that the real estate agent won't be passing out the business cards of those who have screwed up deals.

Real estate agents have a short list, but sometimes people wonder if their agent gets a "cut" of the commission for referrals. Does a loan officer pay an agent for a referral once the deal closes? No. At least they're not supposed to. Referral fees are not allowed. It's the law. Under the Real Estate Settlement Procedures Act of 1986, or RESPA, any fees whatsoever during the course of a real estate transaction must be disclosed. Real estate agents use preferred loan officers knowing the deal will get closed on time and the loan officer will take good care of their clients. Real estate agents work on a commission and if the deal doesn't close, they don't get paid.

Loan officers get their business through a variety of sources. There are loan officers who specialize in making sales calls to financial planners and accountants; when a client of a financial planner asks for help with a mortgage, the client is referred to a particular loan officer. There are other loan officers who like to call on attorneys, others who solicit their friends and family, and yet others who pursue any sphere of influence they think might garner a few mortgage leads. You will also find loan officers advertising in newspapers, on television, on the radio, and on the Internet. There is no one single source from which loan officers get all their business.

12.2 HOW DO I KNOW IF THE LOAN OFFICERS MY REAL ESTATE AGENT SUGGESTS ARE ANY GOOD?

For starters, you need to know how long the agent has been in business. Agents who have only been in business for a year or two and have had only four or five closings really haven't had enough experience to provide a good referral.

TELL ME MORE

If you've got one of the best agents in town, then you can bet they use the best loan officers in town as well. Real estate agents spend most of their time selling homes and very little time tracking down mortgage loans for customers, not to mention tracking down the status of someone's loan application. Top agents use loan officers who will close deals with no problems. They rarely, if ever, call the loan officer to check on the status of a loan. The loan officer has most likely spent a considerable amount of time and effort to get on this agent's short list, so as you can imagine, the loan officer will do anything to make sure you're a happy camper.

I know of loan officers who make over $200,000 a year doing business with no more than three real estate agents. These individuals are experienced and very knowledgeable, and they have competitive pricing with a wide range of products. Top agents like to work with top loan officers. Top loan officers also know that if they mess up a deal, they'll likely never get another lead from that agent. If loan officers who rely on just three sources of business do something to effectively damage one of their referral sources, then they will have effectively put a third of their income in jeopardy.

Additionally, top loan officers find it easier to get into the doors of other top real estate agents. "Oh, you do loans for Ms. (fill in blank here), don't you? Sure, come on in." A top loan officer who keeps doing things right can make a lot of money. If they make mistakes and routinely have problems with mortgage loans, they'll typically be relegated to doing only two or three loans per month. Not a bad income, mind you, but nothing like what they could be making. If your real estate agent is a heavy hitter in town and you get a business card from a local loan officer, keep that card as one of your mortgage loan prospects.

Another way to find a good loan officer is to see how quickly they return your initial telephone calls or emails. If you call them and they don't get back to you for a couple of days, you've got to wonder how they'll respond if you're an actual client of theirs.

12.3 WHAT IF MY AGENT'S NOT A HEAVY HITTER?

There's no reason to discount referral sources at first glance. Some new agents (even experienced ones) don't provide any whatsoever for mortgage loans. Some do, but give out more than one business card. If you get two or three mortgage referrals from your agent, it might not be because she works with three loan officers all of the time. The agent might be doing it for liability purposes. What liability? Not financial liability, but to avoid referring just one loan officer, to give you a choice. If your loan turns sour and you've been given three referrals, your agent can say, "Hey, I gave you three. You just picked the wrong one." If your agent gives you more than one referral source, ask which one they've used the most. They probably have a favorite lender they prefer to work with, even though they throw in two other business cards anyway.

12.4 DO THE BEST LOAN OFFICERS WORK WITH THE BIGGEST LENDERS?

Some of the best loan officers don't work for the megabanks, but instead opt to work for a smaller mortgage banking firm or a mortgage broker. A super-talented loan officer with superior customer service skills can sometimes make more money with a smaller operation. Loan officers who work with national banks typically have the business brought to them simply by taking loan applications from bank customers. Loan officers who go out and bring new business to a mortgage operation get paid more than the loan officer sitting in a bank lobby.

12.5 WHAT QUESTIONS SHOULD I ASK A POTENTIAL LOAN OFFICER?

You want to ask questions that accomplish two things: determine their experience and let them know that you're a savvy borrower who knows all the tricks. You don't need to go over a list of a hundred questions or have them fill out a questionnaire. Just spend a couple of minutes and ask them a few things.

For example:

What is your rate today for a 30-year fixed conventional mortgage? The answer should be quick, precise, and comfortable. Loan officers shouldn't have reluctance quoting an interest rate. You don't want to listen to any hemming and hawing. You want them to get to the point.

What are the lender closing costs on this loan? If you're talking to a mortgage banker, they'll have this number memorized. Usually it's their company that sets the fees, not the loan officer. If you're talking to a mortgage broker, make sure the fees they're quoting include those from the wholesale lender as well as from the mortgage broker. When using a broker there will sometimes be two sets of fees: broker and lender fees. If you just ask for lender fees and don't specifically ask for broker fees, they might not quote them to you because, frankly, you didn't ask. If you're not sure whether the lender is a broker or a banker, you need to ask.

What is the APR for this loan? This question is the setup from the first two questions. By knowing the interest rate, loan amount, and lender closing costs, the *annual percentage rate,* or APR, can be calculated. Most veteran loan officers, and even the good, not-so-veteran loan officers, have been asked this question so many times their heads spin; it should literally fall off the tongue. If you sense some reluctance from the loan officer, or they tell you that the APR is meaningless, this ought to send up a red flag. You need to work with a loan officer who not only can explain APR properly, but can explain when and why that's an important number.

What is the par price for this loan? The term *par* means a rate quote with no discount points charged to the borrower to obtain the advertised rate. The term is hidden deep in lending lingo, and if you use the word when interviewing your loan officers, it immediately tells them that you've not just fallen from the turnip truck. For some strange reason you know some obscure lending jargon, so they better not mess with you.

How long have you been in the business? This seems like a fair question, one that should be asked of almost anyone in a profession. But in the mortgage business it takes on an additional meaning. Let's say you set up a doctor's appointment to see about that nagging cough. You sign in, take your seat, and suddenly you see some kid about 18 years old walking in with your medical chart. Are you going to question this kid's experience? Of course you are. But in reality, physicians spend most of their adult life just getting through medical school, so you won't see any 18-year-olds walking around with a stethoscope. There are requirements for being a doctor.

When interest rates drop and homeowners are refinancing their mortgages, then suddenly there's a surge of new loan officers in the industry. When rates go back up and business slows, those loan officers get out of the business entirely and go back to being accountants or whatever. You want a loan officer who's good enough at his business to make money when rates are high as well as when they're low. Any loan officer can close a loan during a refinance boom, but the experienced loan officers know how to make money during all business cycles. If your loan officer hasn't been in the business for very long, say, only a year or two, I'd rank him a little lower than someone with more experience.

Which lenders do you use? If you ask this question of mortgage brokers, you'll get one of two responses: one straightforward and one vague. The straightforward answer is, "I typically use XYZ Bank, ABC Bank, and HIJ Bank, depending on the loan." The vague answer is, "I really won't know until I review all of our lenders. You see, we're signed up with over 100 national lenders and I'd like to find you the best deal possible."

While that second answer sounds terrific, it's not what you want to hear. Your loan officer should be able to tell you who they're doing business with. Maybe there will be some names you won't recognize, but that shouldn't necessarily cause you any concern. There are lenders who do nothing else besides whole-sale lending. But if your loan officer won't tell you who they're working with, they're not being straight with you. Okay, I'll admit that a loan officer may not know exactly where they'll send your loan, but they should have a fairly good idea. If they fail to answer your question, you might want to lower their ranking.

How much money will you make on my loan? Ouch. This issue of how much a broker will make off you has been around for quite some time, and it's still not fully resolved. But ask your loan officer how much the company will make on your deal. I know that sounds weird, but your loan officer will ask you the very same question, right? Mortgage brokers are required to disclose how much they're going to make on your mortgage loan and will provide you with a good-faith estimate, disclos-ing who charges what. Most will tell you right away that "we charge an origination fee and a processing fee," for instance, and they will disclose other third-party loan costs as well.

12.6 HOW DO LOAN OFFICERS GET TRAINED?

Most loan officers will tell you that they never intended to get into the business, that they just ended up there somehow. There are a few colleges that offer degrees in mortgage banking, but not many. Sure, there are degrees in finance or accounting, but not in mortgage banking. At least they are not as widely available as other business degrees. Loan officers get trained by experience, by their company, and through courses, as in many other lines of work.

TELL ME MORE

In general, there are two types of loan officers. One typically has a financial background or is good with numbers, and that person gravitates to home lending. The other is someone who is good in sales or marketing and learns the mortgage business from that angle.

There's some good money to be made in the mortgage business. If you find a loan officer who's been in the business for more than five years, it's likely that they're making $100,000 or more a year.

That kind of income potential attracts lots of folks, but it takes a particular type of person to be a good loan officer. First, it takes attention to detail. Loan applications can't be taken haphazardly. There are too many things that can go wrong. Second, and perhaps most important, it takes an individual who can find the business in the first place. If the loan officer doesn't develop a client base, then all the attention to detail doesn't matter.

Many loan officers start in the real estate business, while others start in the financial services industry. Still others come from a solid sales or marketing background, which they can use to help them establish a client base. There is no bona fide career path; usually it just happens.

12.7 ARE THERE REQUIREMENTS FOR BEING A LOAN OFFICER?

Yes, there are. Following the financial crisis in 2008, Congress passed the Secure and Fair Enforcement for Mortgage Licensing Act, or SAFE.

As of August 1, 2009, a mortgage loan officer employed by a federally insured bank or credit union must be federally registered and all other mortgage loan officers, including mortgage bankers and mortgage brokers, must also be state licensed. Each state has its own licensing system but must comply with SAFE standards.

The law requires loan officers to go through and successfully pass a criminal history and credit background check, take a 20-hour pre-license education class, and pass the exam as well as complete eight hours of approved continuing education each year.

Residential mortgage loan officers must register with the National Mortgage Licensing System and Registry, or NMLS, and be assigned an identification number.

12.8 HOW DO LOAN OFFICERS GET PAID?

Some very handsomely, some not. It depends on whom they work for. If they work for a national bank, they typically get paid a salary.

For a mortgage broker or banker, they, too, get a base salary and then a certain amount of basis points based upon loan volume each month.

TELL ME MORE

The national prominence of a mortgage lender helps bring in the business on its own, so the loan officer spends less time developing new business. In exchange for the lender doing most of the prospecting and coming up with the mortgage applicants, the pay structure is typically reduced.

Loan officer compensation is fairly standard with a few tweaks perhaps between different mortgage operations. A common compensation structure is a base salary plus an additional bonus based upon loan volume each month. For example, a loan officer gets a standard salary each month and then gets a certain amount of basis points based upon volume. A basis point is 1/100th of a percent. A loan officer might have a base salary of, say, $30,000 plus 90 basis points of the total loan volume for that month.

Say that a loan officer closes $2 million in loans. Ninety basis points of $2 million is $18,000. Some mortgage companies offer "tiered" pricing where the amount of basis points increases as loan volume increases. On the other hand, there might be a month or even two throughout the year when a loan officer has no closings for a month and only gets the base salary. The mortgage company still pays the loan office a base salary regardless of any production. However, if there are too many months where production is extremely low or nonexistent, the loan officer will likely soon be out of a job because the mortgage company cannot afford the pay with no production.

Good loan officers can stay in business for a long time if they so choose. Bad ones can't, because they are unable to bring in the deals fast enough or are too inept to close the ones they do get. After a few months of no income, it's quite possible the loan officer will choose a different career path, don't you think?

12.9 DO ALL LOAN OFFICERS CHARGE 1 PERCENT ON EVERY LOAN?

That depends entirely on company policy. What loan officers cannot do, however, is charge an interest rate for one client and then another rate for another borrower. Under the exact same scenario, a loan officer is prohibited from charging different rates.

Say there are two borrowers, both with a 740 FICO with a 20 percent down payment and borrowing $400,000 and they both want to lock their rate on the same day. The loan officer must charge each customer the very same rate and term.

Before the introduction of Dodd-Frank (see Chapter 7 for more information), loan officers could be paid on a straight commission with no base salary. Mortgage loan officers could steer borrowers to higher-rate loans in order to get more commission. Or, loan officers might accept a rate lock from a customer but don't officially lock in the loan at the time of the request and internally "float" the loan to see if rates get any better and then lock in the customer's requested rate. Loan officers can no longer be compensated based upon the rate and loan program selected.

12.10 MY LOAN OFFICER ISN'T ANY GOOD. CAN I CHANGE LOAN OFFICERS?

Sure you can. Just because you made a decision to work with one loan officer doesn't mean you're required to stay with him. Especially if this individual is not doing a very good job for you or, worse yet, is trying to take advantage of you.

When you cancel a loan application, you'll typically be asked to send in a written cancellation notice saying that you want to cancel your loan and transfer it to another mortgage company. This written notice might not be a legal requirement, and in fact, you don't have to do anything at all other than apply somewhere else. You can do that without your current loan officer knowing about your doing so. The written cancellation will be required, though, should you want some of your documents that your old loan officer has that you want to send to the new loan officer. The appraisal, for instance, will have to have the new company's name on it.

12.11 WHERE DO I COMPLAIN ABOUT MY LOAN OFFICER?

Each state regulates and licenses its own loan officers, so there is no national database of complaints. Instead, you need to find out who regulates mortgage loan officers in your state and make the complaint with them. Some states have different regulatory agencies depending on whether the loan officer is licensed as a mortgage broker or mortgage banker.

You can file your complaint at the state regulatory agency and also file a complaint with the Better Business Bureau. Too often, when people get shoddy service or they feel taken advantage of, they don't register their feelings with the proper agencies. If you have a legitimate complaint about a loan officer, then by all means make your case with the regulatory agency that watches over him. You could be doing someone a great favor by helping to weed out ineffective and/or potentially corrupt loan officers.

Finding the Best Interest Rate

Ah, the Holy Grail. After getting all your finances together, finding a home, finding a loan program, finding a lender, and finding a loan officer, it all boils down to this, doesn't it? Knowing how rates are set, how they can move, and when they move can help you nail down a rock-bottom rate.

13.1 WHO SETS MORTGAGE RATES?

Lenders set interest rates every business morning as markets open. There are various indexes, but for fixed-rate mortgages they're set to a mortgage bond and priced accordingly. A 30-year fixed-rate price will be tied to the current 30-year Fannie Mae coupon being traded that day. If the yield on that mortgage bond (coupon) goes down, lenders will drop their interest rates. If that yield goes up, the rate goes up.

For adjustable-rate mortgages they do the very same thing. If your ARM is based on the one-year treasury, then your rate will move up or down depending upon the current price of a one-year treasury. So it goes with any other loans that track a particular index. If that index goes up or down, your rate will move along with it.

13.2 HOW DOES MY LOAN OFFICER QUOTE RATES?

Your loan officer will have more direct influence on your mortgage rate than the lender will. At major retail banks and national mortgage bankers, loan officers are required to quote a specific rate for a specific product without variance. If a lender says, "For loans between $300,000 and $417,000 the interest rate will be 4 percent with one point," that's what you'll be quoted.

National lenders have a database that the loan officer uses to review all your parameters, such as credit scores, loan amounts, amount of down payment, debt ratios, and so on. The loan officer will ask you the appropriate questions to enter those variables into the mortgage rate pricing system and your rate will be quoted based on your answers.

If you're not working with one of these national lenders or retail banks, it's your loan officer that determines your interest rate. Each day as lenders set their rates, they're really only setting the "wholesale" price of each rate and program, and it's up to the loan officer to quote the rate to you.

13.3 BUT DOESN'T THE FED SET INTEREST RATES?

Sure, the Federal Reserve chair along with the Federal Open Market Committee, or FOMC, set interest rates, but they don't set mortgage rates. What the Fed sets is either the Federal Funds rate or the discount rate or both. They provide cheaper or more expensive money to the markets by making money more expensive or less expensive. These two rates that the Fed sets are short-term rates. Very short term, as in overnight.

TELL ME MORE

The *Federal Funds rate* is the rate banks charge one another to borrow money overnight. Why do banks do this? They have certain reserve requirements that keep them liquid. If a bank makes a loan, they have to adjust their reserves at the same time. If they don't have enough money in reserve at the end of a business day, they have to go borrow it—fast. So they borrow from one another at deeply discounted rates. If the Fed wants to stimulate a sluggish economy, they make money cheaper by reducing these rates. The theory is that since money is so cheap, lenders and investors are more likely to make more loans to businesses that want to buy new factory equipment or invest in new products.

The Fed plays a role in interest rates, just not one tied to your mortgage. Instead, what happens is that investors anticipate future Fed moves and hope to profit from them. And when it comes to bonds, it sometimes depends on whether these investors think the economy will be white-hot with consumer demand, driving up prices (which raises interest rates), or stone-cold, with all the money leaving the stock market and being placed in bonds, thereby driving up the bond prices and reducing interest rates.

When the Fed reduces rates, they hope to stimulate the economy. When they increase rates, they want to slow the economy down. The Fed looks at the overall economy and pays attention to various reports that may help guide them in keeping the economy from overheating or going into a recession. If a report comes out that suggests the economy is gaining steam, then the likelihood of higher interest rates looms larger. Not just one report by itself, but perhaps several reports over an extended period. Exactly what the Fed watches is a mystery, but there are plenty of pundits that watch the same data and try to guess what the Fed's next move might be.

13.4 ARE MORTGAGE RATES TIED TO THE 30-YEAR TREASURY AND THE 10-YEAR TREASURY?

Sorry, they're not. You can't track mortgage rates against the 10-year or 30-year treasury. While they're both fixed investments, they're not tied to mortgage rates. Trying to tie mortgage rates to either of these rates is like trying to track Wal-Mart stock to the Dow Jones average. You might see some coincidental moves, but there is no direct correlation.

But let's look a moment at what can influence the price of a bond in general. When investors have money to invest, they can do it in stocks or equities that may provide a greater return on their invest-ment than bonds. Or if investors want to avoid more risk but get a steady return, they will choose a bond. In the case of mortgages, they might choose a mortgage bond. It's less risky than a stock, and the return is guaranteed. That's the reason why, during soft economic times, people invest less in a stock market they perceive as risky and park their money in bonds instead. If more people have the same feeling and buy the same bond, they then push up the price of that bond. Higher demand equals higher price, right? When the price of a bond goes up, the rate goes down.

TELL ME MORE

Here's how it works. Let's say a note seller has some $1,000 notes that pay 5 percent in interest over a preset term. At the same time, the Dow Jones Industrial Average has been taking a beating as of late and some investors are getting a little weary of losing money by the bucket. So instead of investing in stocks, they look at these $1,000 notes. Sure, they only pay 5 percent, but that's a lot better than los-ing 20 percent, right? These investors begin buying the bonds at $1,000 a clip.

Because of the increase in demand, the seller soon begins raising the price of that bond, and those same $1,000 bonds now cost $1,100 for the same 5 percent return. Sure, the 5 percent is still nice, but it costs a little more now, doesn't it? Because of that rise in price, the *effective* interest rate then drops from 5 percent to 4.55 percent. That's how mortgage bonds work as well. When the price increases, the rates fall.

13.5 WHO INVESTS IN BONDS?

Most every institutional investor does. It's a guaranteed rate of return for them. But there's a bugaboo when investing in bonds: inflation. Inflation will eat into the value of the bond by reducing the value of the return. A bond will guarantee a certain yield, say, $5,000. If inflation creeps into the picture and prices rise across the board by, say, 10 percent, then that same $5,000 isn't worth what it was when it was first issued. Inflation ate away at the final value.

That's one of the reasons that when the stock markets are doing well, the bond market is not.

TELL ME MORE

As an economy picks up steam, a couple of dynamics come into play. First, people pull money out of bonds (reducing the price and raising the interest rate of the bonds) and put it into stocks. Second, a stimulated economy can increase consumer demand, which will increase consumer prices. This situation can cause inflation, which again reduces the value of a mortgage bond, raising rates. Historically, when bonds are doing well, the stock market isn't. At least that's the theory. And in practice?

Overall, yes, when the stock markets are doing poorly, then people invest more in safer fixed instruments like bonds, resulting in lower interest rates. There are times, however, when the bond and stock markets are doing well at the same time. How does that work? Toward the end of an economic slowdown and at the beginning of an economic upturn, lower rates encourage businesses to borrow more and then use that money to hire more workers and expand factories. As people begin to gain more confidence in the stock market, they start to invest in lower-priced stocks, anticipating an upturn. Sound confusing? It can be, but in general if the economy isn't doing very well for any extended time, then you will see interest rates gradually move downward.

13.6 WHERE ARE RATES HEADED?

I have probably been asked that question more than a thousand times. Literally. It's the question everyone wants answered. The fact is that no one knows where rates are headed. No one. Yeah, there may be long-term trends over the course of a month or a year, but when you're closing at the end of the month that's not much help, is it? Trying to determine what rates are going to do over the next few weeks or months is a nightmarish prospect. I don't know, your neighbor doesn't know, and the financial gurus on television don't know, either. They might guess, but they don't know.

When I'm asked where rates are headed, I always respond, "I can't tell you where they're going, but I can tell you where they've been and where they are now." If that sounds a little smart-alecky, it's not supposed to.

Anyone who is advising you on interest rates and tells you where they think rates are going is being irresponsible. They're not the ones closing on a home loan, after all. If they predict wrongly, so what? No harm. But if someone tries to tell you what's going to happen in the interest rate environment, ask them if they'll guarantee their predictions with a little moolah. I promise you that you'll get no takers.

13.7 WHAT TYPES OF ECONOMIC REPORTS SHOULD I PAY ATTENTION TO?

Some reports may impact interest rates more than others. Some reports might cause a reaction in the markets one day and then be completely meaningless the following day. It's only important that you understand how daily economic data can make an interest rate move in the course of a few minutes after a report's release. Any report that suggests good economic news will be portrayed as bad for the bond market, causing interest rates to rise. Reports that foretell a future recession may cause rates to fall. Here are some reports that might cause rates to swing one way or the other after their monthly release. In essence, the better the economic report, the greater the likelihood of higher rates.

Report	What It Means
Construction Spending	More spending means more jobs, recovering economy, and the possibility for higher rates.
Consumer Confidence	A confident consumer buys more and acquires more debt, which creates higher prices and higher rates.
CPI	Consumer Price Index: an inflation indicator. Higher inflation means higher rates.
Durable Goods Orders	More goods sold means more jobs, strong economy, and higher rates.

Existing Home Sales	More homes sold means more jobs and a better economy, which can lead to higher rates.
Factory Orders	More orders, higher rates.
GDP	Gross Domestic Product: More goods produced means a strong economy, which leads to higher rates.
ISM	Institute for Supply Management (formerly called the Purchasing Managers Index): More goods sold means good economy and higher rates.
LEI	Leading Economic Indicators: used to forecast future economic growth. High indicators mean higher rates.
NFPN	Non-farm Payroll Number: This is the net gain or loss of full-time private and government jobs from the previous month. Job gains indicate a strong economy, rates will rise.
PPI	Producer Price Index: wholesale inflation numbers. Higher prices for goods mean higher rates.
Retail Sales	Strong retail sales figures mean a strong economy and higher rates.
Unemployment Numbers	Low unemployment and lots of new jobs being created mean higher rates.

Note that all of these reports can cause higher rates. But these same reports can also have the opposite effect. If unemployment goes up, and more and more people lose their jobs, that's a negative for the economy. A negative for the economy can mean lower interest rates. Just as reports can point to a booming economy, they can also point to a weakening one. And here's an additional twist: The report can also be reported as neutral and having no effect at all because the new economic data reflected a "steady as she goes" economy.

13.8 DO I FOLLOW ALL OF THE ECONOMIC REPORTS?

Of course not, but you need to understand how economic reports can affect mortgage rates. And you must understand how mortgage rates are priced before you can begin to negotiate. Otherwise, you won't know why interest rates went up, down, or sideways for no apparent reason. There are plenty of things that can impact interest rates, such as a speech by a key political figure, a natural disaster, the threat of war, oil shortages, the value of the dollar, the trade deficit, or a foreign country investing heavily in U.S. bonds. But as you and I are at work all day, it's impossible to keep track of all of them.

13.9 WHEN IS THE BEST TIME TO GET A RATE QUOTE?

The best time to get rate quotes is in the morning after any governmental reports on the economy are released. Most reports are released by 9:00 a.m. (EST), though some come before and some come a little after. If you check interest rates late in the day the markets may be closed, and if you check too early in the morning lenders may not have had time to price their rates for that day.

There are some very smart people in the mortgage business whose sole job is to price mortgage rates. They scan all the economic data, watch the various mortgage bond prices, and price their interest rates for their loan officers to use. If mortgage bonds are up, then rates for that day will be down. Sometimes, during the course of a business day, mortgage bonds will make a sudden move. If the move is dramatic enough, the lender will reprice mortgage rates during the business day. If the move is only slight, the lender may do nothing at all, waiting until the following day to see if a price change is necessary.

Interest rate prices are set by *basis points,* and a basis point is 1/100th of 1 percent. If the cost of a mortgage bond rises by 20 or 30 basis points, you can expect the cost of that bond to adjust accordingly. A move of 50 basis points would cause a 30-year fixed mortgage rate to adjust by 0.125 percent. A move of 100 basis points would cause a rate adjustment of 0.25 percent, and so on.

13.10 CAN I TRUST THE INTEREST RATES IN THE NEWSPAPER OR ONLINE?

Interest rates in newspapers are days old. Many newspapers around the country publish their "interest rate surveys" in the Sunday paper, usually in the real estate or business section. Many papers cut off their advertisements for businesses on Thursday mornings, so the interest rates you see aren't from that Sunday; they're from the previous Thursday morning. Not only that, but by the time you contact a lender the following Monday morning, new pricing has already come out for that day as well.

Don't expect to get the same rate you see in the newspaper when you make your telephone call. You might be able to get that rate if rates haven't changed for several days, but just know that published rates are old news. For that matter, any published rate advertisements have to be understood in the same context, whether they are in newspapers, on the radio, on television, in business magazines, or even on the Internet.

Over the years, the Internet has been the place where lenders advertise their rates where a service will publish a list of mortgage companies and their associated interest rates. These are updated typically every day by the individual lender. But still, by the time you research the rate and place a phone call, the rate might very well have moved.

13.11 WHY ARE SOME LENDERS SO MUCH LOWER THAN EVERYONE ELSE?

They can't be. Okay, someone might be a little lower, but lenders and brokers all get their mortgage money from the same place, so any differences will be marginal. When I was a mortgage broker, I would get interest rate sheets faxed to us each and every day from our wholesale lenders. Probably 40 to 50 different lenders would solicit our business that way. When I first started in the business, I would painstakingly pore over dozens and dozens of rate sheets, hoping to find the lender that would have the absolute lowest rate on the planet so I could get all the business I wanted. What I didn't realize was that I wasn't the only mortgage broker in town doing the exact same thing. In fact, I lived in San Diego, where there were thousands of loan officers getting the very same rate sheets.

I soon discovered that there was no reason for me to scour 40 rate sheets every day for the best interest rate. There was no such thing. Almost to a lender, each rate sheet was within 25 to 50 basis points of one another. That works out to rates being about 1/8 percent or so apart (since 50 basis points buy 1/8 percent). That means 4 percent and 4.125 percent. Nothing like the 5 percent or 6 percent I was looking for. It just didn't work out that way. On occasion a lender might run a promotion and offer better pricing or lower fees to gain market share, but even then such promotions were relatively tame and short-lived. Instead, I discovered that I used maybe three or four wholesale lenders on a daily basis, not 40 or 50. What does that mean? It means that if someone's quoting a rate that is hands-down 1/2 percent better than anyone else's, then there's something wrong. Either something is wrong with the quote or it's a misprint.

13.12 HOW DO I GET A GOOD RATE QUOTE FROM ALL MY COMPETING LENDERS?

There are four things you must absolutely do in order to compare apples to apples, or mortgage quote to mortgage quote:

1. Get your rate quotes on the same day, at the same time of day.
2. Get a rate quote on one loan program only.
3. Get a rate quote for a time frame long enough to cover your transaction.
4. Get a quote for all the lender fees associated with that rate.

TELL ME MORE

1. Get your rate quotes on the same day, at the same time of day.

If you don't do it at the same time, then at 9:00 a.m. in the morning you may get a rate quote from one lender and at 4:00 p.m. another quote from a different lender. If there's been a price increase during the day, then the rate the lender quoted in the afternoon may be higher than the rate you got in the morning. The fact is that both lenders' rates are higher if rates went up during the day. During times of high market volatility, I've seen interest rates change as much as three times a day. Maybe more. This means that the interest rate quotes I made in the morning are no longer any good. Lenders price their competing loans on the very same index. You won't find one lender at 6 percent and another at 7 percent on the exact same loan under the very same terms. Forget what the advertisements tell you; it just won't happen.

2. Get a rate quote on only one loan program.

There is no way to compare a 30-year fixed loan with a hybrid. They're two different animals. You must determine beforehand, absolutely, the mortgage loan program you need and get quotes on that exact loan. Some loan officers can't compete on certain loan programs, or one lender might have a promotion on a particular type of loan that they'll try and steer you toward. If you call a lender and ask for their rate on a 30-year fixed rate, but that lender hasn't been very competitive in that market, they may try and suggest another product. They'll ask, "Tell me, how long do you intend to keep this mortgage?" or some other question to try and find an alternate product you might be interested in. For instance, you tell the loan officer you're only going to be in the house for three to four years and guess what, the loan officer says, "I have a special loan program (a hybrid) that's fixed for three or four years at a much lower rate. Would you like me to quote you on that instead?"

When the interest rate on hybrids is much lower than a 30-year fixed, it's tempting to sign up immediately and feel lucky at finding such a great deal. But your journey of finding the best rate just ended there because you changed the course of your search. If you get a low hybrid quote instead of a 30-year fixed rate, make absolutely certain you immediately contact other lenders and get their quote for that same hybrid as well. You may find that when one lender is competitive at one program they're competitive on others, too.

3. Get a rate quote for a time frame long enough to cover your transaction.

Today's rate quote might be a steal, but it will only last for a short time, say, five days. If you can't get your loan approved and closed within five days, then what good is the rate quote? No good at all. That's a common trick some loan officers use when quoting interest rates. "My rate today is 3 percent, but that's only good for loans currently in our system ready to go to closing. If I had your loan in my closing department today, I could offer you that rate, but alas, I don't."

Don't fall for it. In your head you're thinking, "Wow! This company has super-low rates! I'd better get my loan in with them as soon as I can!" But you're forgetting that lenders can't be that much better than everyone else because they set their pricing using the same index. If you do fall for the trick, you'll also find that when you get ready to go to closing, the lender's rates turn out to be just like everyone else's. And probably a little higher. Instead, get a rate quote that will cover your transaction. If you close within 30 days, then get rate quotes covering a 30-day period. If you need 45 days, get 45-day quotes.

4. Get a quote for all the lender fees associated with that rate.

A lower rate means little if it costs you more to get the rate. Some lenders and brokers offer lower rates but stack the transaction with closing fees. Who cares if the money comes from an origination fee or from a variety of junk fees? It still costs you the same. Getting a quote with associated fees is perhaps the most difficult part of comparing various offerings. It can get confusing, especially when you're comparing to no-point quotes and one-point quotes.

For instance, you call lender A and you get a quote of 7 percent with 2 points, and then you get another quote from lender B at 7.5 percent with zero points. Still later, lender C quotes you 7.25 percent with one point, and finally lender D quotes you 7.375 percent with 1.5 points. Confused yet? Sometimes a loan officer will do just that— try to confuse you. And try to convince you they have the better deal simply by trying to muck up the process.

To keep this from happening, simply ask each lender for their 30-day quote and 30-year fixed rate, and then specify for:

❑ Your rate with no points and all lender/broker fees
❑ Your rate with one point and all lender/broker fees
❑ Your rate with 1.5 points and all lender/broker fees
❑ Your rate with 2 points and all lender/broker fees

Notice I didn't say anything about nonlender fees, such as title policies or tax escrows. Nonlender charges will remain the same regardless of who places the mortgage. Your hazard insurance policy will be priced the same whether you choose lender A or lender B. The same is true for other nonlender fees, such as a document stamp or settlement charges. These charges will be what they will be, so don't confuse the issue by including them in your lender comparison.

Now you finally can compare apples and apples. You have a quote from each lender covering the exact same type of loan. Take your two best quotes and move forward.

13.13 WHAT DO I DO WITH MY TWO BEST QUOTES?

Compare the APRs on each offering, then ask for concessions. Yes, you've worn them down and made them compete against other lenders, but you still need to negotiate one more time. Approach them like this, saying, "I really like your rate and your company, but I'm not ready to pick a lender. If you'll waive your $300 processing and $300 administration fees, I'll lock with you today."

13.14 HOW DO I LOCK IN MY MORTGAGE RATE?

You have to specifically request an interest rate *lock,* because it's not automatic. Just because your good-faith estimate has a rate on it doesn't mean that's what you're getting. Getting your interest rate guaranteed means that you "lock" that rate in. It's set. Throw away the key and get on with life.

Your interest rate quote is no good unless it's locked in with your lender or broker. And there may be as many ways to lock in a loan as there are loan programs, because there is no universal policy. If you call lender A and ask for a rate quote, don't expect to get that rate until you get a lock agreement from them. You also need to lock in the rate allowing for enough time to close the deal, and you must follow your lender's lock instructions.

TELL ME MORE

Lenders are required to provide you with a document explaining their interest rate lock guidelines; the document spells out when you can lock and under what circumstances. Once you do lock your loan, you will receive your lock agreement.

A lock agreement is an understanding that the interest rate you agreed to will be presented to you at closing. But there's a little more to it than that. There is some due diligence required on both the lender's and borrower's part.

The lender or broker will most likely require a loan application from you, signed by you and placed on file. This loan application must be "official" as we explained previously (see Chapter 1). It needs to include your name, Social Security number, income, property address, loan amount, and estimated value of the subject property. Many years ago, consumers could call different lenders and lock in at one place, lock in at another, and lock in later on at still a third—without even having to turn in a loan application. Not so anymore. Mortgage rate lock-ins are serious business for lenders.

Once you lock in a rate for a mortgage loan, there are people down the pike who know about it. They're the people working in the mortgage company's *secondary market* department. One of their jobs is to reserve a place for you at the mortgage rate table you requested. Many secondary departments intend to sell your loan later on, and when you lock in an interest rate at, say, 5 percent, then they count it. If they lose your lock, they have to replace you with someone else.

Still other secondary departments have no intention of selling your loan, but they need to know what rate you've locked in at so that they can better manage their loan portfolio. Lenders take locks just as seriously as you do, if not more so. Getting your loan application in with the lender or broker is a typical requirement.

Some lenders or brokers will ask for money at this point, either as an "application fee" or to pay for your appraisal before they lock in your loan. Appraisals can cost $400 or more, and if you don't pay the fee and end up closing with someone else, that lender has lost the $400 right out of the gate.

There are also performance issues a lender wants to see. In lock agreements, you will be asked to provide information in a timely manner to give the lender time to process your loan. If you apply on the first of the month for a loan scheduled to close on the fifteenth, then you'll be asked to provide your documentation immediately. If you don't turn in your pay stubs or bank statements until the fourteenth, your lock agreement won't be enforceable. You didn't perform.

13.15 DOES MY LOCK MEAN I'M APPROVED?

No. A common misconception is that a lock agreement is also a loan approval. It's not; it's an interest rate guarantee. If you lock in a mortgage for 8 percent and then get declined for the loan, you don't get the loan or the rate. A rate lock isn't a commitment to lend, but rather an agreement that should your loan be approved you'll get the agreed-upon interest rate. It's also an agreement to offer a rate that's not just based on an approval, but on the specific loan program you're requesting. If you lock in a 30-year rate but the lender later discovers the purchase is a four-unit investment property, then your rates will change. Or perhaps there's a credit issue that needs to be addressed. Whatever the case, understand that a lock agreement and a loan approval are two different things.

13.16 WHAT HAPPENS IF MY RATE LOCK EXPIRES AND I STILL HAVEN'T CLOSED MY LOAN?

Be prepared to get the higher rate, either whatever rate you locked in or the prevailing rate. Most lock agreements will explain this requirement, but you need to understand it before you get much further. Several years ago I had a closing scheduled for the end of the month for a client who was a little tardy in getting his documentation in. And that's putting it nicely. He locked in for 30 days, but a few days after his lock he saw that rates were drifting downward. When our office called him and encouraged him to send in his pay stubs, bank statements, and so on, somehow he never got around to it. With about 10 days left until closing, I called to warn him that we were getting dangerously close to missing his closing date. He said, "Yeah, that's what I'm counting on. I want my lock to expire so I can get the lower rate." I reminded him to read his lock agreement and, sure enough, it said, "If your lock expires you will get the higher of your locked rate or the prevailing rate at time of expiration." He wasn't all that pleased about that, but you can bet he got his documentation in within hours.

13.17 WHAT HAPPENS IF I LOCK AND RATES GO DOWN?

There are a few options available to you when you lock in your interest rate and rates move down immediately afterward. If you have a *float-down* feature in your lock, you can use it. If not, you can try to negotiate with the lender or broker.

TELL ME MORE

Again, lenders take locks just as seriously as you do. If you locked in your rate and rates jumped up immediately afterward, I can guarantee that you won't get a call from your loan officer wanting you to break your lock and relock at the new, higher rate. But there are programs designed to protect the consumer when rates fall after locking in.

Some loan programs have what is called a float-down feature that allows you to lock in one rate but, if rates fall during your lock period, to relock the lower rates sometime during your loan process. There are a few variations on this theme, but typically you can relock your loan just one time during the lock period. Some lenders require this relock period to be during a specific window during the lock and not just any old time during the loan approval process; others ask for a fee when relocking a rate, and some won't let you relock unless the interest rate falls by a certain percentage. Some lenders do all three.

Many lenders offer a float-down feature on almost any loan they offer, but your starting interest rate might be higher than their best offering. In other words, "Yeah, I've got a float-down for ya, but the rate's a little higher." This is not uncommon. Lenders are fairly good about risk—that's their business. If they're going to give the consumer a little extra, you can bet they'll try and offset that risk with a little more yield. If you talk to a lender who offers a float-down, ask if the rate would be reduced if you didn't want the feature.

When you work with a mortgage broker, there is another way to get out of a lock. When you lock with a broker, the broker then locks with a lender. If you lock at 8 percent with a broker and rates fall to 7.5 percent thereafter, ask the broker to lock you with another lender. The broker may or may not be inclined to do that. Brokers maintain special business relationships with their wholesale lenders. In fact, wholesale lenders track something called a *pull-through* rate, which is the percentage of loans that close that have been locked by a broker. If a broker locks with one lender and sends the loan somewhere else, you can bet the broker will be asked about that loan. If brokers break a lock too many times with a wholesale lender or don't send them the loans they promised, it's possible the wholesale lender won't do business with them again. But if rates do drop after you've locked with a broker, then why not ask? It's your mortgage, not theirs.

In practice, simply asking the broker to break your lock can be used in other circumstances as well. If you locked with a mortgage banker and rates have dropped, ask them for the new lower rate. Why not, right? But there are a few things that have to come into play before your lender will get your rate reduced. The rate drop must be more than a few basis points. Lenders won't negotiate with you after you've locked if rates have only come down 1/8 percent or so. Even a 1/4 percent drop isn't enough. But if rates have dropped 1/2 percent or more, then you'll probably get a favorable ear. Why?

Lenders know that if you stop your approval process with one lender and move it somewhere else, that takes time. Time you may not have to move a loan around. There is also some risk involved. Since most lenders or brokers won't lock you in without a loan application, rates might shoot back up in the time it takes to make a new application somewhere else. Another reason a lender might not negotiate is due to the proximity of your closing date. If your closing is within the next week, it's likely you won't have enough time to close elsewhere. If your closing is a couple of weeks away, then your lender might find some room somewhere to reduce your rate.

Lenders and brokers do a significant amount of work on a loan closing before they ever see any money. If the loan doesn't close, they've lost money on the deal. In fact, due to the initial overhead lenders incur during the loan approval process, it sometimes takes a year or more after the loan closes before the lender breaks even on the entire loan. That said, if rates drop, perhaps the easiest way to get the lower rate is simply to ask. It goes something like this: "Hey, I know you've already done a lot of work on my loan, but rates have dropped by almost 1/2 percent since we've started. I understand our lock agreement, but you also have to understand my position. I still have plenty of time to take my loan elsewhere. What do you say we break my old lock and get a new, lower rate?"

Simple enough, right? One of two things will happen. One, nothing will happen. Your lender declines your offer, and now you have to decide if you want to start all over somewhere else. Two, and perhaps the more likely scenario: Your lender agrees with your logic, breaks your lock, and gives you a lower rate. It may not be at the lowest rate currently available, but the lender may meet you halfway, or drop the rate somewhat and charge you a relock fee.

One final note on locks. You have much more freedom with regard to rates and fees during a refinance period compared to buying a house. If your initial purchase contract says that you'll close within 30 days, you don't have the luxury of shopping your mortgage around till the cows come home. At maximum, you should give yourself two full weeks of mortgage processing time. And this is only if you've already been approved by your lender and provided them with all required documentation. On the other hand, if you're thinking of refinancing, then you pretty much control the entire process. If you want to lock this week and close the next, fine. If you don't want to lock and are willing to wait another six months for your target interest rate, then that's fine, too.

All the rate lock strategies in the world are constricted by time when you're talking about a purchase. Remember to keep yourself from being under the gun, so to speak. If you mess around too much, trying to outsmart everybody, you might find that you got a terrible deal only because you waited too long to choose a lender. Then the rate is less important than missing your closing date—and possibly your earnest money.

13.18 WILL LENDERS DRAG THEIR FEET TO MAKE A LOCK EXPIRE?

You may be the victim of someone trying to squeeze a little bit more out of you by using market gains. If you've been cruising along with your 30-day lock agreement and you're at day 20 and haven't heard from anyone like the appraiser, attorney, or settlement agent, it's possible your lock is going to expire before you can get to your closing. Market gains only work for the loan officer if mortgage rates have fallen since you locked in. If you're suspicious about your loan delays after you've locked, then call your loan officer and ask them directly: "You locked my loan in at 7 percent. Have you officially locked me in, or are you trying to make a little extra money?" Believe me, if your loan officer has indeed been playing the market with your loan, this question will put a stop to that nonsense.

Closing Costs and How to Save on Them

Closing costs are a necessary evil when buying a house. Sorry, that's the way it is. There are lots of people involved in your transaction; most you'll never even meet. And they're all doing stuff needed to close your deal.

14.1 WHAT TYPES OF CLOSING COSTS CAN I EXPECT?

You can expect a lot of them, most of which you will never pay again until you get another mortgage. Closing costs can vary based upon locale, but generally you can anticipate your closing costs to average just about 3 percent of your loan amount, more if you pay points or origination fees to your lender.

TELL ME MORE

Here is a list of potential charges and services, divided between lender and nonlender fees, that you can anticipate when you get a mortgage loan. Not all lenders charge them all. The fees are estimates and can vary according to where the property is located.

Lender Fees

Discount Point	1 percent of the loan amount
Origination Fee	1 percent of the loan amount
Administration	$200–$300
Application	$200–$400
Appraisal	$300–$500 (some lenders require two appraisals for jumbo loans)
Credit Report	$10–$65
Flood Certificate	$17–$20
Lender's Inspection	$50–$100 per inspection (used to measure progress for construction loans)
Processing	$300–$500
Tax Service	$60–$70
Underwriting	$300–$500

Nonlender Fees

Title Examination	$125–$200
Title Insurance	Ranges from $1.00 per thousand financed to 1 percent of the loan amount (varies by state)
Attorney Fee	$225–$500
Abstract Fee	$50–$300
Document Prep	$100–$300
Document Stamp	1 to 3 percent of the loan amount
Escrow	$150–$350
Intangible Tax	1 to 3 percent of the loan amount
Pest Inspection	$100–$200
Recording	$50–$85
Settlement/Closing	$150–$350
Survey	$250–$350

Real estate agent fees are not part of the good-faith estimate that is sent to the borrower. Depending on where you live, there may also be fees for miscellaneous inspections, such as radon testing or termite inspections, but those requirements vary from state to state.

14.2 WHY ARE THERE SO MANY CHARGES?

Because there are a lot of different businesses that are active in your account. Nonlenders charge to cover their services. So do lenders.

But lenders charge fees at the beginning of a loan to help offset some of their initial overhead when processing a new loan file.

TELL ME MORE

Lenders can make money in three basic ways from a new mortgage:

1. Collecting lender or broker fees at the very beginning of the loan. This is the only way a mortgage broker makes money. Once the loan closes, the broker makes no more money on that file.
2. Collecting the interest payments on the loan.
3. Selling the loan to another lender.

Only lenders can make money on interest payments or selling the loan.

14.3 WHY DO LENDERS CHARGE FEES?

Because they can. If your local market has established that most lenders charge a $200 application fee, then you can expect that fee. Lenders charge fees to offset the initial expenses of finding and funding a mortgage loan request.

In addition, due to the initial overhead of finding and closing a mortgage, the mortgage company may not begin to show a profit on any particular loan until well past the first year of the new loan's life. Yes, the lender is collecting interest payments, but the lender also paid the salaries and benefits of the loan officers, loan processors, underwriters, and managers of the company, along with rent, payroll taxes, and any other associated costs of doing business. Sometimes lenders attempt to offset such costs with these other fees.

14.4 ON WHICH CLOSING COSTS CAN I SAVE AND WHICH ONES CAN I FORGET ABOUT?

You can only save on closing fees that can be negotiated. Your loan officer is bound to quote a standard set of fees the lender charges. If a lender charges a \$350 processing fee and a \$400 administrative fee, there is very little leeway, if any, to have a lender fee waived. Loan officers are required to provide the same set of fees to borrowers under the same set of circumstances. Just as loan officers cannot quote different interest rates to different borrowers under the same scenario, loan officers cannot waive a \$350 processing fee in order to get the deal in-house. Rules require any fee waiver to be applied universally.

There can be provisions when the loan officer can in fact waive a particular fee based upon "competitiveness," which means the loan officer was forced into a competitive situation and the only way to get the loan was to match another lender's offer.

14.5 ARE FEES FOR PURCHASES AND REFINANCES THE SAME?

They can be, but some of them will be different. When refinancing, you can get discounts for reissued title policies, and if your lender requires a survey you can sometimes use your old survey instead of paying for a new one. If you're buying a home, then you may not have much luck negotiating reduced fees for title work or lawyer fees. Your sales contract will identify who will be holding your loan closing, where it will be held, and who will issue your title insurance.

14.6 HOW CAN I SAVE ON MY APPRAISAL FEES?

A typical fee for a conventional appraisal is \$300. But with the advent of AUS applications, sometimes those approvals also come back with reduced appraisal requirements. Appraisals come in five varieties:

1. A full-blown appraisal with interior and exterior photos, costing around \$300.
2. An exterior appraisal only with photos, costing around \$250.
3. A "drive by" appraisal that might cost \$100.
4. An *automated valuation model* (AVM) costing under \$100. An AVM electronically scours public records for recent home

sales in the subject property's area to estimate approximate value.

5. An appraisal "waiver," which eliminates the need for an appraisal altogether.

What determines the type of appraisal you'll need? It's determined by your approval from your AUS. If you have little or no down payment and average credit, don't expect any reduced appraisal requirements. However, if you're a high-FICO borrower with 20 percent or more down, ask your lender if your approval qualifies you for a reduced appraisal, which will allow you to save a couple of hundred bucks. For an appraisal waiver, this can only be issued by the Automated Underwriting System and is based on a variety of factors such as credit, equity, income, and assets.

14.7 HOW CAN I SAVE ON MY CREDIT REPORT?

Your credit report, offered by an AUS, can be the source of another cost savings. In the past, the Residential Mortgage Credit Report (RMCR) would cost $70 or more and would take three to five days to get from the credit reporting company. But with automated underwriting, many of these systems pull their own reports and provide a credit report to the lender utilizing the AUS for a loan decision. Ask your lender if they really need an RMCR and your $70, or if they can get what they need with an AUS credit report.

14.8 HOW CAN I SAVE ON TITLE INSURANCE?

If you're refinancing, there may be discounts if you use the same title agency. Some call this a *reissue* of an original title report, which can cost much less than a full title insurance policy. This is something you need to ask for. Don't assume the lower policy premium will be offered automatically because a full title policy costs more than a reissue.

In several parts of the country, one business will offer several services, especially when it comes to title insurance. One office might be able to hold your closing, research your title, issue a title insurance policy, and make sure all your documents are properly recorded. While you may not be required to have everything done at one business, you'll get package discounts for these settlement services if you choose to do everything under one roof.

14.9 WHAT EXACTLY IS THE GOOD FAITH ESTIMATE?

The Good Faith Estimate has had a name change and is now referred to as the Loan Estimate. It's a long form, divided into six sections that are numbered—strangely I might add. The section numbers are 800, 900, 1000, 1100, 1200, and 1300, and they are assigned as follows:

800 All the items payable in connection with the loan, or lender fees, which can include appraisals, credit reports, and origination fees, among others.

900 Items required by your lender to be paid in advance. Examples are your hazard insurance policy, interest on your new loan, or other premiums.

1000 Reserves that are to be deposited with your lender—your escrow or impound accounts, for example.

1100 Fees for your title charges, attorney, and settlement work.

1200 Government recording and transfer fees.

1300 Everything else that didn't go somewhere above, such as survey charges or pest inspection fees.

Because lenders are responsible for producing this estimate, they will typically know exactly what their own fees (800 series) are, but they'll be less certain about third-party charges for title insurance or attorney charges. Most loan officers who have been in business for any length of time should be able to provide you with a fairly accurate quote. The accuracy of the quote will be compared to the Final Closing Disclosure you will receive three business days before you attend your loan closing.

TELL ME MORE

When your loan officer quotes lender fees, they cannot be different than the ones shown on your final closing statement. There is no variance allowed and if the lender fees at settlement are higher than originally quoted, the lender must make up the difference.

Regarding nonlender fees that you do not have the ability to shop around for on your own, there can be a variance of no more than 10 percent of the original quote. Anything more must again be paid for by the loan officer. Finally, closing costs that you do have the ability to shop for can vary by any amount.

When you attend your final settlement, you will then encounter the TRID, or the TILA-RESPA Integrated Disclosure. That's a mouthful but it is a combination of the Truth in Lending and Real Estate Settlement Procedures Act. TRID will list the final closing costs, amount borrowed, annual percentage rate, and other details about your loan. Closing costs listed on the TRID should be the very same as the Final Closing Disclosure.

14.10 HOW DO I USE A LOAN ESTIMATE TO COMPARE LENDERS?

First, you need to identify which fees count and which fees don't. Items in the 900 and 1000 sections—the items the lender wants you to prepay in advance—won't vary from one lender to the next. Why? Lenders have no control over your property taxes. Lenders have no control over the cost of your homeowners insurance policy; likewise, they have no control over your escrow or impound accounts. These numbers will be estimated, and don't be surprised to see three different quotes for taxes and insurance on three different estimates. I'm not kidding. But disregard these fees when comparing closing costs.

Second, you need to ignore other third-party charges, because the lender you select has no impact on tax rates, attorney charges, title insurance, or any nonlender costs. Sure, I know there are controlled business arrangements that might offer settlement charges at a discount if you choose to "bundle" these services together, but those instances are the exception, not the rule. Only compare fees in the 800 section.

TELL ME MORE

I recently had a client who told me that my rates were too high. Not just a little higher, but a solid 1/4 percent higher than a competitor. I asked to see my competitor's Good Faith Estimate and I immediately spotted the culprit. Nearly $2,000 in junk fees.

That's a lot of fees. I would be happy to match that quote if I, too, could charge $1,950 in junk fees.

The loan officer was also low-balling all the other charges, from property taxes to title charges. Instead of taxes being realistically quoted at $350 per month, they were quoted at $100 per month. Hazard insurance was ridiculously low. Title policies were quoted at $150 instead of $600. The list went on. This is a not-uncommon trick. Consumers, when reviewing a Good Faith Estimate, zero in on the bottom line of the closing fees. "Gee, honey, ABC Bank charges $3,500 and XYZ Bank charges $3,000. Let's go with XYZ Bank."

But the line details tell another story. The loan officer increased his lender fees—a lot—while at the same time quoting unusually low third-party fees to offset the increase. If you want to do what many people do, simply pick up the phone and ask the various third parties what their charges are. Pay little attention to any fees other than those listed in section 800 of your quote when comparing one lender to another.

14.11 WHAT IS APR, AND DOES IT REALLY WORK?

If used properly, it works great. The problem is that some loan officers don't know how to calculate the *annual percentage rate* (APR). The big mistake comes in two ways: One, the loan officer may calculate it incorrectly, and two, the APR is only effective when used to compare the exact same loan from two different lenders.

Comparing one loan to another is difficult enough without clouding it with an APR number. The APR is an excellent consumer tool, but all too often it's shoved aside by some loan officer who either doesn't understand it or doesn't want to quote it because his rates are higher. I've often heard consumers say that other loan officers told them that the APR is "just a number crunched from a computer" and to pay little attention to it. Yeah, right.

TELL ME MORE

You should pay attention to the APR and you should pay attention to loan officers who can explain it to you. Some critics of the APR being used as a consumer tool point out that it doesn't work for loans with little or no money down. For instance, most loans with 5 percent down require private mortgage insurance (PMI). But when calculating the APR for loans with PMI, the calculation makes the incorrect assumption that mortgage insurance will be in existence for the life of the loan.

Not true. PMI is only needed when the mortgage balance is more than 80 percent of the value of the home. "Aha!" say the skeptical loan officers. The APR is meaningless because it confuses the PMI issue with loans less than 20 percent down. Or so they say.

But if both lenders use the same loan amount, the same loan, and the same PMI policy, the APRs will still be a useful tool for the consumer. Will there be PMI for the life of the loan? Of course not. But by using the APR quote from both lenders, using the same loan parameters, the consumer can still tell who has the better deal by looking at the lower APR. If both lenders quote under the exact same circumstances, the lower APR is the better deal.

14.12 HOW CAN I GET THE SELLER TO PAY FOR MY CLOSING COSTS?

First and foremost, you have to ask. That's part of your or your agent's job. The seller isn't going to give something up that he doesn't need to give up, but the first thing to do would be to make the request as part of your offer. If a home is for sale at $100,000, make an offer you believe is fair and request that the seller pay X percent of your closing costs. What do you have to lose? If the seller says "no" and you still need or want the seller to pay your closing costs, change your offer.

TELL ME MORE

If you want the seller to pay $2,000 of your closing costs and the seller refuses, increase your offer by $2,000. That way the seller still gets the same amount, the sales concession is within guide-lines, so as not to affect the value of the home, and you've saved $2,000. If you planned to put 20 percent down, your sales price would increase by $2,000, and your loan would increase by $1,600 (80 percent of $2,000). Sure, your principal balance goes up, but your monthly payment only rises by $27 on a 30-year mortgage at 7 percent.

There are those who wouldn't advise this strategy, complaining that a $27 extra payment adds up to over $9,700 over the life of the loan. And that complainer would be right. But in reality, who keeps a mortgage for 30 years?

Why not ask the seller to pay for a discount point or two in the very same fashion? If the seller declines to pay points on your behalf, simply increase the offer by a similar amount. Using a $200,000 offer, have the seller pay for two discount points to buy down your interest rate. You might pay $3,000 in closing costs, but the seller is now buying down your interest by nearly 1/2 percent. If you were getting quoted 5 percent at par from your loan officer and your seller agreed to pay two discount points to buy down your rate to 3.5 per-cent on a 30-year fixed-rate mortgage, the math works out this way: With a $200,000 loan, 30-year fixed at 4 percent, the monthly pay-ment is $1,176. A rate cut to 3.5 percent drops that payment to $1,140, or a savings of $36 per month. After the first five years, the buydown saves you more than $2,100 in mortgage interest. And over the life of the loan? You save $12,960.

14.13 CAN A LENDER PAY ALL MY FEES?

Certainly, and there are lenders who advertise that they will pay all fees for you. And not by increasing your interest rate in order to do so. This is a different promotion than simply covering closing costs with higher rates. How?

Good question. The fact is that people in a real estate transaction want their money. People like attorneys or title insurance companies. Still, you may see advertisements where the lender does offer to pay all those costs without increasing your rate. But it doesn't wash. When a lender advertises they have a mortgage loan with no closing costs, all you need to do is call up that lender, get their rate quote, then compare that quote with other mortgage lenders and brokers for the exact-same scenario. Every time I see those ads, I call up that lender, pretend I'm a borrower, and see what their quotes are. And they're nothing special. In fact, they are higher, albeit slightly. It doesn't take a whole lot in a rate increase to offset loan costs. Sometimes as little as 1/8 percent is enough.

CHAPTER 15

Using the Internet
the Right Way

The Internet provides unprecedented speed and access to information. Your loan closes in a matter of days, not weeks. Because of the Internet, "Google" is now a real word. Thanks to the Internet, it takes just a few seconds to get a question answered. Encyclopedia? Ha! Nothing is as fast and as handy as the World Wide Web, right? Doing things faster and with fewer people keeps costs down and helps to keep rates lower than they otherwise might be.

15.1 HOW HAS THE INTERNET HELPED MORTGAGE LENDING?

As with other industries, it's changed the landscape. It's fast, efficient, and highly productive. Just a few short years ago, even though people had the option of applying for a mortgage online, just a small percentage would do so. There were two obstacles that prevented lenders from getting the full benefit of using the Internet to speed up the process: universal language and consumer attitude. Now, however, there are two standards in electronic loan processing: Fannie Mae's and the Mortgage Industry Standards and Maintenance Organization, or MISMO (mizz-mo), standard.

Do you recall, as discussed in the first chapter, how loans are now digitized? Under the same universal guidelines as established by

Fannie Mae and MISMO, your loan is delivered electronically rather than manually.

When you apply for a home loan at a mortgage company's website, your loan is downloaded and read by a universal protocol using these standards. Even though different loan companies may have different-looking websites and different loan origination systems, those loans are still based upon the very same language. These standards ensure that mortgage companies don't have to have a particular brand of software or online application in order to read and review the application itself. Once the application is downloaded to the loan officer's computer, she can do a multitude of things that would normally take days to do. In the course of about five minutes, a loan officer with a downloaded file can:

Order the credit report.

Order title insurance.

Order hazard insurance.

Submit for an AUS approval.

Third parties can also deliver documentation electronically to mortgage companies and closing offices because everyone now operates under the same MISMO standards—for electronic document delivery, electronic loan delivery, and storage.

15.2 SHOULD I APPLY FOR A MORTGAGE ONLINE OR MEET WITH A LOAN OFFICER?

That's entirely up to you but you'll likely do both. There is no right or wrong way, just personal preference. Some people feel more comfortable when they sit across the desk from a loan officer, while others would rather be eaten by ants than sit through a boring old 1003 interview. But for convenience's sake, applying online is certainly faster and easier as long as you're comfortable with the online process. Once you've selected your loan officer, you'll be asked to apply, typically online. Few lenders today even issue paper loan applications to clients. The convenience of the web has slowly eliminated much of the paperwork required and the emergence of an entirely "paper free" environment is here.

When you complete an online application, you'll get hard copies of everything you filled out on the website, as well as other required disclosures and closing cost estimates. Applying online doesn't mean everything is electronic; it only means your lender or loan officer has taken your loan application in a way that was different from what it was just a few years ago.

If you feel uncomfortable applying online, there's no reason to. Just ask to come into the office or have the loan officer fax or mail an application to you. If you fax or mail in a loan application, your loan officer will take that information and turn it into an electronic file to begin the loan process. Fax machines are quickly becoming a thing of the past in the mortgage industry as items are either digitized or scanned. I've heard of some loan officers who actually require the customer to apply online.

15.3 HOW CAN I USE THE INTERNET TO FIND THE BEST MORTGAGE RATE?

Carefully. But there are some good places to start. One of the best-known websites for interest rates in general and for mortgages specifically is BankRate Monitor, found at *www.bankrate.com*. BankRate Monitor both surveys area lenders for mortgage rates and provides a venue for mortgage companies—brokers as well as bankers—to advertise on the same page.

The mortgage section lets you select which major city and state your property is located in, and whether you want a conforming or jumbo quote. It also breaks down fixed- and adjustable-rate mortgages. If you live in San Diego, you would fill in your city and state, then click on your mortgage requirements, and *voilà*, lists upon lists of mortgage rate quotes appear on your screen. On these rate quotes you'll see loan parameters, such as the rate, the APR, how long the rate is good for, and when the rate was posted, as well as any other comments lenders may add, such as, "We specialize in loans for hamster farmers!"

The problem with websites such as bankrate.com or other rate comparison sites is that there is no quality control check in place. You will see interest rates that seem too good to be true, and they always are. Such lenders have one thing in mind and one thing only: to get their telephone to ring so they can begin the sales pitch. And if their rates aren't the absolute lowest, then why would you call them? Online advertisers know that and quote rates as such. You can certainly begin your rate quest on bankrate.com, but you'll most likely end up at a local lender or someone you've been referred to.

One thing you'll notice is that there are a great many lenders who advertise on the Internet, and you've probably never heard of most of them. Is that a bad thing? Of course not, but you do need to scrutinize them with a tad more diligence than lenders who were referred to you by your agent or your friends. Is Big Shot Mortgage offering an interest rate of 4 percent while everyone else is offering 7 percent? Do you think Big Shot Mortgage has a special edge on the mortgage market? Of course they don't. But there are some ways to help qualify those companies you see advertising on the Internet.

TELL ME MORE

First, visit the lender's website. Easy enough, right? But you're not looking for claims such as "We offer great rates" and "We offer great service" or any other such patter. Instead, compare the interest rate quotes on their website with others that are advertised on the Internet. Do they match up? If they do, are they for the same date? You can't compare interest rates unless they're for the same date, and even then the markets may have changed. If you get interest rates that are much different on the company's website than you see advertised in other places, take the advertisement with a grain of salt.

Another thing to determine from lender websites is whether they're in compliance with federal Truth in Lending laws by quoting interest rates in the correct and legal manner. If you see a rate quote, do you also see the corresponding APR quote? Do you see the loan amount used for the quote? If you see a lender or broker quoting interest rates on their website without complying with federal statutes regarding rate quotes, you might think of moving on.

Are they operating legally in your state? Most states have licensing laws for lenders and brokers. If someone is advertising in your state, are they doing so legally? A broker's website usually lists the states where the broker is authorized to do business. If you find no such list or nothing about their licensing, don't consider this lender or broker. I know this sounds a little tough, and quite frankly, there are probably some very good lenders and brokers out there who might get dropped from your list because they didn't advertise properly or disclose their licensing authority. But think about that for a moment if you are tempted to apply with someone you've never heard of just because they advertise a great rate while at the same time they're in flagrant violation of federal Truth in Lending laws. Do you really want to take that chance?

15.4 WHAT ABOUT ONLINE COMPANIES THAT ADVERTISE THEY WILL HAVE LENDERS "BID" ON MY MORTGAGE LOAN?

What a change from just a few years ago. Today you can fill out a single application online and have several lenders or mortgage brokers provide you with their best quote after reviewing your application. You may not get anything better than what you can get locally, but you still get four mortgage quotes without having to complete four different applications.

Lending Tree is perhaps the most famous, but there are countless others that will send you "spam" that says the same thing: "Fill out one application, let lenders fight for your loan." These online companies are nothing more than lead services. If you apply on one of these sites or fill out their online form, you're doing nothing more than letting a lead-generation company know that you're in the market for a home loan. That company, in turn, sells your name and information to a lender—or even another lead company.

TELL ME MORE

Before the advent of various "mortgage bidders," it was unheard of for a consumer to have multiple mortgage applications out at once. Not that it was illegal or anything, it was just that if one lender found out that you had applied somewhere else, then the lender wouldn't approve your loan unless you canceled the other ones.

Not so today. Nowadays, some websites actually encourage you to apply, not using several mortgage applications, but just one. After you complete the application, it is sent to a select group of lenders or brokers for their review. They'll see how much money you make and what your current debt load is, and they'll get your credit report along with your credit scores. After an evaluation, those lenders will make an offering, which you can accept or reject.

This is a relatively easy process for making multiple applications. Sometimes, however, you don't know who's going to be bidding on your loan or who will see it. You might see a list of approved lenders, but you might also come back with a quote from someone you've never heard of or who doesn't have an office in your city.

The mortgage process has been made both easier and harder at the same time. As the loan approval process becomes more efficient, lenders and loan officers can find themselves in a more difficult situation when it comes to marketing. After all, a loan is a loan is a loan. Lenders have turned a mortgage into an off-the-shelf commodity, making it harder for them to differentiate themselves from other lenders. In most cases, anyway.

15.5 WHAT HAPPENS IF I CHOOSE AN ONLINE LENDER BUT THE CLOSING PAPERS ARE ALL WRONG?

That depends upon how "wrong" the papers are. If it's something minor that your settlement agent can change, it might be fixed right there at the closing. But what if you were quoted 3 percent and all of your documents show 5 percent? If you're at the closing table getting ready to move into your new home that day, there isn't a whole lot you can do about it. It might be too late. Sure, you can walk away from the closing, but you also might lose any deposit money you placed up front. You just might be stuck. Why would a lender do this? Maybe because they can. They're totally out of compliance, and the TRID does not reflect the Closing Document.

TELL ME MORE

If you chose an online lender who doesn't have a physical office in your area, then you can bet that office doesn't call on your local bevy of real estate agents. They don't have a local following. They don't have loan officers in your town. They don't have a reputation to uphold. So what if they screw up your deal—what are you going to do about it? Tell the real estate agent? File a complaint with their state agency? Local lenders, or at least lenders you know and trust, keep a keen eye on their marketing and sales efforts. If they continually mess up deals, then guess what? No more referrals. Their business reputation is tarnished and they could find themselves out of business. Not so with an online lender. If they mess up and you're mad at them, so what, right?

When there are things that are not accurate at the settlement table, there's nothing else you can do except reschedule your closing. The offending lender will need to have the closed loan in compliance; otherwise, it won't be eligible for sale in the secondary market.

I am not suggesting that you should never, ever use someone you found online. I ran an online division for several years. It's simply that if you are compelled to use Big Shot Mortgage Company, do your homework and watch your step. You might very well get a better deal, but you just need to make sure they follow through with their offerings. Research the company first, as outlined in Chapter 11.

15.6 SHOULD I AVOID ONLINE-ONLY LENDERS?

When you work with an "online-only" lender, there is no physical office where you might meet your loan officer; instead, you speak to a customer service person at "1-800-whatever" to get your questions answered.

You need to establish a working relationship with your loan officer and have someone who is there when you have questions or things go wrong. You could use an online lender to help the loan officer down the street sharpen her pencil, so to speak, but if the rate quote from the online company is too low, you'll probably not get much cooperation from your in-town loan officer. Your loan officer will simply tell you the rate can't be guaranteed and if you want an online lender then go right ahead.

The trouble with the Internet is that every single lender and mortgage broker has a website, which makes it difficult, if not impossible, to learn about the mortgage company based upon their site. Just as mortgage bankers can spend millions of dollars on marketing only to have an incompetent loan officer ruin it all for them, so, too, can a flashy website make mortgage lenders appear to be more than they are.

There's just no way to evaluate a company by looking at its site. Mortgage websites try to overcome this problem by providing testimonials from previous clients and pictures of happy homeowners, but even those can be faked.

The online-only business model has been tried to some extent, and there are a few national names that command the online-only space, but they have never taken over the market as many once feared. With all the standardization of online applications, instead of online lenders putting traditional lenders out of business, it happened the other way around. Traditional lenders put up their own websites. The best model is using a local loan officer using the company's website to apply for a loan. You want a relationship, not simply a transaction.

15.7 I KEEP GETTING EMAILS FROM COMPANIES WITH SOME VERY COMPETITIVE OFFERS. SHOULDN'T I AT LEAST EXPLORE THEM?

No. You're wasting your time. The emails you get are nothing more than spam. As a matter of fact, they're rarely from mortgage companies. In connection with an article I wrote about the practice of mortgage "spam," I decided to answer one of the many emails that appear in my in-box nearly every day.

TELL ME MORE

I finally responded to one of these emails that guaranteed me the lowest rate and here's what happened. First, I hit the "reply" button and said "thank you," but I got an error message saying the email address wasn't valid. I then clicked on the link embedded in the original spam and went directly to a website quoting interest rates that were a full 1 percent below the market. In clear violation of federal advertising guidelines, I might add.

I then clicked on another link on that site and went to a form that asked me to fill out some information. I filled out the form, saying I wanted a refinance for my home in Austin. About three days later I got three different emails. Two of the emails said "thank you" for the information request and had a link back to their own website. Again, when I tried to reply to the emails, I got an invalid address. I also got a telephone call from a local company I'd never heard of. "Hi, Mr. Reed, I'm Linda Loan Officer and I'm following up on your request." I called her back and she wanted an application, but before I complied I asked for her interest rate quote. Sure enough, it was nowhere near what was quoted in the fake advertisement from the original email. That's because she was only supplied my information when she bought my name and phone number from a mortgage lead service—the owners of the original mortgage spam who kept themselves secret from me. She had no idea about any rate quotes sent through the email but would be more than happy to quote me one from her company. Yeah, right.

If you respond to one of these emails, be wary, and whatever you do, don't complete an application with sensitive data such as your Social Security number or bank account numbers. Identity theft is big business these days, and one of the easiest ways people can steal someone's personal information is to have them complete a phony loan application. That information could then get stolen, sold, or otherwise used and misused. If you don't know whom you're dealing with, don't respond to their email, and certainly don't fill out their "loan" application.

15.8 CAN I GET MY LOAN APPROVAL ONLINE?

You can, but lenders won't hand you the keys. The only thing that's really done online nowadays is taking the loan application; a loan officer will then call you back. Lenders learned a lesson with online loans and "instant" approvals when borrowers began questioning just how good their approvals actually were.

Loans will still have to be documented and lenders will feel better about issuing an approval after review of the physical file. When you see a website that says "Get approved in minutes!" or something similar, understand that they operate in the very same way as anyone else. They don't have a corner on the instant-approval market.

15.9 IS THERE ANY WAY I CAN CHECK ON RATES WITHOUT CONTACTING A LENDER?

Do you want to check current rates or get a history of where interest rates have been for, say, the last 10 years? Do you want to compare interest rate trends or see how volatile an interest rate index has been over the past few years? There are various websites that provide historical rate data at no charge to the consumer. Perhaps one of the most extensive sites is HSH Associates, or *www.hsh.com*.

At this site you can view various ARM indexes and compare them to one another. Are you looking at a one-year treasury ARM and a LIBOR ARM? Then go to the site and compare where the rates have been over the years. This is a valuable tool not only for comparing historical rates but for spotting potential interest rate trends. Are rates currently at a high spot? Then maybe an ARM or a hybrid is a good choice. Do rates appear to have bottomed out? Then perhaps it might be a good time for a fixed-rate mortgage.

The HSH site is for consumers because it offers plenty of tools you can use to help you with your mortgage selection. Besides historical rate trends there is a lot more useful information, including multiple financial calculators, a loan library, and a host of other free stuff. You'll also notice that there is the ubiquitous interest rate survey similar to ones found at BankRate Monitor, where lenders and brokers advertise interest rates. But the real value of this site is to get a sense of where interest rates have been and to be able to compare them side by side.

Do you want to get current interest rate information? There is no single source for you to track mortgage bonds or mortgage-backed security data; in fact, I don't know of any place where mortgage bond pricing can be viewed. Instead, you'll need to follow trends by watching a 10-year treasury or by hooking up with a loan officer who follows mortgage bond pricing. Lenders pay a lot of money to get mortgage bond pricing for use by their secondary market and production managers, so don't expect this kind of information to be lying around on eBay somewhere. You, as a consumer, don't have real-time access to such quotes.

If you want to get national averages on mortgage rates—the same information that's published every week in your newspaper—then log onto Freddie Mac's website at *www.freddiemac.com*. Here is where Freddie publishes its weekly national mortgage survey that compiles the average 30-year and 15-year fixed mortgage rates for different parts of the country. Here you can compare your current rate quotes with interest rate averages found in your area. While this isn't as good as getting real-time mortgage bond pricing, you can at least see if the quotes you've been getting are in the ballpark.

Remember that this is a weekly survey, not a live quote, so keep that in mind when comparing your rate with the regional average.

Both Freddie Mac and Fannie Mae (*www.fanniemae.com*) have excellent websites for home buyers. They won't quote you mortgage rates because they're not mortgage lenders, but they do have a wealth of information about their respective loan programs.

15.10 CAN I TRACK MY LOAN APPROVAL ONLINE?

That depends on whether your lender has the type of system that lets you do that. If a lender or mortgage broker has the ability to let you track the status of your loan application, they'll let you know at the beginning of your loan process. You'll also choose a user name and password to use when you log on. There are variations on this theme, but in practice, most systems allow you to log onto your lender's website, type in your loan number or password, and see a status report on where your loan is in the approval process and what has or has not been done.

Be careful here on two points: First, lenders do a lot of stuff in the background that's considered part of the loan process. They order flood certificates and tax certifications, but you won't necessarily know when and whether they do. All loans have to have a certificate stating whether your house lies in a flood zone. That's pretty important information, fair enough, but it's not necessary for you to ask your loan officer if they've ordered your Flood Cert.

All that being said, online status systems won't reflect absolutely everything that's in your loan process; just expect to see the "biggies" in your file, such as appraisal work being done, approvals issued, loan papers drawn, and so on.

Second, if you log onto a loan status site and see that some things haven't been done yet, don't panic. There will be times when a lender simply makes a mistake and forgets to order your appraisal, but things have to happen in order.

For example, most lenders don't like to order appraisals until the inspection has been completed. After all, there's no sense in ordering an appraisal for a property where the roof is falling in. If you log onto a status website and something's not checked, make sure it's a situation of there not being time to perform a particular loan function rather than someone having forgotten about your deal altogether.

On a similar level, there are web-based applications called transaction management systems (TMS). These Internet applications are usually separate from a lender's software but can be accessed by not just the lender and customer, but also by the title companies and settlement agents. Here you can log onto a website, type in your code, and see a more extensive list of process items and their status.

Such systems are designed to assist the real estate agent, lender, and title company communicate more easily on a loan transaction. When a lender wants to order an appraisal and title report, the lender logs onto the site, uploads the property and borrower information, and all the various orders are placed at once, at one single site. Then, as the other parties in the transaction complete their work, they, too, return to the website and upload their work, and a check is marked next to their name showing everything as "completed."

There are other TMS applications designed for the real estate agent that help track their closings and check the status of their files. There is now an application that combines a *Multiple Listing Service* (MLS) and a TMS at the same time. Now, when an agent lists a home and an offer is accepted on the property, the sales contract is sent to the title agency and the lender automatically. At that point, the lender can forward the contract directly to an appraiser while at the same time ordering the title report. When the appraisal is completed, it's sent as an electronic attachment to the lender.

The customer can log onto a special site that tracks the status of his loan application and tracks various documents floating throughout the system. Is my appraisal in? Check. Is my loan approved? Check. Can I view my closing papers? Check. These systems aren't widely available and not all MLS systems have this feature. In fact, as of this writing, there was only one MLS that also had a TMS embedded in the program.

15.11 WHAT ARE SOME GOOD WEBSITES CONSUMERS CAN USE TO HELP THEM?

There are probably thousands of them. Really. Your own real estate agent's site should be chock-full of consumer information. Besides

Fannie's and Freddie's sites, which I already mentioned, let's review some of the websites that provide useful home loan information without also trying to sell you something.

www.realtor.com This is the official website for the National Association of Realtors and is a good place to start looking for a home if you have no idea where to start. Here you can type in your desired location, how much you want to pay, and so on. You can also find a list of realtors if you don't have one yet. And you can find a lender, or a mover, and pick up some handy consumer information about home buying.

www.hud.gov This is a big site, paid for with taxpayer dollars, which gives you all you need to know about FHA loans—buying, selling, owning, renting, you name it. It's very consumer-friendly and a nice starting place if you're thinking of getting an FHA mortgage loan.

www.nahb.org This is the official website for the National Association of Home Builders. It's very much like the site at *www.realtor.com,* but it only lists new homes or homes under construction. You can view new homes by location and price range, as well as look at new home plans online. Need some names for a builder? You can find that list here as well.

www.va.gov This is the website for VA loans. There's lots of information on VA loans and how to qualify for them, along with forms that qualified veterans might need. This section is actually a subset of the Department of Veterans Affairs, but there's a direct link from the main page to the home loan section.

www.fsbo.com "For Sale by Owner," or FSBO (fizz-bow), homes are listed here from all parts of the country. Here's a place for homes that never make it to an MLS, where people want to save some real estate commission and sell the home themselves.

www.realtytimes.com This consumer site is chock-full of articles and tips, written by industry experts, on everything from how to clear up your credit to what's happening in Washington, D.C., on mortgages. There is also a site specifically for real estate agents, *www.agentnews.com.*

www.myfico.com   This site is owned by Fair Isaac Corporation, the company that developed the FICO score. It has information on credit, credit scores, and credit reports. Even though consumers are allowed to get one free credit report per year, there may be times when you need a second one.

www.aarp.org/revmort   If you're considering a reverse mortgage, you need to start here. This site explains the reverse mortgage process and the Home Equity Conversion Mortgages (HECMs) better than anyone and offers commentary and consumer tips from the AARP.

www.bbb.com   This is the site for the Better Business Bureau. You can type in a company's business name, its website, or its telephone number, and the Better Business Bureau will research records to see if there is any information or complaint on that company. While this isn't foolproof—a scam artist can still be a scam artist whether or not there's a BBB complaint on file—it's a good starting point.

There are countless others. Perhaps too many. But almost all of them carry basic consumer information with tips on their particular area of expertise. You won't get any advertisements on VA and FHA sites, but you'll certainly get your share on other sites. Some sites also have old information that doesn't apply in today's world, so be careful.

A P P E N D I X

Monthly Payment Schedules

The following schedule shows monthly payments per thousand dollars financed. To calculate your monthly payment:

1. Find your interest rate in the first column.
2. Move across to the appropriate column for your term.
3. Multiply that number by the number of thousand dollars financed.

EXAMPLE

If you are borrowing $150,000 at 6.5 percent interest for a 30-year term:

$$\$6.32 \times 150 \text{ (thousands)} = \$948.00 \text{ principal}$$
$$\text{and interest payment}$$

Thus, your monthly payment for both principal and interest is $948.

Rate	40 years	30 years	25 years	20 years	15 years	10 years
2.500	$3.30	$3.95	$4.49	$5.30	$6.67	$9.43
2.625	$3.37	$4.02	$4.55	$5.36	$6.73	$9.48
2.750	$3.44	$4.08	$4.61	$5.42	$6.79	$9.54
2.875	$3.51	$4.15	$4.68	$5.48	$6.85	$9.60
3.000	$3.58	$4.22	$4.74	$5.55	$6.91	$9.66

Rate	40 years	30 years	25 years	20 years	15 years	10 years
3.125	$3.65	$4.28	$4.81	$5.61	$6.97	$9.71
3.250	$3.73	$4.35	$4.87	$5.67	$7.03	$9.77
3.375	$3.80	$4.42	$4.94	$5.74	$7.09	$9.83
3.500	$3.87	$4.49	$5.01	$5.80	$7.15	$9.89
3.625	$3.95	$4.56	$5.07	$5.86	$7.21	$9.95
3.750	$4.03	$4.63	$5.14	$5.93	$7.27	$10.01
3.875	$4.10	$4.70	$5.21	$5.99	$7.33	$10.07
4.000	$4.18	$4.77	$5.28	$6.06	$7.40	$10.12
4.125	$4.26	$4.85	$5.35	$6.13	$7.46	$10.18
4.250	$4.34	$4.92	$5.42	$6.19	$7.52	$10.24
4.375	$4.42	$4.99	$5.49	$6.26	$7.59	$10.30
4.500	$4.50	$5.07	$5.56	$6.33	$7.65	$10.36
4.625	$4.58	$5.14	$5.63	$6.39	$7.71	$10.42
4.750	$4.66	$5.22	$5.70	$6.46	$7.78	$10.48
4.875	$4.74	$5.29	$5.77	$6.53	$7.84	$10.55
5.000	$4.82	$5.37	$5.85	$6.60	$7.91	$10.61
5.125	$4.91	$5.44	$5.92	$6.67	$7.97	$10.67
5.250	$4.99	$5.52	$5.99	$6.74	$8.04	$10.73
5.375	$5.07	$5.60	$6.07	$6.81	$8.10	$10.79
5.500	$5.16	$5.68	$6.14	$6.88	$8.17	$10.85
5.625	$5.24	$5.76	$6.22	$6.95	$8.24	$10.91
5.750	$5.33	$5.84	$6.29	$7.02	$8.30	$10.98
5.875	$5.42	$5.92	$6.37	$7.09	$8.37	$11.04
6.000	$5.50	$6.00	$6.44	$7.16	$8.44	$11.10
6.125	$5.59	$6.08	$6.52	$7.24	$8.51	$11.16
6.250	$5.68	$6.16	$6.60	$7.31	$8.57	$11.23
6.375	$5.77	$6.24	$6.67	$7.38	$8.64	$11.29
6.500	$5.85	$6.32	$6.75	$7.46	$8.71	$11.35
6.625	$5.94	$6.40	$6.83	$7.53	$8.78	$11.42
6.750	$6.03	$6.49	$6.91	$7.60	$8.85	$11.48
6.875	$6.12	$6.57	$6.99	$7.68	$8.92	$11.55
7.000	$6.21	$6.65	$7.07	$7.75	$8.99	$11.61
7.125	$6.31	$6.74	$7.15	$7.83	$9.06	$11.68
7.250	$6.40	$6.82	$7.23	$7.90	$9.13	$11.74
7.375	$6.49	$6.91	$7.31	$7.98	$9.20	$11.81
7.500	$6.58	$6.99	$7.39	$8.06	$9.27	$11.87
7.625	$6.67	$7.08	$7.47	$8.13	$9.34	$11.94
7.750	$6.77	$7.16	$7.55	$8.21	$9.41	$12.00
7.875	$6.86	$7.25	$7.64	$8.29	$9.48	$12.07
8.000	$6.95	$7.34	$7.72	$8.36	$9.56	$12.13
8.125	$7.05	$7.42	$7.80	$8.44	$9.63	$12.20
8.250	$7.14	$7.51	$7.88	$8.52	$9.70	$12.27

Rate	40 years	30 years	25 years	20 years	15 years	10 years
8.375	$7.24	$7.60	$7.97	$8.60	$9.77	$12.33
8.500	$7.33	$7.69	$8.05	$8.68	$9.85	$12.40
8.625	$7.43	$7.78	$8.14	$8.76	$9.92	$12.47
8.750	$7.52	$7.87	$8.22	$8.84	$9.99	$12.53
8.875	$7.62	$7.96	$8.31	$8.92	$10.07	$12.60
9.000	$7.71	$8.05	$8.39	$9.00	$10.14	$12.67
9.125	$7.81	$8.14	$8.48	$9.08	$10.22	$12.74
9.250	$7.91	$8.23	$8.56	$9.16	$10.29	$12.80
9.375	$8.00	$8.32	$8.65	$9.24	$10.37	$12.87
9.500	$8.10	$8.41	$8.74	$9.32	$10.44	$12.94
9.625	$8.20	$8.50	$8.82	$9.40	$10.52	$13.01
9.750	$8.30	$8.59	$8.91	$9.49	$10.59	$13.08
9.875	$8.39	$8.68	$9.00	$9.57	$10.67	$13.15
10.000	$8.49	$8.78	$9.09	$9.65	$10.75	$13.22
10.125	$8.59	$8.87	$9.18	$9.73	$10.82	$13.28
10.250	$8.69	$8.96	$9.26	$9.82	$10.90	$13.35
10.375	$8.79	$9.05	$9.35	$9.90	$10.98	$13.42
10.500	$8.89	$9.15	$9.44	$9.98	$11.05	$13.49
10.625	$8.98	$9.24	$9.53	$10.07	$11.13	$13.56
10.750	$9.08	$9.33	$9.62	$10.15	$11.21	$13.63
10.875	$9.18	$9.43	$9.71	$10.24	$11.29	$13.70
11.000	$9.28	$9.52	$9.80	$10.32	$11.37	$13.78
11.125	$9.38	$9.62	$9.89	$10.41	$11.44	$13.85
11.250	$9.48	$9.71	$9.98	$10.49	$11.52	$13.92
11.375	$9.58	$9.81	$10.07	$10.58	$11.60	$13.99
11.500	$9.68	$9.90	$10.16	$10.66	$11.68	$14.06
11.625	$9.78	$10.00	$10.26	$10.75	$11.75	$14.13
11.750	$9.88	$10.09	$10.35	$10.84	$11.84	$14.20
11.875	$9.98	$10.19	$10.44	$10.92	$11.92	$14.27
12.000	$10.08	$10.29	$10.53	$11.01	$12.00	$14.35
12.125	$10.19	$10.38	$10.62	$11.10	$12.08	$14.42
12.250	$10.29	$10.48	$10.72	$11.19	$12.16	$14.49
12.375	$10.39	$10.58	$10.81	$11.27	$12.24	$14.56
12.500	$10.49	$10.67	$10.90	$11.36	$12.33	$14.64
12.625	$10.59	$10.77	$11.00	$11.45	$12.41	$14.71
12.750	$10.69	$10.87	$11.09	$11.54	$12.49	$14.78
12.875	$10.79	$10.96	$11.18	$11.63	$12.57	$14.86
13.000	$10.90	$11.06	$11.28	$11.72	$12.65	$14.93
13.125	$11.00	$11.16	$11.37	$11.80	$12.73	$15.00
13.250	$11.10	$11.26	$11.47	$11.89	$12.82	$15.08
13.375	$11.20	$11.36	$11.56	$11.98	$12.90	$15.15
13.500	$11.30	$11.45	$11.66	$12.07	$12.98	$15.23

Rate	40 years	30 years	25 years	20 years	15 years	10 years
13.625	$11.40	$11.55	$11.75	$12.16	$13.07	$15.30
13.750	$11.51	$11.65	$11.85	$12.25	$13.15	$15.38
13.875	$11.61	$11.75	$11.94	$12.34	$13.23	$15.45
14.000	$11.71	$11.85	$12.04	$12.44	$13.32	$15.53
14.125	$11.81	$11.95	$12.13	$12.53	$13.40	$15.60
14.250	$11.92	$12.05	$12.23	$12.62	$13.49	$15.68
14.375	$12.02	$12.15	$12.33	$12.71	$13.57	$15.75
14.500	$12.12	$12.25	$12.42	$12.80	$13.66	$15.83
14.625	$12.22	$12.35	$12.52	$12.89	$13.74	$15.90
14.750	$12.33	$12.44	$12.61	$12.98	$13.83	$15.98
14.875	$12.43	$12.54	$12.71	$13.08	$13.91	$16.06
15.000	$12.53	$12.64	$12.81	$13.17	$14.00	$16.13
15.125	$12.64	$12.74	$12.91	$13.26	$14.08	$16.21
15.250	$12.74	$12.84	$13.00	$13.35	$14.17	$16.29
15.375	$12.84	$12.94	$13.10	$13.45	$14.25	$16.36
15.500	$12.94	$13.05	$13.20	$13.54	$14.34	$16.44
15.625	$13.05	$13.15	$13.30	$13.63	$14.43	$16.52
15.750	$13.15	$13.25	$13.39	$13.73	$14.51	$16.60
15.875	$13.25	$13.35	$13.49	$13.82	$14.60	$16.67
16.000	$13.36	$13.45	$13.59	$13.91	$14.69	$16.75
16.125	$13.46	$13.55	$13.69	$14.01	$14.77	$16.83
16.250	$13.56	$13.65	$13.79	$14.10	$14.86	$16.91
16.375	$13.67	$13.75	$13.88	$14.19	$14.95	$16.99
16.500	$13.77	$13.85	$13.98	$14.29	$15.04	$17.06
16.625	$13.87	$13.95	$14.08	$14.38	$15.13	$17.14
16.750	$13.98	$14.05	$14.18	$14.48	$15.21	$17.22
16.875	$14.08	$14.16	$14.28	$14.57	$15.30	$17.30
17.000	$14.18	$14.26	$14.38	$14.67	$15.39	$17.38
17.125	$14.29	$14.36	$14.48	$14.76	$15.48	$17.46
17.250	$14.39	$14.46	$14.58	$14.86	$15.57	$17.54
17.375	$14.49	$14.56	$14.68	$14.95	$15.66	$17.62
17.500	$14.60	$14.66	$14.78	$15.05	$15.75	$17.70
17.625	$14.70	$14.77	$14.87	$15.15	$15.84	$17.78
17.750	$14.80	$14.87	$14.97	$15.24	$15.92	$17.86
17.875	$14.91	$14.97	$15.07	$15.34	$16.01	$17.94
18.000	$15.01	$15.07	$15.17	$15.43	$16.10	$18.02

Glossary

Abstract of Title A written record of the historical ownership of the property that helps to determine whether the property can in fact be transferred from one party to another without any previous claims. An abstract of title is used in certain parts of the country when determining if there are any previous claims on the subject property in question.

Acceleration A loan accelerates when it is paid off early, usually at the request or demand of the lender. An acceleration clause within a loan document states what must happen when a loan must be paid immediately, but usually it applies to nonpayment, late payments, or the transfer of the property without the lender's permission.

Adjustable Rate Mortgage A loan program where the interest rate may change throughout the life of the loan. An ARM adjusts based on terms agreed to between the lender and the borrower, but typically it may only change once or twice a year.

Alternate Credit Items you must pay each month but that won't appear on your credit report. Alternate credit accounts might include your telephone bill. In relation to mortgage loans, while such items aren't reported as installment or revolving credit, they can establish your ability and willingness to make consistent payments in a responsible manner. Sometimes called nonstandard credit.

Alt Loans Alternative loans, so-called because they're not conventional or government loans but step outside the lending box and establish their own lending criteria.

Amortization Amortization is the length of time it takes for a loan to be fully paid off, by predetermined agreement. These payments are at regular intervals. Sometimes called a *fully amortized* loan.

Amortization terms can vary, but generally accepted terms run in five-year increments, from 10 to 40 years.

Annual Percentage Rate   The cost of money borrowed, expressed as an annual rate. The APR is a useful consumer tool to compare different lenders, but unfortunately it is often not used correctly. The APR can only work when comparing the same exact loan type from one lender to another.

Appraisable Asset   Any item whose value can be determined by a third-party expert. That car you want to sell is an appraisable asset. If the item can be appraised, then you can use those funds to buy a house.

Appraisal   A report that helps to determine the market value of a property. An appraisal can be done in various ways, as required by a lender, from simply driving by the property to ordering a full-blown inspection, complete with full-color photographs of the real estate. Appraisals compare similar homes in the area to substantiate the value of the property in question.

APR   *See* Annual Percentage Rate.

ARM   *See* Adjustable Rate Mortgage.

Assumable Mortgage   Homes sold with assumable mortgages let buyers take over the terms of the loan along with the house being sold. Assumable loans may be fully or nonqualifying assumable, meaning buyers take over the loan without being qualified or otherwise evaluated by the original lender. Qualifying assumable loans mean that while buyers may assume terms of the existing note, they must qualify all over again as if they were applying for a brand-new loan.

AUS   *See* Automated Underwriting System.

Automated Underwriting System   A software application that electronically issues a preliminary loan approval. An AUS uses a complex approval matrix that reviews credit reports, debt ratios, and other factors that go into a mortgage loan approval.

Automated Valuation Model   An electronic method of evaluating a property's appraised value, done by scanning public records for recent home sales and other data in the subject property's neighborhood. Although not yet widely accepted as a replacement for full-blown appraisals, many in the industry expect AVMs to eventually replace traditional appraisals altogether.

AVM   *See* Automated Valuation Model.

Balloon Mortgage A type of mortgage where the remaining balance must be paid in full at the end of a preset term. A five-year balloon mortgage might be amortized over a 30-year period, but the remaining balance is due, in full, at the end of five years.

Basis Point A basis point is equal to 1/100 percent. A move of 50 basis points would cause a 30-year fixed mortgage rate to change by 1/8 percent.

Bridge Loan A short-term loan primarily used to pull equity out of one property for a down payment on another. This loan is paid off when the original property sells. Since they are short-term loans, sometimes lasting just a few weeks, usually only retail banks offer them. Usually the borrower doesn't make any monthly payments and only pays off the loan when the property sells.

Bundling Bundling is the act of putting together several real estate or mortgage services in one package. Instead of paying for an appraisal here or an inspection there, some or all of the buyer's services are packaged together. Usually a bundle offers discounts on all services, although when they're bundled it's hard to parse all the services to see whether you're getting a good deal.

Buydown Paying more money to get a lower interest rate is called a *permanent* buydown, and it is used in conjunction with discount points. The more points, the lower the rate. A *temporary* buydown is a fixed-rate mortgage that starts at a reduced rate for the first period, and then gradually increases to its final note rate. A temporary buydown for two years is called a 2–1 buydown. For three years it's called a 3–2–1 buydown.

Cash-Out A refinance mortgage that involves taking equity out of a home in the form of cash during a refinance. Instead of just reducing your interest rate during a refinance and financing your closing costs, you finance even more, putting the additional money in your pocket.

Closer The person who helps prepare the lender's closing documents. The closer forwards those documents to your settlement agent's office, where you will be signing closing papers. In some states, a closer can be the person who holds your loan closing.

Closing Costs The various fees involved when buying a home or obtaining a mortgage. The fees, required to issue a good loan, can come directly from the lender or may come from others in the transactions.

Collateral Collateral is property owned by the borrower that's pledged to the lender as security in case the loan goes bad. A lender makes a mortgage with the house as collateral.

Comparable Sales Comparable sales are that part of an appraisal report that lists recent transfers of similar properties in the immediate vicinity of the house being bought. Also called "comps."

Conforming Loan A conventional conforming loan is a Fannie Mae or Freddie Mac loan that is equal to or less than the maximum allowable loan limits established by Fannie and Freddie. These limits are changed annually.

Conventional Loan A loan mortgage that uses guidelines established by Fannie Mae or Freddie Mac and is issued and guaranteed by lenders.

Correspondent Banker A mortgage banker that doesn't intend to keep your mortgage loan, but instead sells your loan to another preselected mortgage banker. Correspondent bankers are smaller mortgage bankers, those perhaps with a regional presence but not a national one. They can shop various rates from other correspondent mortgage bankers that have set up an established relationship to buy and sell loans from one another. They operate much like a broker, except correspondent bankers use their own money to fund loans.

Credit Report A report that shows the payment histories of a consumer, along with the individual's property addresses and any public records.

Credit Repository A place where credit histories are stored. Merchants and banks agree to store consumers' credit patterns in a central place that other merchants and banks can access.

Credit Score A number derived from a consumer's credit history and based upon various credit details in a consumer's past and upon the likelihood of default. Different credit patterns are assigned different numbers and different credit activity may have a greater or lesser impact on the score. The higher the credit score, the better the credit.

Debt Consolidation Paying off all or part of one's consumer debt with equity from a home. Debt consolidation can be part of a refinanced mortgage or a separate equity loan.

Debt Ratio Gross monthly payments divided by gross monthly income, expressed as a percentage. There are typically two debt ratios to be considered: The *housing ratio*—sometimes called the front-end or front ratio—is the total monthly house payment, plus any monthly tax, insurance, private mortgage insurance, or homeowners association dues, divided by gross monthly income. The *total debt ratio*—also called the back-end or back ratio—is the total housing payment plus other monthly consumer installment or revolving debt, also expressed as a percentage. Loan debt ratio guidelines are usually denoted as 32/38, with 32 being the front ratio and 38 being the back ratio. Ratio guidelines can vary from loan to loan and lender to lender.

Deed A written document evidencing each transfer of ownership in a property.

Deed of Trust A written document giving an interest in the home being bought to a third party, usually the lender, as security to the lender.

Delinquent Being behind on a mortgage payment. Delinquencies typically begin to be recognized as 30+ days delinquent, 60+ days delinquent, and 90+ days delinquent.

Discount Points Also called "points," they are represented as a percentage of a loan amount. One point equals 1 percent of a loan balance. Borrowers pay discount points to reduce the interest rate for a mortgage. Typically each discount point paid reduces the interest rate by 1/4 percent. It is a form of prepaid interest to a lender.

Document Stamp Evidence—usually with an ink stamp—of how much tax was paid upon transfer of ownership of property. Certain states call it a *doc stamp*. Doc stamp tax rates can vary based upon locale, and not all states have doc stamps.

Down Payment The amount of money initially given by the borrower to close a mortgage. The down payment equals the sales price less financing. It's the very first bit of equity you'll have in the new home.

Easement A right of way previously established by a third party. Easement types can vary but typically involve the right of a public utility to cross your land to access an electrical line.

Entitlement The amount the VA will guarantee in order for a VA loan to be made. *See also* VA loan.

Equity The difference between the appraised value of a home and any outstanding loans recorded against the house.

Escrow Depending upon where you live, escrow can mean two things. On the West Coast, for example, when a home goes under contract it "goes into escrow" (*see also* Escrow Agent). In other parts of the country, an escrow is a financial account set up by a lender to collect monthly installments for annual tax bills and/or hazard insurance policy renewals.

Escrow Account *See* Impound Account.

Escrow Agent On the West Coast, the escrow agent is the person or company that handles the home closing, ensuring documents are assigned correctly and property transfer has legitimately changed hands.

FACTA *See* Fair and Accurate Credit Transactions Act.

Fair and Accurate Credit Transactions Act The FACTA is a new law that replaces the Fair Credit Reporting Act, or FCRA, and governs how consumer information can be stored, shared, and monitored for privacy and accuracy.

Fair Credit Reporting Act The FCRA was the first consumer law that emphasized consumer rights and protections relating to credit reports, credit applications, and privacy concerns.

Fannie Mae *See* Federal National Mortgage Association.

Farmers Home Administration The FmHA provides financing to farmers and other qualified borrowers who are unable to obtain loans elsewhere. These loans are typical for rural properties that might be larger in acreage than a suburban home, as well as for working farms.

FCRA *See* Fair Credit Reporting Act.

Fed Shorthand name for the Federal Reserve Board.

Federal Funds Rate The rate banks charge one another to borrow money overnight.

Federal Home Loan Mortgage Corporation The FHLMC, or Freddie Mac, is a corporation established by the U.S. government in 1968 to buy mortgages from lenders made under Freddie Mac guidelines.

Federal Housing Administration The FHA was formed in 1934 and is now a division of the Department of Housing and Urban Development (HUD). It provides loan guarantees to lenders who make loans under FHA guidelines.

Federal National Mortgage Association The FNMA, or Fannie Mae, was originally established in 1938 by the U.S. government to buy FHA mortgages and provide liquidity in the mortgage marketplace. It is similar in function to Freddie Mac. In 1968, its charter was changed and it now purchases conventional mortgages as well as government ones.

Federal Reserve Board The head of the Federal Reverse Banks that, among other things, sets overnight lending rates for banking institutions. The Fed does not set mortgage rates.

Fee Income The closing costs received by a lender or broker that are outside of the interest rate or discount points. Fee income can be in the form of loan processing charges, underwriting fees, and the like.

FHA *See* Federal Housing Administration.

FICO FICO stands for Fair Isaac Corporation, the company that invented the most widely used credit scoring system.

Final Inspection The last inspection of a property, showing that a new home being built is 100 percent complete or that a home improvement is 100 percent complete. It lets lenders know that their collateral and their loan are exactly where they should be.

Financed Premium An alternative to second mortgages and mortgage insurance that allows for the borrower to buy a mortgage insurance premium and roll the cost of the premium into the loan amount, in lieu of paying a mortgage insurance payment every month.

Fixed Rate Mortgage A loan whose interest rate does not change throughout the term of the loan.

Float Actively deciding not to "lock" or guarantee an interest rate while a loan is being processed. A float is usually done because the borrower believes rates will go down.

Float-Down A mortgage loan rate that can drop as mortgage rates drop. Usually a loan comes in two types of float, one being during construction of a home and the other being during the period of an interest rate lock.

Flood Certificate A certificate that shows whether a property or part of a property lies above or below any local flood zones. These flood zones are mapped over the course of several years by the Federal Emergency Management Agency (FEMA). The certificate identifies the property's exact legal location and a flood line's elevation. There is a box that simply asks, "Is the property in a flood zone, yes or no?" If the property is in a flood zone, the lender will require special flood insurance that is not usually carried under a standard homeowners hazard insurance policy.

FmHA   *See* Farmers Home Administration.

Foreclosure   A foreclosure is the bad thing that happens when the mortgage isn't repaid. Lenders begin the process of forcefully recovering their collateral when borrowers fail to make loan payments. The lender takes your house away.

Freddie Mac   See Federal Home Loan Mortgage Corporation.

Fully Indexed Rate   The number reached when adding a loan's index and the margin. This rate is how adjustable note rates are compiled.

Funding   The actual transfer of money from a lender to a borrower.

Funding Fee   A required fee, equal to 2 percent of the sales price of a home, that helps to fund a VA loan guarantee.

Gift   When the down payment and closing costs for a home are given to the borrower instead of the funds coming from their own accounts, it is called a gift. Usually such gifts can only come from family members or foundations established to help new homeowners.

Gift Affidavit   A form signed whereby someone swears that the money they're giving you is indeed a gift, not a loan, and is to be used for the purchase of a home. Lenders like to see that form, as well as a paper trail of the gift funds being added to your own funds.

Gift Funds   Monies given to a borrower for the sole purpose of buying a home. These funds are not to be paid back in any form and are usually given by a family member or a qualified nonprofit organization.

Ginnie Mae   *See* Government National Mortgage Association.

Good Faith Estimate   A list of estimated closing costs on a particular mortgage transaction. This estimate must be provided to the loan applicants within 72 hours after receipt of a mortgage application by the lender or broker.

Government National Mortgage Association   The GNMA, or Ginnie Mae, is a U.S. government corporation formed to purchase government loans like VA and FHA loans from banks and mortgage lenders. Think of it as Fannie or Freddie, only it buys government loans.

Hazard Insurance A specific type of insurance that covers against certain destructive elements such as fire, wind, and hail. It is usually an addition to homeowners insurance, but every home loan has a hazard rider.

HELOC *See* Home Equity Line of Credit.

Hold-Back A contingency fund associated with a construction or remodel. It covers any change orders that might occur during the process. A change order is what happens when you simply change your mind. The hold-back helps pay for the change when changing your mind costs more than the loan. A typical hold-back amount is 10 percent of the original loan.

Home Equity Line of Credit HELOC is a credit line using a home as collateral. Customers write checks on this line of credit whenever they need to and pay only on balances withdrawn. It is much like a credit card, but secured by the property.

Homeowners Insurance An insurance policy that covers not just hazard items, but also other things, such as liability or personal property.

Hybrid Loan A cross between an ARM and a fixed-rate loan. In a hybrid loan, the rate is fixed for a predetermined number of years before turning into an adjustable-rate mortgage, or ARM.

Impound Account An account that is set up by a lender to deposit a monthly portion of annual property taxes or hazard insurance. As taxes or insurance come up for renewal, the lender pays the bill using these funds. Also called an *escrow account.*

Index An index is used as the basis to establish an interest rate, usually associated with a margin. Most anything can be an index, but the most common are U.S. treasuries or similar instruments. *See also* Fully Indexed Rate.

Inspection A structural review of the house to determine defects in workmanship, damage to the property, or required maintenance. An inspection does not determine value of the property. A pest inspection, for example, looks for termites or wood ants.

Installment Account Borrowing one lump sum and agreeing to pay back a certain amount each month until the loan is paid off. A car loan is an example of an installment loan.

Intangible Asset An asset not valuable by itself, but by what it represents. A publicly traded stock is an intangible asset. It's not the stock itself that has the value, but what the stock represents in terms of income.

Intangible Tax A state tax on personal property.

Interest-Only Loan A loan that requires only that you pay the interest on your loan each month, without having to pay any part of the principal.

Interest Rate The amount charged to borrowed money over a specified time.

Interest Rate Reduction Loan An IRRL is a VA refinance loan program that has relaxed credit guidelines. Also called a streamline refinance.

IRRL *See* Interest Rate Reduction Loan.

Jumbo Loan A mortgage that exceeds current conforming loan limits. For 2007, anything above $417,000 is considered jumbo.

Junior Lien A second mortgage or one that subordinates to another loan. Not as common a term as it used to be. You're more likely to hear the terms *second mortgage* or *piggyback*.

Land Contract An arrangement where the buyer makes monthly payments to the seller but the ownership of the property does not change hands until the loan is paid in full.

Land-to-Value An appraisal term that calculates the value of the land as a percentage of the total value of the home. If the land exceeds the value of the home, it's more difficult to find financing without good comparable sales. Also called lot-to-value.

Lease-Purchase Agreement Also known as rent-to-own. An option whereby a buyer leases a home until the buyer has saved up enough money for a down payment to qualify for a conventional mortgage.

Lender Policy Title insurance that protects a mortgage from defects or previous claims of ownership.

Liability An obligation or bill on the part of the borrower. It works like an automobile loan. When you pay off the car, you get the title. Liabilities such as student loans or a car payment can show up on a credit report, but they can also be anything else that you are obligated to pay. Those liabilities on the credit report are used to determine debt ratios.

LIBOR Index *See* London Interbank Offered Rate.

Lien A legal claim or prior interest on the property you're about to buy. Borrowing money from another source in order to buy a house could mean that someone else has a lien on that property.

Loan Money granted to one party with the expectation of it being repaid.

Loan Officer The person typically responsible for helping mortgage applicants get qualified and assisting in loan selection and loan application. Loan officers can work at banks, credit unions, and mortgage brokerage houses or for bankers.

Loan Processor The person who gathers the required documentation for a loan application for loan submission. Along with your loan officer, you'll work with the loan processor quite a bit during your mortgage process.

Loan-to-Value Ratio LTV is expressed as a percentage of the loan amount when compared to the valuation of the home determined by an appraisal. If a home were appraised at $100,000 and the loan amount were $70,000, then the LTV would be 70 percent.

Loan Underwriter The person responsible for ultimately saying "yes" or "no" on a loan file. The underwriter compares loan guidelines with what you have documented in the file.

Lock An agreement guaranteeing an interest rate over a predetermined period. Loan locks are not loan approvals; they're simply the rate your lender has agreed to give you at loan closing.

London Interbank Offered Rate LIBOR is a British index similar to our Federal Funds rate, where British banks borrow money from one another over short periods to adhere to reserve requirements.

LTV *See* Loan-to-Value Ratio.

Margin A number, expressed as a percentage, that is added to a mortgage's index to determine the rate the borrower pays on the note. An index can be a six-month CD at 4 percent and the margin can be 2 percent. The interest rate the borrower pays is 4 + 2, or 6 percent. A *fully indexed rate* is the index plus the margin.

Market Gain The difference between what a mortgage price was when you locked it with the lender and what the mortgage price is when the loan is physically locked with the lender's secondary department or with a mortgage broker's wholesale lender.

Market Value In an open market, the market value of a property is both the highest the borrower is willing to pay and the least the seller is willing to accept at the time of the contract. Property appraisals help justify market value by comparing similar home sales in the subject property's neighborhood.

Modifiable Mortgage A mortgage loan that allows its interest rate to be modified, even if it's at another lender.

Mortgage A loan with the property being pledged as collateral. The mortgage is retired when the loan is paid in full.

Mortgage-Backed Securities Investment securities issued by Wall Street firms that are guaranteed, or collateralized, with home mortgages taken out by consumers. These securities can then be bought and sold on Wall Street.

Mortgage Bankers Lenders who use their own funds to lend money. Historically, these funds would have come from the savings accounts of other bank customers. But with the evolution of mortgage banking, that's the old way of doing business. Even though bankers use their own money, it may come from other sources such as lines of credit or through selling loans to other institutions.

Mortgage Brokers Companies that set up a home loan between a banker and a borrower. Brokers don't have money to lend directly, but they have experience in finding various loan programs that can suit the borrower, similar to how an independent insurance agent operates. Brokers don't work for the borrower but instead provide mortgage loan choices from other mortgage lenders.

Mortgagee The person or business making the loan; also called the lender.

Mortgage Insurance (MI) *See* Private Mortgage Insurance.

Mortgagor The person(s) getting the loan; also called the borrower.

Multiple Listing Service MLS is a central repository where real estate brokers and agents show homes and search for homes that are for sale.

Negative Amortization A neg-am loan is an adjustable-rate mortgage that can have two interest rates, the contract rate or the fully indexed rate. The contract rate is the minimum agreed-upon rate the consumer may pay; sometimes the contract rate is lower than the fully indexed rate. The borrower has a choice of which rate to pay, but if the contract rate is lower than the fully indexed rate, that difference is added back to the loan. If your contract payments are only $500 but the fully indexed rate is $700 and you pay only the contract rate, $200 is added back into your original loan amount. Not for the fainthearted, nor for those with little money down.

NINA No Income, No Asset mortgage. This type of loan does not require that the borrower prove or otherwise document any income or asset whatsoever.

No-Fee Loan A loan where your lender pays closing costs for you, if you agree to a slightly higher interest rate.

Nonconforming Loans whose amounts are above current Fannie or Freddie limits. *See also* Jumbo Loan.

Note A promise to repay. It may or may not have property involved and may or may not be a mortgage.

Note Modification Taking the original terms of a note, and without changing any other part of the obligation or title, reducing the interest rate for the remaining term of the loan. A note modification means you can't "shop around" for the best rate to reduce your rate; instead, you must work with your original lender who still services your mortgage. In a modification, nothing can change except the rate.

One-Time Close Loan A construction loan whereby you obtain construction financing and permanent financing, and lock in a permanent mortgage rate at the same time. *See also* Two-Time Close Loan.

Origination Fee A fee charged to cover costs associated with finding, documenting, and preparing a mortgage application, and usually expressed as a percentage of the loan amount.

Owner's Policy Title insurance made for the benefit of the homeowner.

Par An interest rate that can be obtained without paying any discount points and that does not have any additional yield beyond its rate. For instance, you get a 30-year quote of 7 percent with one point, or 7.25 percent with zero points, or 7.5 percent with zero points plus an additional yield to you of $1,000 toward closing costs. Here the 7.25 percent at zero points is the par rate.

Payment Option ARM A type of negative amortization loan where you have a choice as to what you'd like to pay each month. The choice is between an initial contract rate, an interest-only, or a fully indexed, fully amortized loan.

Payment Shock   A term used by lenders referring to the percentage difference between what you're paying now for housing and what your new payment would be. Most loan programs don't have a payment shock provision, but for those that do, a common percentage increase is 150 percent.

Permanent Buydown   *See* Buydown.

Piggyback Mortgage   *See* Second Mortgage.

PITI   Principal, Interest, Taxes, and Insurance. These figures are used to help determine front debt ratios.

Pledged Asset   An appraisable property or security that is collateralized to make a mortgage loan. Sometimes a pledged asset can be a stock or mutual fund. A lender can make a mortgage loan and use the mutual fund as part of the collateral. If the borrower fails to make the payments, all or part of the pledged asset can go to the lender.

PMI   *See* Private Mortgage Insurance.

Points   *See* Discount Points.

Portfolio Loan   A loan made by a direct lender, usually a bank, and kept in the lender's loan portfolio instead of being sold or underwritten to any external guidelines.

Predatory Loan   A loan designed to take advantage of people by charging either too many fees or too high of an interest rate, or both, while also stripping that homeowner of his equity.

Prepaid Interest   Daily interest collected from the day of loan closing to the first of the following month.

Prepayment Penalty   An amount is paid to the lender if the loan is paid off before its maturity or if extra payments are made on the loan. A *hard penalty* is automatic if the loan is paid off early or if extra payments are made at any time or for any amount whatsoever. A *soft penalty* only lasts for a couple of years and may allow extra payments on the loan not to exceed a certain amount.

Principal   The outstanding amount owed on a loan, not including any interest due.

Private Mortgage Insurance   PMI is typically required on all mortgage loans with less than 20 percent down. It is an insurance policy, paid by the borrower with benefits paid to the lender. It covers the difference between the borrower's down payment and 20 percent of the sales price. If the borrower defaults on the mortgage, this difference is paid to the lender.

Pull-Through Rate   A term, used by wholesale lenders, to track the percentage of loans that close that have been locked by a broker.

Quit Claim   A release of any interest in a property from one party to another. A quit claim does not, however, release the obligation on the mortgage.

Rate-and-Term Refinance   Refinancing to get a new rate. You're changing the interest rate and changing the term, or length, of the new note.

Rate Cap   How high your ARM rate is permitted to change each adjustment period. There are three possible caps on an adjustable-rate mortgage: the adjustment cap, the lifetime rate cap, and the initial rate cap.

Real Estate Account   A mortgage secured by real estate.

Realtor   A member of the National Association of REALTORS and a registered trademark. Not all real estate agents are Realtors.

Recast   A term applied to ARMs and used when extra payments are made to the principal balance. When your note is recast, your monthly payment is calculated for you.

Refinance   Obtaining a new mortgage to replace an existing one. There is also a "rate-and-term refinance," where only the outstanding principal balance, interest due, and closing costs are included in the loan.

Reissue   When refinancing, there may be discounts if you use the same title agency. This "reissue" of an original title report can cost much less than a full title insurance policy.

Rescission   Withdrawal from a mortgage agreement. Refinanced mortgage loans for a primary residence have a required three-day "cooling off" period before the loan becomes official. If for any reason you decide not to take the mortgage, you can "rescind" and the whole deal's off.

Reserves   A borrower's assets after closing. Reserves can include cash in the bank, stocks, mutual funds, retirement accounts, IRAs, and 401(k) accounts.

Reverse Mortgage   A mortgage designed to help older Americans who own their homes by paying the homeowner cash in exchange for the equity in his home. When he no longer owns the home by selling or moving out or dying, then the reverse mortgage lender is paid back all the money borrowed, plus interest.

Revolving Account   A credit card or department store account on which you typically have a limit and don't make any payments until you charge something.

Sales Contract   Your written agreement to sell or purchase a home, signed by both the seller and buyer.

Secondary Market   A financial arena where mortgages are bought and sold, either individually or grouped together into securities backed by those mortgages. Fannie Mae and Freddie Mac are the backbone for the conventional secondary market. Other secondary markets exist for nonconforming loans, subprime loans, and others.

Second Mortgage   Sometimes called a "piggyback" mortgage, a second mortgage assumes a subordinate position behind a first mortgage. If the home goes into foreclosure, the first mortgage would be settled before the second could lay claim. *See also* Junior Lien.

Seller   The person transferring ownership and all rights for his home in exchange for cash or trade.

Settlement Statement   Also called the Final HUD-1. It shows all financial entries during the home sale, including sales price, closing costs, loan amounts, and property taxes. Your initial Good Faith Estimate will be your first glimpse of your settlement statement. This statement is one of the final documents put together before you go to closing and is prepared by your attorney or settlement agent.

Subprime Loan   A loan made to people with less than "prime" credit. There are various stages of subprime credit, from loans for those with simply "tarnished" credit who can't quite get a conventional mortgage, to those with seriously damaged credit who may be in or just out of bankruptcy or have collection accounts or judgments and liens against them.

Survey   A map that shows the physical location of the structure and where it sits on the property. A survey also designates any easements that run across or through the property.

Temporary Buydown   *See* Buydown.

Title   Legal ownership in a property.

Title Exam/Title Search   The process where public records are reviewed to research any previous liens on the property.

Title Insurance   Protection for the lender, the seller, and/or the borrower against any defects or previous claims to the property being transferred or sold.

Two-Time Close Loan   In a construction financing, when you first get a construction loan and then get another mortgage at the end of construction. You'll go to two different closings for a two-time close loan. *See also* One-Time Close Loan.

VA Loan   Government mortgage guaranteed by the Department of Veterans Affairs.

VA No-No   A type of VA loan where the borrower not only puts *no* money down, but also pays *no* closing costs.

Verification of Deposit   A VOD is a form mailed to a bank or credit union that asks the institution to verify that a borrower's bank account exists, how much is in it, how long the borrower has had it, and what the average balance was over the previous two months.

VOD   *See* Verification of Deposit.

Wraparound Mortgage   A method of financing where the borrower pays the former owner of the property each month in the form of a mortgage payment. The former owner will then make a mortgage payment to the original mortgage holder.

Index

Printed in the USA
CPSIA information can be obtained
at www.ICGtesting.com
JSHW030511040823
45943JS00008B/264